THE
GREAT BEAR
AT WAR

OSPREY
PUBLISHING

THE
GREAT BEAR
AT WAR

THE RUSSIAN AND SOVIET ARMY 1917–PRESENT

EDITED BY

CHRIS McNAB

OSPREY PUBLISHING
Bloomsbury Publishing Plc
PO Box 883, Oxford, OX1 9PL, UK
1385 Broadway, 5th Floor, New York, NY 10018, USA

E-mail: info@ospreypublishing.com

www.ospreypublishing.com

OSPREY is a trademark of Osprey Publishing Ltd

First published in Great Britain in 2019

Material in this book is adapted from the following Osprey publications: ELI 5 *Soviet Bloc Elite Forces*, ELI 10 *Warsaw Pact Ground Forces*, ELI 12 *Inside the Soviet Army*, ELI 197 *Russian Security and Paramilitary Forces since 1991*, ELI 217 *The Modern Russian Army 1992–2016*, ESS 69 *The Russian Civil War 1918–22*, ESS 75 *The Soviet–Afghan War 1979–89*, ESS 78 *Russia's Wars in Chechnya 1994–2009*, MAA 29 *The Soviet Army*, MAA 216 *The Red Army of the Great Patriotic War 1941–45*, MAA 293 *The Russian Civil War (1)*, MAA 464 *World War II Soviet Armed Forces (1)*, MAA 468 *World War II Soviet Armed Forces (2)*, MAA 469 *World War II Soviet Armed Forces (3)* and *WAR 123 Soviet Rifleman 1941–45*.
Artwork by Ronald Volstad, Andrei Karachtchouk, Johnny Shumate, Michael Roffe and Howard Gerrard © Osprey Publishing.

A catalogue record for this book is available from the British Library.
ISBN: HB 9781472836533; eBook 9781472836526; ePDF 9781472836540; XML 9781472836557

19 20 21 22 23   10 9 8 7 6 5 4 3 2 1

Maps by Peter Bull Art Studio
Index by Fionbar Lyons
Layouts by Myriam Bell Design, Shrewsbury, UK
Originated by PDQ Digital Media Solutions, Bungay, UK
Printed and bound in India by Replika Press Private Ltd.

Front cover: Shubenmer/iStock
Back cover, from the top: A unit of the NKVD on parade, shortly after its formation in 1934. (Courtesy of the Central Museum of the Armed Forces, Moscow via www.Stavka.org.uk); A platoon commander reads excerpts from a newspaper to his SVT-40 rifle-armed men. (Courtesy of the Central Museum of the Armed Forces, Moscow via www.Stavka.org.uk); During a May Day parade, a formation of ASU-85 self-propelled guns rolls through Moscow. (Cody/AirSeaLand); A Russian Airborne soldier trains his full-camo AK-103 during an exercise. (Ministry of Defence of the Russian Federation/ Mil.ru/ CC-BY-4.0)

Osprey Publishing supports the Woodland Trust, the UK's leading woodland conservation charity. To find out more about our authors and books visit www.ospreypublishing.com. Here you will find extracts, author interviews, details of forthcoming events and the option to sign up for our newsletter.

CONTENTS

FOREWORD:
A NATION FORGED BY WAR

ALL NATIONS HAVE BEEN TEMPERED by war, but few have been so forged in the fires of conflict as Russia. Indeed, the very concept of 'Russia' as a nation is a product of conquest, as Viking warrior-traders looking for land routes to fabled Byzantium decided to carve themselves out their own principalities ruling over scattered Slav tribes. Over the years, Slav and Varyag ('Varangian') would intermarry, and the Rurikid dynasty of invaders would become the backbone of the country's aristocratic families.

War was never far from Russia, though. With no obvious natural borders to hem them in, its people would drift south and east, soon to be followed by the tax collectors and soldiers and governors of the state. More to the point, Russia's position as a Eurasian nation, at the crossroads of Europe and Asia, north and south, meant that it was perennially on the path of each generation's conquerors. In the thirteenth century, it was the Mongols from the east who would dominate the cities of the Rus for more than two centuries. Later the Russians would have to face Poles and Lithuanians from the west, Swedes from the north, Turks from the south. Napoleon was able to take a Moscow the Russians were willing to burn rather than let him enjoy, and then he had to watch his Grande Armée harried in the long, painful, frozen retreat. Hitler broke his Wehrmacht on the gates of Moscow, Leningrad and Stalingrad.

'No one and nothing is forgotten' runs their minatory slogan of World War II – tellingly known to the Russians as the Great Patriotic War – and

A Red Army soldier, wearing the classic greatcoat and fur cap of the World War II era, March 1946. Notably, he has armed himself with a captured German MP 40. (Photo by William Vandivert/ The LIFE Picture Collection/ Getty Images)

the lesson that the world is a dangerous place and that weakness means vulnerability is one successive leaders – tsars, general secretaries and now presidents – have encouraged and exploited. Head to the new Russia – My History museum in Moscow and you will be treated to a version of the national story that explicitly draws this connection. 'Atomization!' screams the caption across a map of early Russia that shows its division into myriad princely domains, each feuding with its neighbour and thus easy pickings for the Mongols. Just in case the message is lost on the crocodiles of schoolchildren being guided through the exhibit, later Russian martial triumphs, from the victory over the Golden Horde at Kulikovo in 1380 to rolling into Berlin in 1945 are presented as the fruits of unity, determination and a necessary ruthlessness.

Today, this is a country where a school might have an old World War II-vintage anti-tank gun on display in the playground, where children are encouraged to join the 'Young Army' and learn soldierly skills, and where, on the annual Victory Day celebrations, veterans parade in their medals. There is, of course, much more to Russia than war, but the shadow it throws over the nation is long and deep.

Over the years, Russia has presented itself as – and believed itself to be – a peace-loving country, one that arms for war in the hope of averting it. Yet the legacy of its history means that its notion of defence has often taken distinctly offensive forms. Potential invaders must be neutralized before they set their boots on the soil of Mother Russia, and if this looks like unprovoked aggression, then so be it. The paradox of talking to Russian soldiers is precisely this, that they see themselves often as men of peace, but forced to earn peace for Russia at the price of war for others.

Certainly they have not lacked for work. In the early modern era, their predecessors fought wars of conquest and defence, civil strife and imperial adventure. Later, they followed Napoleon all the way back to France (leaving one very distinctive mark: the word bistro comes from bystro, 'quickly', an order snapped to their waiters by impatient Russian aristocrat-officers enjoying the perks of being conquerors in Paris). They brought Tsarist rule to the Caucasus with fire and the sword through to the nineteenth century. In the twentieth century they fought and lost in both the Russo-Japanese War and World War I and then in their new incarnation as Red Guards and then Red Army, tried and failed to spread 'socialist internationalism' to Poland, but would then bring it to Central Europe on the back of T-34 tanks in and after World War II. They kept it there until 1989 with force when needed, in East Germany in 1953, Hungary in 1956 and Czechoslovakia in 1968. They sent guns and men to join anti-colonial wars around the globe, then in 1979 launched their own imperial adventure in Afghanistan. (They should have asked the British: this never turns out well. Then again, arguably the Americans should later have asked the Russians.) Later, under a Russian rather than Soviet flag, they would fight two bloody imperial wars in Chechnya, others in Georgia and Syria, and an undeclared intervention in Ukraine.

But now? This foreword is being written, fittingly enough, in Moscow. A thriving, lively, modern and even fun city, distant from the gloomy Soviet capital I remember from my very first visits to the USSR. There are familiar café chains on the street corner; young people dress the same as in the West, and are as glued to their mobile phones. Nonetheless, Russians still march in their thousands in the main cities on Victory Day to commemorate the 'immortal regiments' who fell in World War II, they consider the annexation of Crimea a national triumph rather than an act of geopolitical piracy, and the defence ministry even has its own TV channel delivering a diet of war films and glossy odes to Russian military power. You can go into the same shop and buy a Manchester United football shirt or one glorifying the 'polite people' (as the Russians call them), the 'little green men' who seized Crimea at Kalashnikov-point in 2014.

Which is the real Russia? Of course, it is both, but as thoughts begin to turn to what may follow Vladimir Putin's increasingly assertive and confrontational regime, at a time when Russia's economy is suffering from both the level of defence spending and the sanctions levelled on it as a result of its adventurism in Ukraine, the country is nearing a crossroads. Can it, will it, move beyond its fears of foreign conquest and its exaggerated, aggressive response? We will all have to see.

Mark Galeotti
Moscow, 2019

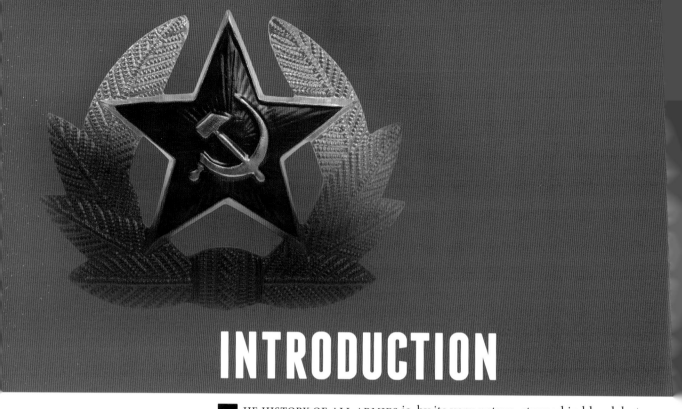

INTRODUCTION

THE HISTORY OF ALL ARMIES is, by its very nature, steeped in blood, but that of the Soviet and then the Russian Army especially so. Born out of revolution, ideology and the catastrophic fighting on the Eastern Front in World War I, the Red Army fought for its existence from the outset, first in the brutal Civil War (1917–22) and then in another world war just two decades later. Between those wars, it also had to endure the madness of Stalin's purges, which eviscerated the army's command structure.

Nevertheless, the very hardness of existence in the Soviet Army bred a resilience and ferocity that was deep seated and, for opponents, profoundly unsettling. According to Colonel (later Marshal of the Soviet Union) Nikolai Krylov, 'The Russian soldier loves a fight and scorns death. He was given the order: "If you are wounded, pretend to be dead; wait until the Germans come up; then select one of them and kill him! Kill him with gun, bayonet or knife. Tear his throat with your teeth. Do not die without leaving behind you a German corpse"' (quoted in Clark 1985: 43). Such bloodthirsty exhortations were a part of the life of the Soviet Armed Forces (RKKA), where the language of command, training and education was entirely subsumed into the political vernacular of the state. In such an environment, duty was to the Party, the state and the *Rodina* (Motherland), in that order; regimental or divisional pride, such a marked characteristic of German and other armies of the time, was discouraged.

Though the Red Army of World War II was largely a conscript force, the fierceness with which its personnel fought the invaders from the very first was a cause for comment and (for the Germans) concern. Although the German High Command, blinded to a degree by its own peculiar political ideology, believed that the RKKA was poorly led and filled with degenerate Slavs who had been weakened morally and intellectually by their sufferance under Bolshevism, the men of the RKKA were 'average Soviet citizens [who] fought for the USSR for several basic reasons: loyalty to the idea of historic Russia; normal obedience to the state; the fact that the USSR had been invaded, making it a 'just war'; the realization that life would not be any better under Nazi German rule; because the war represented a great societal and historical task for the first post-revolution generation; and out of self-interest, hoping to improve their place in society through wartime service.' (Reese 2011: 10) The positive sense of defending one's homeland against a monstrous aggressor would not be fully adopted by the Stavka (the Soviet High Command) or the state until 1942. In the interim, endless exhortations to do one's duty were compounded with savage discipline and punishment for those who seemed unwilling to give all they had for the state. Executions of men at the very highest level, such as General of the Army Dmitry Pavlov, were matched in a more rudimentary way throughout the RKKA; patrols from the NKVD (People's Commissariat of Internal Affairs) hunted for 'deserters' among the detritus of shattered divisions, and officers at all levels could avail themselves of on-the-spot shootings if they felt them appropriate.

Structurally speaking, the RKKA, barely capable of supporting itself in peacetime, was disastrously unprepared for a conflict on the scale of Operation *Barbarossa*, the Nazi invasion of the Soviet Union in 1941. The existing supply structure was complex, sluggish and corrupt; it failed at almost every level from the supply of bullets and boots through to tanks and train cars, leaving the RKKA short of vital support weapons and ammunition. Vehicles, when they were available, suffered from constant shortages of fuel, and when they broke down – which they often did due to poor maintenance and hard use – had to be abandoned as there were no spare parts with which to fix them. The result was a military disaster in 1941, with millions of Soviet men lost, equal materiel decimation and a German advance that took it to the gates of Moscow.

What then occurred was little short of a miracle. Through titanic and often tactically crude and humanly costly efforts, the German juggernaut was, eventually, stopped and reversed. Inch by painful inch, the Soviet Army learned how to fight the modern war, galvanized by a surging war industry that began producing tanks, aircraft and weapons in vast quantities. German defeats at Stalingrad and then Kursk began the Red Army's offensive momentum that, in 1945, took it into the streets of Berlin itself and final victory.

To this day, the epic narrative of the Great Patriotic War – as it is known in the former Soviet Union – remains an emotional and sombre frame of reference for those serving in the Russian military. Yet the army of today is the product of profound and repeated changes in both the politics of the Soviet Union/Russia, and the military that has reflected those changes. From 1945 until 1991, the armed forces were the Soviets' nuclear-tipped instrument of the Cold War, both within the Soviet Union and in the countries of the Warsaw Pact that mirrored Soviet tactics and equipment. For a time, at least until the removal of Nikita Khrushchev from power in 1964, the Cold War Soviet military was dominated by a strategic nuclear focus, at the expense of its wider conventional forces, which had been heavily demobilized following the end of World War II in 1945. Yet from the mid 1960s, the conventional forces surged onwards in strength and capability. They were still a somewhat blunt instrument. Training could be poor, conditions for soldiers spartan and technology often lagged behind that of the relatively cash-rich United States and NATO alliance forces. Soviet tactics were also illustrative of those of a heavily command-centralized army; the main emphasis was on fast and piercing advances by armoured and mechanized forces, or great pushes across broad fronts. The sophisticated fire-and-manoeuvre and decentralized command structures of the Western armies did not always mesh with the Soviet military mentality, as was often painfully revealed in the defeats of Soviet allies in the Arab–Israeli 'proxy wars' of the Middle East. Just in terms of scale and muscle alone, however, the Soviet Army was undoubtedly a towering presence to be respected, with a long and broad shadow over Western Europe.

Ultimately, the military Great Bear of communism was to be humbled. In 1979–89, the Soviet Armed Forces embarked upon a tragically unsuccessful attempt to keep Afghanistan within the communist sphere of influence. Over ten grinding years, Soviet forces were steadily eroded – militarily, politically and morally – by the counter-insurgency warfare of the *mujahideen* guerrillas. It was a conflict that the Soviets had neither prepared for nor understood, conducted at a time when the failing Soviet economy and weakening political will deprived the frontline soldier of proper training, equipment and tactics.

Shortly after the final withdrawal of Soviet forces from Afghanistan in 1989, the Soviet Union collapsed. In Russia, there was a period of chaos in its armed forces. Soldiers went unpaid or poorly fed. Barracks bullying reached epidemic and occasionally fatal proportions. Equipment degenerated or was stolen. The decline of the Russian Armed Forces is nowhere better represented than in the First Chechen War (1994–99), resulting in a humiliating defeat and the deaths of at least 5,500 soldiers. And yet, from the late 1990s onwards, and particularly under the political rule of Vladimir Putin from 1999, the Russian Army has been resurgent. Reforms during the 2000s have brought the federal forces into the modern era of warfighting, at both tactical and technological levels. The Russian military establishment, smarter and more capable, has somewhat laid the ghosts of Afghanistan and the First Chechen War to rest, illustrating new capabilities in later more confident fighting in Chechnya and in places such as Georgia, Ukraine and Syria. Through a combination of new combat technology allied to a ruthless and intelligent political will, the Russian military once more exercises international authority.

This book is an exploration of the Soviet and Russian Armed Forces from the Russian Revolution to the present day. In its chapters, we will explore not only the larger structural and strategic composition of the armed forces, but also focus the microscope down to the level of the humble frontline soldier, what he wore and ate, how he was treated and trained, and how he fought. The chapter on World War II is naturally a major element of this story, but I do not attempt to retell the story of that conflict – that is better left to full-length studies of the conflict. In the post-war era, however, three chapters consider the history of the wars in Afghanistan and Chechnya, both because these are generally less well known to the non-Russian audience, and because they illustrate key moments in the evolution of the Soviet to the Russian military. What emerges from this history is that the post-communist army shares much of the resilience, adaptation and, to varying degrees, patriotism and defiance that was displayed in the army of a century ago.

Bolshevik soldiers march through Red Square near the Kremlin, c.1917. In the foreground is a mounted Cossack officer. (CORBIS/Corbis via Getty Images)

CHAPTER I

THE EMERGENCE OF THE RED ARMY, 1917–39

THE RED ARMY WAS BORN directly out of war – both global and civil – and revolution. By March 1917, when the first major strikes and demonstrations began to ripple through Petrograd, the Russian Army had been at war for three ghastly years. The losses on the Eastern Front during World War I had dealt the Russian armed forces a staggering blow, with around five million casualties by the end of October 1916, including 1.8 million dead and two million captured. This devastation, combined with wartime crises in the domestic economy, stoked the flames of revolutionary disorder, flames that rose to full strength in 1917 with the overthrow of Tsarist rule and the establishment of a socialist government, albeit one contested in civil war. With the triumph of the communists in this war in 1922, the Soviet Union was born. What it now needed was a new army, militarily powerful enough to survive in a hostile world, but also ideologically aligned with the new regime.

THE TSARIST HERITAGE

In 1874, following the lead of the Prussians, Imperial Russia abandoned its large long-service standing army, for which recruits were selected by lot for 25 years with the colours, in favour of general short-term conscription.

A mixed group of armoured cars operated by the Red Army, pictured at Yaroslav in 1918. Such vehicles would have provided armoured protection against only up to rifle-calibre ammunition; they could be obliterated by a common field artillery or mortar shell. (Courtesy of the Central Museum of the Armed Forces, Moscow via www.Stavka.org.uk)

Service was originally set at six years, but by 1914 it had been reduced to three years for infantry and artillery and four years for all other arms. Conscripted recruits came principally from the Slav nationals, Russians, Ukrainians, White Russians and Poles, but included also natives of the Baltic States and certain parts of the Lower Volga and Caucasia. Finns from the Duchy of Finland and the Asian and Siberian peoples, with a few exceptions, were not accepted for conscripted military service.

As Russia teetered on the brink of a world war, the 1914 order of battle contained only a handful of minority national formations – a few brigades of Lettish and Finnish Rifles and some Turkestan and Caucasian cavalry and infantry divisions. The 11 divisions of Siberian Rifles consisted mostly of Russian settlers. The great majority of the formations that made up the Imperial Army were, in effect, ethnic Russian. Many Russian units, however, had a subsidiary recruiting area in a non-Russian (that is to say, Ukrainian or Polish) territory. And so, two nationalities might be found in a single regiment, the non-Russian element being limited in size to 30 per cent of the total establishment. For political reasons, neither the Russians nor the minority subject races were allowed to serve in their home areas.

Formerly the greater part of the officer corps came from the hereditary nobility and was linked with intellectual and ruling circles. Reforms in 1874, however, opened the officer's career to all classes, the qualifications for entry being nationality, education and ability, so that the social origin of the Tsarist officer in the period from 1880 to 1914 became much more diverse. The guards and cavalry of the line continued, admittedly, to be officered by the wealthy, whether from noble, merchant or industrialist background, since the officer's pay in these regiments could cover only a small part of the necessary expenses. But officers of the main arms and technical corps came from the middle and lower middle classes and some were even of serf origin. Ninety per cent of infantry officers lived on their modest pay. As retirement ages were high, promotion was slow.

Whether of noble or plebeian origin, wealthy or poor, all officers had much in common, since long service in the *corps des pages* or the cadet and military *Junker* schools established a pattern even before commissioning. The strength of these regimental officers lay in their insight into the mentality of the Russian *muzhik* (peasant) soldier, from whom by long and close proximity, or by birth, they were not far removed. As a class the professional regular officers were loyal to the Tsar.

Although the 1874 reforms made the officer corps more professional and created a strong trained reserve of other ranks which could be called back to the colours in time of war, they raised other difficulties and problems. The new officer society was very narrow in its outlook and was cut off from the court, the professions and political and intellectual circles, indeed from everyday life. The system of giving accelerated promotion to officers of Guard units and the General Staff at the expense of the line officer, and of permitting over-age and inefficient chair-borne officers to remain in the service, had a depressing effect on the junior and more energetic. Even fighting units were infected with the Russian bureaucracy of the times, so that officers became scribblers, spending hours every day on a multitude of inconsequential or unnecessary reports and returns. These deficiencies were brought to light during the heavy defeats in the Russo-Japanese War (1904–05).

For these reasons, the military career was not popular and by 1910 the officer strength was more than 5,000 short of establishment. Since all officers served on long-service permanent commissions, there was virtually no officer reserve. In time of war, officer replacements had to be found

Tsar Nicholas II, accompanied by his young son, Alexei, presents medals to his bodyguard unit in the spring of 1916. The entire royal family would be brutally assassinated in July 1918, with the young Tsarevich only 13 years old. (From the fonds of the RGAKFD in Krasnogorsk via www.Stavka.org.uk)

by calling up *praporshchiki* (ensigns of the reserve), former junior non-commissioned officer (NCO) conscripts with less than two years' service. A *praporshchik* had no training or experience as an officer, but had earned an early discharge from the ranks merely by virtue of having completed secondary education and becoming so-called 'officer material'.

Another weakness of the short-term conscript army lay in the difficulty of recruiting a reliable and experienced corps of long-service NCOs. There was no permanent cadre and despite every encouragement it proved difficult to induce the conscript NCOs to prolong their service. In consequence, the majority of the NCOs were found by promotion from the intake of conscripts. From 1914 onwards casualties, particularly in the infantry, were very heavy among regimental officers and senior NCOs.

Many of the replacement officers were *praporshchiki* or officer candidates from the intelligentsia, many with socialist revolutionary or egalitarian sympathies. Whereas the old type of regular officer, notwithstanding his many faults, was a simple soul who maintained his own rough and ready peasant discipline by fist or cudgel, his replacement generally hated military life and was often too lazy or too lacking in purpose to enforce orders or look after the welfare of the troops. And so after 1914 there rapidly grew a yawning gulf between officers and men. Contemporary World War I sources have stressed that the Russian soldier required more leading and driving than any other soldier in Europe. Well led, he was formidable; without leaders of quality, he struggled to make account of himself. The

The British had a significant training influence over the Russian Army, and therefore also on the men who fought the Civil War. Here we see British sailors of the Royal Navy Armoured Car Division teaching men of the Caucasian Cavalry Corps how to use Maxim-type heavy machine guns in the summer of 1917. (Nik Cornish at www. Stavka.org.uk)

soldiers, naturally enough, had the faults and the virtues of their history. Centuries of Tartar domination and Muscovite serfdom had robbed many of them of initiative. On the other hand, as though in compensation, history and environment had left them hardy, stoical and with great endurance. They were subject to sudden changes of mood for which they themselves could not account; they could be stolid or mercurial, good-humoured or grim, peaceable or aggressive, heroic or cowardly, kindly and generous or unbelievably brutal and cruel.

Before 1914, one recruit out of four had no knowledge whatever of the Russian language. Of the Russian recruits, four out of five could not read or write; all orders had to be read aloud to them. By German standards the 1914 Tsarist Army was inadequately trained and indifferently led. And yet the Russian soldier was undoubtedly superior to many of the troops of the Austro-Hungarian Empire and the efficiency of the Tsarist High Command compared favourably with that of the Habsburgs. The most reliable and probably the most efficient troops of the Russian Army were the artillery and the cavalry, and these maintained their morale and discipline long after the other arms were in a state of dissolution. At the other end of the scale were the sappers and miners, recruited mainly from industrial workers, a corps with a long record of disorder and mutiny in the years between 1905 and 1914.

A Russian Army machine-gun team at the end of World War I. They are firing the 7.62×54mmR PM-10 machine gun, the Russian version of the Maxim machine gun. It fired at 600rpm and was water cooled. Such was its reliability that it would serve on through both world wars. (Courtesy of the Central Museum of the Armed Forces, Moscow via www.Stavka.org.uk)

The Tsarist Army entered World War I unprepared and poorly equipped. Sufficient munitions and supplies were never produced for the 15.5 million men mobilized during the war; Imperial Russia had reserves of men but no rifles, horses but no saddles or sabres, and little ammunition for the guns available. Only six million rifles were manufactured against a requirement of 17 million; Britain, Japan and the United States could not make good the deficiency in time. Wave upon wave of Russian infantry attacked German positions with little or no artillery support, only to be driven back when just short of their objectives by the devastating weight of the defensive fire of the enemy.

THE REVOLUTION

By 1915, Russian losses had mounted to 2.3 million men and, at a secret ministerial meeting held early that summer, General Alexei Polivanov, the Minister for War, described the situation in the gloomiest terms, placing his hopes 'on the immeasurable distances, the impassable roads, the deep mud and the grace of St Nicolas'. The heavy losses had diluted and transformed both the commissioned and the non-commissioned officers' corps, and within the army a social revolution had already taken place. Yet the fate of the Romanovs was to depend not on the constancy of the army in the field, but on the draft and training units and the rear installations in the area of the capital. These rear units had one overriding motive, that of avoiding frontline service.

Tsar Nicolas II, the last of the Romanovs, had once more ignored the advice of his ministers when in September 1915 he had personally taken over the supreme command of the Russian forces and the field command in the West. The field command or Stavka was located not in Petrograd or Moscow, but in the Belorussian city of Mogilev. In neither Mogilev nor Petrograd itself was there a single trained and disciplined regiment with any experience of war, even of the Imperial Guard. On 8 March 1917, there began in Petrograd a series of mass civil demonstrations, sparked off by a shortage of bread, protesting against the war, the government and the police. Socialist Revolutionary, Menshevik and anarchist agitators took advantage of the situation and the police were deliberately singled out for attack. The Cossacks, instead of supporting the civil authority, remained passive. On Monday 12 March, a training draft of the Volinsky Life Guard Regiment killed its commander and,

1) Infantryman, 3rd Petrograd City Guard Rifle Regiment, 1918. The 3rd Petrograd Rifle Regiment was formed from the disbanded Semenovsky Lifeguard Reserve Regiment, which had been stationed in Petrograd. 2) Infantryman, Epifan Kovtiukh's Detachment, Army of Taman, 1918. The Army of Taman was a typical early Civil War formation, dressed in all imaginable types of clothing, from ex-Tsarist uniforms to civilian attire. 3) Commander, Naval Infantry Regiment, 1918–22. Naval infantry saw widespread land service, often in the hottest of actions, since sailors were renowned for their high morale and loyalty to communist ideals. (Andrei Karachtchouk © Osprey Publishing)

calling on men from the Preobrazhensky and Litovsky Guard Regiments to join it, mutinied. Petrograd was given over to anarchy and a few days later the Tsar abdicated.

The period between the first March Revolution and the Bolshevik November Revolution saw the desertion or self-disbandment of most of the old Imperial Army. The reins of administration had been taken up firstly by Georgy Lvov's Provisional Government and then by Alexander Kerensky's, although in truth both governments were accountable neither to themselves nor to the people but to the self-appointed Petrograd Soviet of Workers' and Soldiers' Deputies, one of the chairmen of which was Leon Trotsky. The many Soviets that sprang up all over the country would obey no order from the Provisional Government unless the Petrograd Soviet was in agreement. By the same token, the armed forces owed their allegiance not to Kerensky but to the Petrograd Soviet.

At this stage the revolution was still bloodless, but a heady spirit of liberalism was in the air. This quickly spread to the troops. By Military Order No. 1, published in *Izvestia*, the newspaper of the Petrograd Soviet, and by the 'Declaration of the Rights of Soldiers' that followed it, the armed forces were isolated from the parliamentary Duma and the Stavka, the control of military operations and warlike equipment being handed over to the soldiers' elected committees. Officers were not to be issued with arms, and troops were encouraged to refer complaints against officers to the soldiers' committees. Saluting and standing to attention outside duty hours were stopped, and the accepted modes of address such as 'Your Excellency' and 'Your Honour' when talking to higher-ranking officers were forbidden. The fanning of a mistrust of all officers as a reactionary class, and the removal of their authority over their men, equipment and arms, could lead only to the rapid disintegration of the Russian Army. A deep rift had already been driven between officers and the rank and file, and agitators were already urging, sometimes in the crudest and most violent terms, the replacement of officers by commanders elected from the ranks. Desertion was rife, the numbers running to millions.

If it had not been for the Bolshevik November Revolution and the civil war that followed, it is probable that the old Russian Army would have entirely disappeared. It was owing to Trotsky that the remnants were salvaged, and the new revolutionary Red Army owed its foundations to the Imperial Army of the Tsar; it was, as Lenin expressed it, 'built out of the bricks of the old'.

THE BIRTH OF THE RED ARMY

When the Bolsheviks seized power in Petrograd, they relied neither on the bulk of the mutinous soldiery nor on the peasants. Instead they created a situation in which industry and government organs were paralyzed and the armed forces were benevolently or apathetically passive. In the final outcome, the *coup d'état* rested on a few armed detachments sympathetic to the Bolsheviks, usually foreign units such as the Lettish Rifles, some turbulent revolutionary naval detachments and a hard core of armed factory levies known as Red Guards.

Lenin's views on the establishing of regular armed forces within the communist state were by no means clear. At one time he appears to have favoured a part-time armed militia and to have been against a permanent standing army. Before the March Revolution and during the short-lived period of the Kerensky government, his policy towards the military was in some respects parallel to that which he adopted towards industry. Lenin professed to believe that capitalism must be smashed, if necessary by anarchy, before it could be replaced by his own brand of socialism. And so he appears to have given his support to the system of soldiers' committees, probably because it destroyed the authority of the military commanders and broke down discipline. Without a disciplined military there could be no counter-revolution.

Lenin could not fail to learn the lesson of Kerensky's grossest error, namely, that of his neglect to win the allegiance of a reliable and disciplined body of troops. No sooner had the Bolsheviks seized power than they formed their own secret police, the Cheka, together with its own subordinate military detachments usually made up of Latvians, Serbs, Chinese or other foreign mercenaries

S. Kubelis, a member of the White Army's 1st Workers' Officer Company, who was awarded the St George's Cross for capturing a Bolshevik machine gun during the fighting for Kiev in the summer of 1919. (From the fonds of the RGAKFD in Krasnogorsk via www.Stavka.org.uk)

indifferent to Russian politics and largely impervious to White counter-propaganda. And so the kernel of the highly centralized police state was already in being.

Although Lenin professed pacifism when Kerensky was in office, the reality of power either revealed him in his true colours or forced upon him a complete change of policy; for, having done his utmost to discredit and subvert the Imperial Army, he was soon obliged to repair the damage and rebuild a regular armed force powerful enough to safeguard the new Bolshevik regime against counter-revolution and the steady eastward advance of the troops of the Central Powers. For the Kronstadt and Helsinki bluejackets, sailors of the Baltic Fleet who had been early supporters of the Soviets, had been penetrated by anarchists and were not amenable to discipline, whether Tsarist or Bolshevik, and the Petrograd Red Guards, although said to number about 20,000 at this time, had only very limited military value.

At the time, the Bolshevik November coup had appeared to be the final straw in breaking up what remained of the Russian Army. Large numbers of officers, alarmed at the bitter class hatred preached by the Bolsheviks and their allies, made their way either as armed bodies of men or individually in disguise, to the south-east, to the territories of the traditionally conservative Don Cossacks, to form there the first of the White armies. Yet many of the formations of the old Russian Army still in contact with the German or Austro-Hungarian enemy kept their organization and their cohesion in spite of their lowered efficiency and relatively poor morale. A proportion of the former officers still remained and these formations, providing part of what was known as the Western screens, were to form the core of the new Red Army. Elsewhere many former Tsarist officers, particularly those in the ministries and the larger headquarters, passed into the Bolshevik command organization without a break in their service. In this way part of the heritage of the old army was transferred to the new. Yet the new Red Army was not formally brought into existence until the official decree of January 1918, nor was there any clear pattern in its establishment. Side by side with the regular field formations providing the bulk of the screens, there was a mass induction of Red Guard members by the voluntary recruitment of industrial workers on an extendable three months' engagement at a fixed rate of pay of 150 rubles (150R) a month.

Although numbers of these must have included idealistic party workers, the majority came from the unemployed, anxious to get a meal ticket, together with a criminal minority. Elsewhere, outside Moscow and Petrograd, local soviets raised and paid their own military formations and detachments, recruiting them either from industrial workers or from former military units. The methods of command and administration varied from place to place and the commanders were either elected or appointed arbitrarily by local committees. Many of the new military commanders were Red Guard Bolsheviks or soldiers from the rank and file.

Lenin was forced to come to terms with the Central Powers at the Peace of Brest-Litovsk, signed in March 1918. This lost the Bolsheviks the whole of the Ukraine and part of south-east Russia in the area of Rostov-on-Don. General Lavr Kornilov's White Volunteer Army, the rank and file of which was made up largely of former officers, had begun to overrun the Kuban and the Caucasus. Finland, Poland and the Baltic States had already seceded from Russia and a counter-revolutionary movement in Siberia under Admiral Alexander Kolchak, aided by a Czecho-Slovak corps recruited from former prisoners of war, began to move steadily eastwards along the axis of the Trans-Siberian railway. Japanese troops were already in Vladivostok, and Britain, France and the United States, in an effort to bring Russia back into the war against Germany, began to ship materiel and military aid to the Whites in Odessa, the Caucasus, Siberia, Arkhangelsk and the Baltic States. The German military occupation authorities in the Ukraine, despite the fact that the Empire was now at peace with the new Soviet state, gave arms and moral support to their eastern neighbour, General Pyotr Krasnov, the *Ataman* of the Don Cossacks, in his struggle to maintain his newly found independence from Russia.

During the summer and early autumn of 1918, it looked as if the new Soviet regime would be extinguished. The majority, some of them probably the best, of the officers of the old Russian Army had either been driven out, often into the arms of the Whites, or murdered. Although the Reds were vastly superior to the Whites in numbers of men and materiel, their discipline and leadership were poor; command by committee and revolutionary fervour were not enough. Lenin and Trotsky, however, were hard-headed realists. The naval officer staffs who first came into contact with Lenin as early as December 1917 were surprised at his insistence on restoring discipline; the unquestioning acceptance of centralized authority had always been Lenin's credo.

In March 1918 Trotsky, the brilliant and impetuous Ukrainian, had left his post as Commissar for Foreign Affairs to become Commissar for War.

Equipping himself with an armoured train hauled by two locomotives and provided with a radio centre, a library and military headquarters, automobiles and a large military escort, he set off on his lightning tours of the various fronts, rarely at rest, covering thousands of miles in his travels.

Lenin, meanwhile, had no clear military policy except in his insistence on a military discipline that was eventually to prove even more exacting than the Bolshevik political discipline. He would not admit defeat and was prepared to pay a ruthless price for success in the lives of others, though the cost might be reckoned in millions. Yet, despite his lack of military experience, he closely followed the day-to-day conduct of the Civil War,

Red Army artillery officer cadets conduct training with a 122mm howitzer. Overall, the Whites had a nearly five-to-four numerical advantage in manpower over their enemy's 118,000 men. However, the Reds had greater artillery and machine-gun assets and much larger reserves in their immediate interior. (Courtesy of the Central Museum of the Armed Forces, Moscow via www.Stavka.org.uk)

Red Army artillerymen prepare to load and fire a Soviet-made Vickers 8in howitzer. The Russian Army had made extensive use of British-made artillery during World War I, and based some of its artillery instruction methodology on that of the Royal Artillery. (Courtesy of the Central Museum of the Armed Forces, Moscow via www.Stavka.org.uk)

threatening, chiding, often directly interfering with the details of the High Command. Trotsky, on the other hand, originally no better informed than Lenin in military matters, was closer to the military staffs and the actual conduct of operations in the field, and thus soon amassed a fund of knowledge as well as acquiring a certain expertise and flair for strategy and for military training and organization. Ruthless, vain and unfeeling, he was nevertheless a highly educated or at least a quick-witted man, and had the knack of getting on with the former officer staffs still in Red Army service, whose abilities he used to the full.

Both Lenin and Trotsky were of one mind in suppressing all command by committee. They soon sent the elected commanders packing. But Trotsky went even further. He had little faith in territorial or part-time soldiers or in partisan or guerrilla bands as a substitute for a permanent regular army. Repeated defeats in the field convinced him that the new Red Army would not win through to victory without the aid of professional officers and of NCOs. He won Lenin's reluctant support and on 29 May 1918 a resolution was agreed by the All-Russian Executive Committee changing the voluntary recruitment of the armed forces to one of enforced mobilization of workers and poor peasants. Former officers and NCOs of the old army, although hardly within this mobilization category, were subjected to compulsory call-up and, before the following November, 23,000 former officers and officials, including military doctors, veterinary surgeons and paymasters, and 110,000 former NCOs already formed part of the new Red Army.

1) Cavalryman, Vatman's Red Hussars Brigade, 1918–19. The black leather peak of the cavalryman's cap was somewhat smaller than the infantry version, and, following the period fashion, worn crumpled in a foppish manner. 2) Cavalryman, Bashkir Cavalry Division, Petrograd 1918–19. The Bashkir Division was composed, as its name suggests, of Bashkirs. This cavalryman's appearance is fairly characteristic of the period. He has the usual soldier's cap, khaki cotton *gymnastyorka* pullover tunic and *sharovary* breeches. 3) Kuban Cossack, Budenny's First Cavalry Army, 1918–20. This figure wears traditional Kuban Cossack attire: a small fur *kubanka* hat, a linen *beshmet* undershirt and a cloth *cherkeska* coat. (Andrei Karachtchouk © Osprey Publishing)

Trotsky, like Stalin, had a marked ability to make good use of the instrument left by his predecessors and adapt it to his own needs. Although he has been given the credit for introducing into the Red Army the system of political *komissari* (commissars), what he did was to continue and extend the innovations already introduced by Kerensky. Kerensky had been so antagonistic to and suspicious of the military that he had introduced into the armed forces political commissars to act as watchdogs on the generals and to serve as intermediaries between the commanders and the soldiers' committees. Other communist-appointed commissars were to be found in the Collegium for the Organization of the Red Army in Petrograd as early as December 1917.

Under Trotsky the appointment of all political commissars was regulated from the centre and their role was to protect the new regime from counter-revolution by keeping a check on the reliability of the commanders. In this way the commissar became the military commander's shadow and exercised what was in effect a dual command in that no military order of any consequence was valid unless it bore his countersignature.

At first, commissars were appointed down to the level of divisions, but eventually, before the end of the Civil War, they were to be found in all major units. This commissar system, although originally intended as a temporary political counterweight to the re-employed military officer, was permanently retained as part of the organization of both the Red Army and the Soviet Army.

The early commissar was not necessarily a Communist Party member. More often than not he was an applicant considered suitable for the job simply on the strength of his proletarian background and Bolshevik sympathies. His degree of military experience was of secondary importance, and many of the original positions were filled by ruffians in quest of power or loot. But, as Trotsky's fanatical and ruthless grip took increasing hold, not even the commissars were safe, and numbers were shot for the failure of their troops. Thus there came into being a new race of army political workers, callous, ambitious party members, full of tireless energy, driven on by fear of failure and dread of consequent denunciation.

The commissar, then as in the Cold War, was also responsible 'for the cultural enlightenment and the political, as well as the general, education of the troops'. He was expected to be the best-informed man in his formation or unit. He could never hope to have close ties with his subordinates and with the men themselves, without the presence in the

1) Commissar, Special Task Unit, 1919–20. Special task units, or ChONs, could be distinguished from ordinary Red Army units by their banners, which were covered with slogans and communist symbols, and by the youth of the men – mostly between 14 and 20 years old. All members of special task units also wore large red cloth stars on their left sleeves. 2) Commissar, Army of the Far Eastern Republic, 1921–22. The Far Eastern Republic (FER) was a semiautonomous territory with its own communist-influenced army known as the People's Revolutionary Army (PRA). The uniforms of the PRA were a combination of Russian, Japanese and American. In place of red star cap-badges, PRA men wore a yellow five-pointed star. 3) Member of the Soviet General Staff, 1919–22. The Soviet General Staff uniform for formal wear was garish in the extreme. The most colourful garment was a crimson cloth *gymnastyorka* (tunic) with black velvet collar patches, tabs and star on the left sleeve and silver aiguillettes on the right shoulder. With this were worn (despite the clashing colours): scarlet ridingbreeches with yellow side-stripes, a scarlet peaked cap with yellow piping ('borrowed' from the Lifeguard Hussar Regiment) and kid-leather jackboots with spurs. (Andrei Karachtchouk © Osprey Publishing)

ranks of communist agitators, party members whose task it was to talk with the troops hour by hour and day by day, on parade ground or in the barrack room, spreading the directed line of propaganda and carefully noting each soldier's reactions and views. Since the communist soldier was trained as an agitator-spy, all information picked up was carefully redirected to the commissar. In 1918, however, Trotsky's insistence on close control from the centre was bitterly opposed by many of the regional soviets, some of whom were scandalized by his use of 'the Tsar's flunkeys', the former officers. Most of these had come back to the army unwillingly, many of them only awaiting the opportunity to desert to the Whites. But the alternative to service was death or incarceration in a concentration camp, and their families were already held hostage for their loyalty. Trotsky seems to have treated the former officers on his staff, superficially at least, with tact and to have made good use of their talents; but elsewhere the re-employed officer, particularly if returning to command or regimental appointments in the field, was met with hostility and resentment alike from the elected soldier or party man whom he displaced and from the rank and file who regarded him with suspicion as a bar to their own advancement.

The commissar with whom the former officer was obliged to work most closely was in all probability the same agitator who had done his utmost to destroy the old Tsarist Army, one of the Bolsheviks who were believed by many officers to be in the pay of the Germans. Among the rank and file even the word 'officer' was anathema, so that the re-employed and rankless officers became known as 'military specialists'.

THE CIVIL WAR

The first threat to the new Bolshevik regime came in May 1918 from south-east Russia and the Caucasus. The rich, industrial, grain- and coal-producing area of the Ukraine had been lost to Russia by the signing of the Treaty of Brest-Litovsk, and the Politburo, now housed in the new capital of Moscow, was forced to rely on the corn from the rich farming areas of the North Caucasus. General Kornilov's White Volunteer Army, though only 5,000 strong, had already begun the conquest of the Kuban. Further to the north, Krasnov's Don Cossacks had ended their long flirtation with Moscow and were beginning to press northward into the Voronezh *guberniya* (province) and eastward towards the Lower Volga in order to round off the Don Cossack territories which, they fondly imagined, would remain an autonomous region independent of Russia. The Volunteer Army had already broken the railway from Rostov and Tsaritsyn (later Stalingrad) to Novorossiysk on the Black Sea, and the movement of the Don Cossacks towards the Lower Volga threatened to cut the rail and river communications between the North Caucasus and the capital. Both Moscow and Petrograd were already on very scant rations and were virtually without reserves of food.

At the beginning of June, Joseph Stalin, a comparatively little-known member of the Politburo, was sent to Tsaritsyn to organize the food supplies from the North Caucasus. From there he was to proceed to Novorossiysk. Circumstances kept him at Tsaritsyn where, at his own insistence, he was made the principal political commissar to both Tenth Army, which was holding the Tsaritsyn area, and the North Caucasus Front, the headquarters of which was based on the same city. Virtually dismissing General Andrei Snesarev, a former Cossack officer commanding the North Caucasus Front, together with his commissar, Stalin was for several months the *de facto* front commander, although his command was so scattered and his communications so uncertain that his control did not extend far beyond the territorial limits of Tenth Army.

These Russian Army troops are equipped with a 37mm Rosenberg trench gun, a light artillery piece that could be broken down into three sections for easy transportation during infantry advances or retreats. All told it weighed only 180kg but had a maximum firing range of 3.2km. (From the fonds of the RGAKFD in Krasnogorsk via www.Stavka.org.uk)

In Tsaritsyn, Stalin became closely acquainted with a number of military commanders whom he subsequently selected for the highest ranks in the Red Army: these included Kliment Voroshilov, the commander of Tenth Army, an old Bolshevik without military experience; Efim Shchadenko, the commissar; and Semyon Budenny, a cavalry sergeant-major who was second-in-command of the 1st (Socialist) Cavalry Regiment. Motivated by ambition and jealousy, Stalin secretly supported and intrigued with what was to become known as Voroshilov's 'Tsaritsyn opposition' to Trotsky's reforms and organizational methods. Trotsky's use of the former officer specialists was a measure that came under special attack, Stalin taking it upon himself to have the Cheka secret police arrest the officers as they arrived from Moscow. This widened the rift, not merely between Stalin and Trotsky, but more particularly between Stalin and those senior Red Army officers who were of the Trotsky school. When Stalin eventually came to power, nearly all of them paid the extreme penalty.

Although many years later Voroshilov, when Stalin's Commissar for Defence, extolled Stalin's military ability and the part played by the Tsaritsyn defenders during the Civil War, in reality the only threat to the revolution in the area of the Lower Volga came from the probes of the Don Cossack cavalry. In one of these thrusts, General Konstantin Mamontov actually penetrated to the outskirts of the city. But the Cossacks had always lacked staying power and they disliked being separated from their own territories and the support of infantry. Their discipline was too loose and their mounted training somewhat too specialized to turn them into regular fighting men.

Stalin's main contribution to the fighting was probably in supply, transport and equipment matters, for which he had some ability, and in the repressive police measures that, together with his Cheka colleague Felix Dzerzhinsky, he took against both the military and the civil organizations. Much more bitter fighting took place further to the south in the Kuban and the Caucasus where the White Volunteer Army, since Kornilov's death under the command of Anton Denikin, together with the Kuban Cossacks waged a bloody war against Red Guards and irregulars, estimated to have a strength of 100,000–200,000 men. There Russian committed against Russian, brother against brother, father against son, every kind of brutal and bestial atrocity. Whole populations of towns and villages were often butchered.

Further to the north in Siberia, Admiral Kolchak relied heavily on the support given him by the disciplined and trained Czecho-Slovak corps, but his relationship with the Czech commanders was bedevilled by politics, intrigue and petty jealousies. By the end of 1918 he had become dictator in the east, and had raised large White Russian forces by the conscription of former officers and other ranks back into the service. At first he achieved some striking successes, taking the great city of Perm, 1,130km east of Moscow, on Christmas Day; it appeared that he might join up with the counter-revolutionary forces near Archangel. But Kolchak was to fail because he lacked the determination and cold-blooded ruthlessness of his Red opponents and had no experience of handling troops in the field. His choice of subordinates was unfortunate and, even with sufficient armament and stores at his disposal, he was unable to overcome the problems of administration, movement and supply. His troops went hungry and unsupported.

Moreover, like the other White generals, Kolchak lacked popular appeal. To the Russian peasant and worker he represented the old discredited order of Tsardom. The Bolsheviks, on the other hand, enjoyed some popularity,

A *tachanka* (machine-gun wagon) operated by the Red First Cavalry Army. The machine gun is canted upwards to fire in the anti-aircraft role. Sailors, given their greater technical skills, often provided experienced cadres for the artillery, armoured car and armoured trains units. (From the fonds of the RGAKFD in Krasnogorsk via www.Stavka.org.uk)

even though limited and short-lived, among the workers and peasants because of their golden promises of redistributed land and workers' participation in the profits of industry. Even the non-Russian minorities had been promised autonomy.

But the population was for the most part tired and apathetic, and heartily sick of shortages and war. With the exception of the fanatical communists and the die-hard officer loyalists, men had to be dragooned into both the Red and the White services, and the figures for desertions on both sides ran into millions. Sometimes the men took to the woods and became bandits; but more usually they simply threw their weapons away and made off home. Both sides came to realize that prisoners, rather than being put to death or kept in captivity, could more profitably be offered the choice of death or enlistment with their captors. Their new recruits, however, were usually unreliable material; units frequently changed sides taking their arms with them, and then, liking their new conditions of service no better than the old, changed back again. Yet even in this problem of loyalty, the Reds had an advantage over the Whites in that the communists were better fitted, both by mentality and training and by their party and Cheka police organization, to keep a closer check on their military subordinates and a more repressive hand on their troops.

Numbers of Red commanders distinguished themselves in the fighting against Kolchak on the eastern front. Stalin was there on the northern flank for about three weeks after the fall of Perm, but his role was restricted to that for which he was suited, a Cheka purge of unsuccessful and unlucky military commanders and civil functionaries. Mikhail Frunze, an old Bolshevik and revolutionary assassin and later Commissar for War, commanded the right flank with some success. But the predominant role was played by Trotsky and his two principal military advisers, firstly Jukums Vatsetis, a Lettish soldier of the old Imperial Army, and then Sergei Kamenev, a former colonel of the General Staff who was the military specialist commander of the East Front and later, after July 1918, the titular Red Army Commander-in-Chief. With the withdrawal of the Czechs, Kolchak's forces began slowly to disintegrate, and in the following year he himself was caught and shot by the Reds.

The next heavy blow made against the Bolsheviks came from the Baltic shore, where a former Imperial general by the name of Nikolai Yudenich, with Estonian military and financial support, collected a White Russian force hardly stronger than an army corps and in the autumn of 1919 advanced eastward towards Narva and Petrograd. His success was immediate and within weeks White cavalry had reached the outskirts of the former capital. Trotsky was sent by the Politburo to organize the Red defences, and reinforcements were rushed by rail from the Moscow area. At the time, the world confidently expected Petrograd to fall within a matter of days. But Yudenich failed in his mission for two simple reasons. First, a subordinate neglected to cut the Petrograd–Moscow railway along which Red troop trains were racing into the city; and second, because Yudenich's communications were broken by the demolition of viaducts, and he was unable to overcome the well-nigh insuperable problem of supplying his own troops. With the onset of winter his men were near starvation and a few weeks later his troops fell back rapidly into Estonia.

The efforts of the White generals had hitherto been largely unco-ordinated, succeeding one another rather than concerted. The first campaign had been the operations of Kornilov's and Denikin's Volunteer Army in the far-away Kuban and Caucasus and Krasnov's thrusts on the Lower Volga. Then followed Kolchak's movement westward towards Moscow. Only when Kolchak was in retreat in the east did Yudenich attack from the north-west. Yet Yudenich's offensive was mounted at the same time as that of Denikin from the south.

It was at the time of Yudenich's thrust on Petrograd that the Soviet state appeared to be in danger of obliteration. Denikin, now the Commander-in-

A rather staged photograph of Red Army soldiers, taken on the Polish Front in 1920. The Red Army, in its early days, was a coalition of factions content to fight the Whites, and then each other when the Whites were no longer a threat. As the Civil War progressed, the Red Army became more homogenous, more Bolshevik in nature. (Courtesy of the Central Museum of the Armed Forces, Moscow via www.Stavka.org.uk)

Chief in south Russia, controlled the Volunteer Army under the command of General Vladimir Mae-Maevsky, Sidorin's Don Cossacks and General Pyotr Wrangel's Caucasian Army. Denikin had begun to advance in May 1919 from the Caucasus and the Don Cossack territory to the north of Rostov into Central Russia and the Ukraine. For the Ukraine had been re-occupied by the Reds after the withdrawal of the Austro-German troops in the previous November, and was torn by warring factions and armed banditry.

Denikin was fighting against the odds; he was greatly outnumbered by Bolshevik troops and had been unable to bring the Poles in on his side. He was, however, relatively well provided with British equipment and he numbered among his commanders some of the best leaders in any of the Russian armies, Red or White. His failure was one not of resources or of supply, but of strategy. His principal and probably correct aim was to take Moscow. But he dispersed his troops in a great 180-degree arc, and ordered them on to objectives as far apart as Odessa and Kiev to the west and Tsaritsyn and Saratov to the east. His subsequent success was admittedly remarkable in that by October of that year, very much at about the same time as Yudenich was nearing Petrograd, White troops had overrun almost the whole of the Ukraine and had moved into Central Russia, taking Kursk, Voronezh and Orel, little more than 320km from the capital; in the east, Sidorin and Wrangel had taken Tsaritsyn and were on the road to Saratov. The troops of the Bolshevik South Front had simply melted away. But Denikin's command had already been fatally over-extended and dispersed and now covered a frontage of about 2,575km. Winter was approaching and the presence of bandits, partisans and armed Ukrainian nationalists made the areas to his rear insecure.

The Soviet military commander of the South Front, a former officer by name of Gittis, was replaced firstly by Vladimir Yegorev and then, some weeks later, by Alexander Yegorov. Stalin was transferred from the West to the South Front as political commissar where he was joined temporarily by Trotsky.

From about this time dated the bitter controversy as to whether Denikin should be counter-attacked from the area of the Lower Volga in the east or from the north in the area of Voronezh and thence southward down the Donets Basin. The latter course proved the successful one and the credit for it was claimed by both Trotsky and Stalin. Much of Denikin's success had been due to his use of raiding cavalry columns under the Cossack generals Konstantin Mamontov and Andrei Shkuro, deep in the Red Army

"Генералъ Шкуро"

rear. Budenny's cavalry corps, reorganized as First Cavalry Army, was transferred from the Volga to the area of Voronezh in order to engage the White raiders. The Reds took their tactics from the pattern of the Whites and penetrated between the Volunteer Army and the Don Cossacks. By the end of October 1919, First Cavalry Army, which included in its columns the future cavalry leaders Semyon Timoshenko and Georgy Zhukov, had taken Voronezh and was moving rapidly southward towards Rostov-on-Don, hoping to envelop Sidorin and Wrangel in the Don bend and on the Lower Volga between Tsaritsyn and Astrakhan. To escape being cut off, Denikin began his long retreat to the Crimea and the North Caucasus; amid cruel scenes of violence and disorder the Whites were driven out of the Caucasus, but held on temporarily to the area of the Crimea. Denikin gave up his command to Wrangel. The last of the Whites were now doomed.

THE RUSSO-POLISH WAR

In 1914 Poland had long been partitioned between Germany, Austro-Hungary and Russia, eastern Poland being a province of the Russian Empire. Following the Russian Revolution and the collapse of the Central Powers, the new Polish Republic had come into being.

A Polish armoured train captured and repurposed by the Bolsheviks in 1919. Stalin later ordered that the train be renamed 'People's Hero Budenny', after the Red Army cavalry commander Semyon Budenny, one of Stalin's closest political allies. (From the fonds of the RGAKFD in Krasnogorsk via www.Stavka.org.uk)

A fervently nationalist Poland, bitterly anti-Russian rather than anti-Bolshevik, had no wish to see a strong Russia on its eastern frontier since it regarded this as a threat to its own existence. Józef Piłsudski, Poland's leader, trusted Denikin as little as he did Lenin, and in 1919 he had ignored Denikin's overtures for a joint Russo-Polish campaign against the Bolsheviks. Meanwhile, however, he was, through intermediaries, in secret correspondence with Trotsky. Piłsudski took no notice of Moscow's efforts to secure an armistice; he did not want peace. Nor, for the moment, did he want war; so he contented himself with awaiting the outcome of the Red/White struggle. In the long term he hoped to secure for Poland the White Russian and Ukrainian territories once held by the powerful 18th-century Kingdom of Poland. At the same time, he probably hoped to detach from Russia the remainder of the Ukraine and Caucasia, and make them into puppet states dependent for their existence on an alliance with Poland.

Meanwhile skirmishing and border fighting continued between the Poles and the Red Army and by 1919 Polish troops had already established themselves in Belorussia and Galicia as far east as Vilna, Minsk and Lvov. In April 1920, Third Polish Army suddenly attacked in great strength into the Ukraine. Advancing rapidly eastward, it reached the Dnieper and seized Kiev, the capital, in the first week in May.

The invasion caused a wave of indignation and national fervour among the Russian people and large numbers of volunteers, irrespective of class or political belief, offered their services to the Red Army. Once more there was a frantic reorganization of the Soviet High Command. Troops already deployed against Wrangel were withdrawn from the South Ukraine. Gittis was removed from the command of the West Front, making way for a former *leitenant* (lieutenant) of the Imperial Guards named Mikhail Tukhachevsky, an ambitious and energetic young officer, commissioned only in 1914, who had spent three years in German captivity before returning to Russia and joining the Bolshevik Party. Stalin, as political commissar, rejoined the old South Front, now redesignated the South-West Front, and still under the leadership of the military specialist Yegorov. Budenny's First Cavalry Army, with Voroshilov as its political commissar, was ordered back from the Caucasus to the area of the Middle Dnieper, arriving there at the end of May.

Yegorov's initial successes were due in no small part to the mobility of First Cavalry Army. Although this force numbered little more than 16,000

men it was boldly handled by Budenny; some success was due also to Timoshenko's 6th Cavalry Division. By the second week in June, the cavalry, together with Twelfth Soviet Army, had started to outflank the enemy and it looked as if Third Polish Army would be surrounded in the area of Kiev. The Poles fell back quickly, however, to escape the encirclement and Yegorov's South-West Front took up the pursuit westwards into Galicia.

Tukhachevsky was originally separated from Yegorov by the almost impenetrable belt of the Pripet Marshes, running nearly 500km from west to east and 240km from north to south. But the marshland gave way to firm and open country as the two Soviet fronts entered Poland. Tukhachevsky, with a force of over 100,000 men, comprising four armies and a cavalry corps, had already begun his own offensive in the north in the first week in July. The Poles were in full retreat. Vilna, Minsk and Brest-Litovsk were taken, and the West Front began to close on Warsaw. It appeared as if Poland itself were about to be overrun.

Yet the Red Army, standing on the threshold of victory, was decisively defeated. As many contemporary photographs show, a large proportion of the Soviet fighting men were little more than civilians hurriedly equipped

A mounted scout detachment of the 2nd Kornilov Regiment, 1919. The early Whites on all fronts were volunteers almost to a man. Heavily outnumbered, they survived through an intense commitment to their cause and by fundamental military competence. (From the fonds of the RGAKFD in Krasnogorsk via www.Stavka.org.uk)

with rifles. Units were apt to disintegrate at the first serious check, and there was a very high rate of desertion. Overmuch reliance had been placed on the revolutionary spirit of the Polish proletariat, but these, instead of going over to the Reds, resisted the Bolsheviks with all their might, fighting, sometimes in the Soviet rear, with shot-guns and hunting rifles. A French military mission had already arrived in Warsaw to assist the Polish High Command, and when the Poles counter-attacked, the Red Army troops began to give way.

Tukhachevsky had hardly three years' military experience of any sort and his deployment followed some half-learned school copy-book theme. His troops stood on the Vistula immediately east of the Polish capital and he had successfully contrived to envelop Warsaw from the north and north-west by extending forward his right shoulder. On this flank also he had deployed Gai's cavalry corps. But he had no uncommitted reserve and his own left flank, which had formerly enjoyed the protection of the Pripet Marshes, was open and vulnerable.

Sergei Kamenev, the military specialist commander-in-chief, in a directive issued in the first week in August, was said to have ordered Tukhachevsky's West Front on to Warsaw. Yegorov's South-West Front was ordered to move troops north-westward to close on Tukhachevsky's exposed left flank. It was later argued that Kamenev's directive to the South-West Front ordering First Cavalry Army and Twelfth Army away from Lvov and on to Warsaw was not clear. This may have been so. Certain it is that Stalin, Budenny and Voroshilov deliberately chose to misunderstand it, for even as late as the third week in August they were still resisting any orders that moved the cavalry army away from the Lvov axis. When they did move it was already too late. The Poles had enveloped Tukhachevsky's open southern flank and began to roll up the West Front from south to north. Hemmed in to the north by German East Prussian territory, the Red Army men either passed over the frontier to be interned *en masse* or took to their heels eastward in an attempt to escape the encircling pincer. By September all the Russian forces were in retreat and the Poles, following up, reoccupied most of Belorussia and Galicia.

Hostilities ended with the signing of the Treaty of Riga in October 1920. The Red Army had come out of the Polish War with little credit and its relatively poor showing was one of the factors which caused it to be much underestimated in Western Europe in the period between the two world wars.

1) Rifleman in winter clothing, 1919–21. This is the typical Red Army uniform of the last years of the Civil War. The *budyonovka* cloth helmet has rolldown sides and a star in the dark crimson infantry branch colour. 2) Sergeant-major of Artillery, 1919–21. The rank of *starshina* is denoted by triangles on the left sleeve. 3) Company commander, 1919–21. This commander is one of the so-called *voyenspetsy* (military specialists), former Tsarist officers and generals who, despite political opposition, were encouraged to rejoin the Red Army at a time when their skills were badly needed. (Andrei Karachtchouk © Osprey Publishing)

THE END OF THE CIVIL WAR

While the Russo-Polish War was being fought, Wrangel had attempted to take advantage of the situation by breaking out of the Crimea back into the former territories of the Don and Kuban Cossacks. At first he had some success but, after the signing of the Treaty of Riga, Red Army troops began to arrive from the Western Theatre. The South Front, commanded

Seen here during the 1920s, a Red Army digging machine at work. Mechanization of menial tasks was relatively rare, however, and the Soviets generally used their massive manpower for such labours. (Courtesy of the Central Museum of the Armed Forces, Moscow via www.Stavka.org.uk)

by Frunze, began a late October counter-offensive which drove the Whites back into the Crimean Peninsula. During November 1920 a final offensive was made into the Crimea across the shallow salt marshes of the Lazy Sea and the remnants of Wrangel's force were destroyed. Only the fortunate escaped with their families by ship from the terrible vengeance of the commissar and the Cheka.

A few months later Vasily Blyukher, one of the successful Red commanders in the Crimea, undertook the reduction of the last counter-revolutionary force in the Far East Maritime Provinces where the White general Grigory Semyonov, a brigand and puppet of the Japanese, held the railway between Khabarovsk and Vladivostok. It was not, however, until the end of 1922, after the evacuation of the Japanese, that Semyonov's forces were finally driven over the border into Manchuria.

AN ARMY WITHOUT CONFIDENCE

The Red Army at the end of the Civil War was a mass of partially trained, poorly equipped and ill-disciplined conscripts whose only wish was to go home. Its muster rolls numbered several million, but the desertion rate was very high and the bureaucratic army system so inefficient and cumbersome that the order of battle never totalled more than about 70 divisions. Many of these formations were divisions only in name, having strengths no greater than those of the establishment of regiments. Like the Whites, they were accomplished looters, having lived off the countryside for so long that the peasants and townspeople had been reduced to starvation.

Once more the communist leaders could not make up their minds what sort of defence forces they wanted. The Red Army in 1922 contained the old

NKVD Border Guards here train with a DP light machine gun, visually distinguished by its 47-round flat pan magazine, hence its nickname the 'record player' by Soviet troops. (Courtesy of the Central Museum of the Armed Forces, Moscow via www.Stavka.org.uk)

Stalin (left) and Kliment Voroshilov observe a military parade during the 1930s. Voroshilov was one of the original five marshals of the Soviet Union, and managed to steer his career past Stalin's persecutory gaze, finally retiring from public life in 1960. (Courtesy of the Central Museum of the Armed Forces, Moscow via www.Stavka.org.uk)

and the new: Tsarist generals of the doctrinaire kind, senior commanders who were formerly young officers or NCOs, together with others, often barely literate, who had come from factory floor or field; old Bolsheviks and fanatical communists, former White officers, some foreign-trained, others the recent output from Red military schools. The equipment varied from the modern to the long obsolete, and was of Russian, Japanese, US and British pattern. A few favoured a standing army, but most wanted a militia or loose guerrilla-type force under temporary or elected commanders.

Trotsky, possibly influenced by his military specialist advisers, wanted a return to an orthodox and regular army backed up by territorial reserve formations which in peacetime were to exist in a cadre form. But he was opposed both by the younger group of officer specialists such as Tukhachevsky and Ieronim Uborevich, and, more importantly, by Frunze and other older revolutionaries with a military interest. The 'Tsaritsyn Group', led by Voroshilov and Budenny, were Trotsky's enemies, and when, after Lenin's death, Stalin used Lev Kamenev and Grigory Zinoviev, his two colleagues in the governing triumvirate, to isolate Trotsky politically, the days of the Jewish Commissar for War were numbered. In 1924 Ephraim Sklyansky, the Deputy Commissar for War and Trotsky's trusted aide, was replaced by Frunze. Vladimir Antonov-Ovseyenko, another of Trotsky's close collaborators, was replaced as chief commissar by Stalin's nominee Andrei

Bubnov, formerly of First Cavalry Army. Stalin's henchman Voroshilov took over the command of the troops in the capital and together with Bubnov and Budenny was appointed to the Revolutionary Military Council.

Trotsky was now unprotected and in January 1925 was forced to hand over his post to Frunze. Tukhachevsky and Boris Shaposhnikov, a former colonel of the Imperial General Staff, were appointed as Frunze's deputies and Sergei Kamenev, until recently the Commander-in-Chief, became Chief of the Inspectorate. That year Frunze died unexpectedly. His death was certainly convenient to Stalin, for Voroshilov became the Commissar for War, a post he was to hold until 1940, and from 1928 onwards Shaposhnikov was chief of the newly redesignated General Staff.

Yet the opposition to Trotsky was based on personal and ideological grounds rather than on military logic; Trotsky's successors left the Red Army very much as they found it. In the 1920s the Soviet defence forces were restricted to a ceiling of 562,000 men organized into 31 regular rifle divisions, ten regular cavalry divisions and 46 territorial reserve cadre

An M1931 twin-turreted T26 tank conducts manoeuvres during a training exercise in August 1934. Such light and vulnerable vehicles would later be destroyed in their thousands during Germany's invasion of the Soviet Union in 1941. (Courtesy of the Central Museum of the Armed Forces, Moscow via www.Stavka.org.uk)

Red Army nurses during the 1930s. Large numbers of women served in the Soviet Army in both combat and non-combat roles. Indeed, women's frontline battalions were formed in the last year of Russian fighting in World War I, in 1917. (Courtesy of the Central Museum of the Armed Forces, Moscow via www.Stavka.org.uk)

divisions. There was neither the money nor the equipment for more. The officer in particular occupied a very depressed position; officer ranks, as such, were not in use, the very word 'officer' still being forbidden. Poorly paid, the officer messed with the rank and file and was expected to remove his commander's insignia when not on duty. The 1924–25 experiment of returning to the principle of one-man command in the event came to nothing, and real authority remained with the commissar.

Germany and the Soviet Union, friendless in a very hostile world, were drawn together. Both distrusted a Poland reinforced by the Franco-Polish Entente. Thus, from 1921 there came about a fairly close collaboration between the Red and German armies and between Moscow and the German armament industry. In exchange for training facilities in the Soviet Union, the Germans provided information, equipment and instructors, and the Red Army, like the Imperial Russian Army before it, began to take on a very heavy German bias in its organization, methods and terminology.

From 1927 onwards the Soviet Union professed to believe that it was once again threatened with foreign intervention and war. Its relationship with the West, particularly with Britain, was bad. The communist missions had been evicted from Nationalist China and the Chinese border clashes involving Blyukher's Far East Forces were to become more numerous. Stalin intended at all costs to concentrate on the expansion of heavy industry and the re-equipment of his forces; and so the first of the Five Year Plans was born, aimed at establishing the Soviet Union among the foremost of the world's industrial powers. A large part of the new or redeployed industry was sited in the area of the Urals nearly 1,600km to the east of Moscow, outside the reach of potential foreign interventionists. Soviet agriculture, at that time relatively inefficient, was later to be collectivized under state control in order to increase production, to redirect the surplus labour force into the factories and finally to break down the conservatism of a peasantry which was continually holding the nation to ransom by withholding its food supplies. This at least is how Stalin and the Soviet planners saw the problem. Their solution brought confiscations and deportations with mass starvation to the Ukraine and the North Caucasus. The Red Army was used to quell the riots which followed.

The early 1930s saw the gradual re-equipping and mechanization of the Red Army and its steady increase in size. Tukhachevsky had become

The T-26 was one of a new generation of Red Army light tanks to emerge during the 1930s. It was relatively fast and mobile, and armed with a 45mm main gun plus 7.62×54R DT machine gun. Its main problem was its light armour, which left the vehicle horribly exposed to German armour-piercing guns during World War II. (Wolf DW/CC/PD)

Inspector of Armaments and Yegorov had replaced Shaposhnikov as Chief of the General Staff. In Germany Hitler was in power and Europe was in a state of political turmoil. By 1934 all collaboration with Germany had been stopped. The Red Army now stood at nearly one million men and the Soviet government began to take an even closer and more urgent interest in strengthening the morale and efficiency of its armed forces. That year the Commissariat of the Army and Navy was renamed the Commissariat of Defence and, in an effort to improve the morale and status of the military commanders, political commissars (except where they were members of the military councils of higher formations) were made subordinate to the military specialists.

By 1935, in which year the Red Army had increased to 1.3 million men, officers' ranks were reintroduced, except that the Red Army still had no generals, general officers being designated as 'brigade, division, corps or army commanders'. For the very word 'general', like that of 'officer', was still anathema to the old Bolsheviks. The officers' pay and conditions were greatly improved, and all but junior officers were granted immunity

A unit of the NKVD on parade, shortly after its formation in 1934. The authority of the NKVD reached far across Soviet civil and military society; it was the central instrument of Stalin's purges between 1936 and 1938. (Courtesy of the Central Museum of the Armed Forces, Moscow via www.Stavka.org.uk)

from civil arrest unless the arrest should be approved by the Commissar for Defence. This was the restoration of a dignity enjoyed by the officer in Tsarist times, but in the Soviet state it was meaningless, as subsequent purges were to show. Five Marshals of the Soviet Union were created during 1935: Voroshilov, Budenny, Tukhachevsky, Yegorov and Blyukher. Meanwhile the mechanization and re-equipment of the armed forces were continued, and the leaders of the Red Army, uncertain of themselves and their military thinking, were urgently seeking contact with, and even reassurance from, military circles in Germany and France.

Red Army ski troops conduct cross-country manoeuvres during the 1930s. Ski troops gave some measure of mobility in circumstances where vehicular forces could not operate over wintery terrain. (Courtesy of the Central Museum of the Armed Forces, Moscow via www.Stavka.org.uk)

THE GREAT PURGES

Trotsky had been banished some years before, but Stalin still appeared intent upon ridding himself not only of those who at one time had been close to Trotsky and Lenin, but of any who might be in a position to challenge or undermine his own authority. To these were added those who in the past had done anything to incur his jealousy or displeasure. Yet the Great

Purges, which probably destroyed millions of Soviet and foreign citizens, involved for the most part people in all walks of life of whose existence he was totally ignorant.

From the very earliest days Stalin's fortunes had rested in some degree on the influence he had over the Cheka secret police organization, renamed the OGPU in 1922, and then in 1934 the NKVD. So in 1936 Stalin, by now supreme dictator, instructed the NKVD to undertake its widespread investigation into the state of the Soviet Union. Arrests followed investigations, with torture and execution or deportation, the NKVD being policeman, warder, judge and executioner, apparently accountable to no one but Stalin (indeed, shortly afterwards he decided that much of the NKVD itself should be liquidated). Investigations led to confessions and denunciations, most of them false and intended only to protect the victim's family; and so the purge spread like wildfire and became the terror which Stalin probably intended it to be.

The first of the public trials opened in 1936, and Tukhachevsky was named, as if in an aside, in one of the confessions. Almost immediately Red Army leaders began to be arrested by the NKVD. Any senior leader who had criticized or crossed Stalin in earlier years was doomed, together with any who had been on friendly terms with the so-called opposition elements. Many commanders were arrested for no apparent reason. Tukhachevsky was executed and, of the eight members of the military tribunal who condemned him, six were to follow him to the death chamber. Only Budenny and Shaposhnikov survived. The other two of the five marshals, Yegorov and Blyukher, were done away with. Thirteen army commanders and more than 400 corps, divisional and brigade commanders were arrested and disappeared. Yet it is significant that the small Tsaritsyn Group and those associated with Budenny's First Cavalry Army in the Civil War were, with a few exceptions, retained in their posts. Another reaction associated with the purge of the Red Army was the restoration of the political commissar to his pre-1934 position of equality with the military commander. Once more he could veto all orders.

World opinion of the power and effectiveness of the Red Army was not high. Not unnaturally, the prestige of the Soviet Armed Forces suffered further as a result of the purges. It was argued that the loss of so many of its high-ranking commanders must inevitably lead to a break in continuity and a grave loss in combat efficiency. Nor could the foreign policy or the political proposals of a dictator who appeared determined on slaughtering his own armed forces be taken seriously. In 1937 Shaposhnikov returned to the post of Chief of General Staff and the following year the control of the Soviet Navy was separated from that of the Red Army and put under its own defence commissariat. The Red Air Force, however, remained as an integral part of the Red Army.

SOVIET EXPANSIONISM AND THE THREAT OF WAR

In 1938 border fighting had broken out between the Japanese and troops of Blyukher's Far East Front in the area of Lake Khasan near Vladivostok. In August of that year, Blyukher had been purged, in spite of the fact that his troops had been not unsuccessful. The Far East Front was broken up into two separate armies, one under Ivan Konev and the other under Grigory Shtern, who, shortly afterwards, was arrested in his turn. More fighting flared up, this time to the west of Manchuria in the area of Khalkhin-Gol. There Georgy Zhukov, a former Tsarist cavalry junior NCO but by now an army commander, had been sent to the area to take command of operations. Fighting continued intermittently until September 1939.

The outbreak of war that month between Germany on the one side and Great Britain and France on the other brought to a head a number of outstanding military and political problems in the Soviet Union.

In September 1939 it was announced that henceforth the Red Army would be recruited from national servicemen who would be taken into the forces irrespective of their social origin. Previously, particularly in the late 1920s and early 1930s, recruits from a noble or middle-class background were discriminated against in that they were drafted into unarmed labour units where conditions of service were often particularly harsh. National service had been set at only two years, although NCOs had to serve for three, and the strength of the armed forces stood at just over two million men. That September, however, the conscription age was lowered from 21 to 19 years so that a further two annual intakes each of about 1,400,000 men became eligible for service. Their call-up over the next two years had the effect of increasing Soviet armed strength, actually with the colours, to nearly five million men.

By the terms of the secret protocol signed by Vyacheslav Molotov, the Soviet Commissar for Foreign Affairs, and Joachim von Ribbentrop, the German Foreign Minister, in Moscow on the night of 23 August 1939,

1) Trooper of Cavalry, summer home service uniform, c.1938. In 1938 the Soviet Union had the largest cavalry force in the world. and, together with the artillery, it was probably the best disciplined and trained arm of the Red Army. The cavalryman no longer carried the Tsarist lance but was armed with the M20 7.62mm Mosin-Nagant carbine, which was a shorter version of the M1891/30 rifle, and, like the Tsarist cavalryman, carried a bayonet as well as the Tsarist (or the later Universal Pattern 27) sabre. When fighting dismounted, he usually left`the sword on the saddle. Some soldiers, whose duties required it, were armed with the Nagant revolver rather than the carbine. The French-pattern steel helmet was very common at about this time. Horse furniture consisted of leather Tsarist dragoon saddles, numnahs and webbing girths, sometimes leather surcingles, and the double bridle Pelham port-mouth bits similar to those used by British cavalry. Rifles were always slung over the left shoulder to distinguish cavalry from Cossacks. **2)** Private of Infantry, winter field service uniform, c.1917. This typical conscript on the march is equipped with the M1891/30 Mosin-Nagant rifle. His right and left ammunition pouches do not match and

he has removed his water bottle from the hooks at the back of his belt, thrusting the cover flap through his waistband. A respirator is slung over his right shoulder. One of the features of the Red Army at this time (as of the old Imperial Army) was lack of uniformity of pattern of equipment and dress, even within the same unit. Several patterns of steel helmet existed, but the type shown here later became the standard type. **3)** Private of Infantry, summer field service uniform, c.1937. Except for his forage-cap (*pilotka*), this infantry private is hardly to be distinguished from a soldier in Tsarist times. The *gymnastyorka* was used before World War I and the belt and equipment are of Tsarist pattern, together with the method of carrying the rolled greatcoat either strapped to the pack or thrown across the left shoulder. The ammunition pouches are, however, of Soviet pattern although these also are very similar to those used in 1914. The rifle is of the 0.299in M1891 pattern (mounted type) with a bolt action and five-round magazine, which in 1930 was mass-produced as the Mosin-Nagant M1891/30 taking the 7.62mm round. It was effective up to about 550m. The bayonet was normally carried fixed and not in a scabbard. The steel helmet was not a general issue even in wartime. (Michael Roffe © Osprey Publishing) the Balkans, Finland and the Baltic States were declared to be within the sphere of interest of the Soviet Union. Poland was to be partitioned between Germany and the USSR, the Soviet Union claiming those areas to the east where the population were of Ukrainian or White Russian stock. On 17 September 1939, the Red Army invaded Poland, the troops being deployed in two army groups or fronts, the Belorussian Front under Mikhail Kovalev, and the Ukrainian Front under a Bessarabian Ukrainian, a former cavalry soldier of First Cavalry Army, by the name of Semyon Timoshenko. The war that would come to define the Red Army had just begun.

Soviet Army soldiers parade in 1941, the year in which they faced the crushing onslaught of the German invasion. All the men here are armed with the 7.62 × 54R SVT-40, one of history's first standard-issue semi-automatic rifles. (Sovfoto/Getty)

CHAPTER 2

DEFINING MOMENT, 1939-45

I N THE SUMMER OF 1941, the Red Army was the largest in the world;
but its enormous size could not disguise its serious weaknesses. It had
performed well against Japan in the Far East at Khalkin-Gol in 1939,
but its performance during its unopposed invasion of eastern Poland in
September 1939 was lacklustre. It gave the Germans the impression of an
army ill suited to modern, mechanized warfare. This impression proved
all too accurate in the winter of 1939–40, when the Soviet Union tried to
bully its tiny neighbour, Finland, into unilateral territorial concessions. The
small Finnish army humiliated the Soviets in one of the most embarrassing
fiascos of twentieth-century warfare. The Russo-Finnish War whetted
Hitler's appetite for invasion.

The sorry state of the Red Army was mostly due to Stalin's political
repression. As we have seen, the Red Army had been decapitated in the
purges of the late 1930s. It was not only the large number of officers killed
that proved so devastating: it was the quality of the victims. The cowed
remnants proved ill-suited to prepare the Red Army for its greatest
challenge. In the late 1930s, European armies were trying to develop the
new skills of mechanized warfare. The Red Army had all the spanking new

Recruits undergo rifle
training, despite there
being no uniforms issued.
Presenting instruction on the
Mosin-Nagant MI891/30 rifle
is a *starshy leitenant* (senior
lieutenant). Lectures were
the standard means of giving
training, and the troops stand
to attention to keep them
from dozing off. (Courtesy of
the Central Museum of the
Armed Forces, Moscow via
www.Stavka.org.uk)

tools: tanks, trucks and radios. But the loss of most of the experienced and far-sighted leaders in the Great Purge, and continuing political interference and executions, undermined these efforts. It is worth noting that the units which successfully fought the Japanese in 1939 had escaped the worst ravages of the purges, while the units in Finland were more typical of Red Army units in Europe.

The most visible evidence of political interference was the continuing efforts of the *komissar*. Each unit of battalion size and above had a commissar in addition to the usual unit commander. The commissar had to give his approval for any major order by the unit commander. Commissars did not need to have any particular military skills and were selected above all for their loyalty to the Communist Party. Many commissars kept their noses out of military business and concentrated on their main tasks of political indoctrination, morale-building and training; but many used their post to intimidate loyal officers, and to interfere in military matters of which they had no experience.

The situation was further exacerbated by the use of the Komsomol as an additional tool of the Party during the purges. The Komsomol was a youth organization that young soldiers could join before they reached the age required to enter the Communist Party itself. Membership in the Komsomol during 1937–38 increased dramatically due to Party encouragement. Komsomol members in military units were expected to hold meetings during which officers and commissars could be criticized and denounced. It became impossible to discipline soldiers in some units, since they would be provoked by the reproach to denounce the officer. Normal military discipline began to collapse, and severe demoralization took place. In the wake of the Finland fiasco, reforms began to be instituted, including a reduction in the role of the commissar in August 1940. But the damage was too extensive to repair in the few months that remained before the German invasion. The Red Army was also plagued by a lack of experienced officers; leadership was too often in the hands of incompetent, timid men who had been cowed into submission, and boot-licking opportunists.

THE *BARBAROSSA* CATASTROPHE

The German invasion of the Soviet Union, Operation *Barbarossa*, on Sunday, 22 June 1941 led to a series of staggering defeats and catastrophic losses. In the five months of fighting in 1941, the Soviets lost about four

Workers' Militia troops move through a wrecked factory. They went into battle bearing only one piece of military equipment, a rifle. In the early days regular Red Army units sometimes entered combat wearing working clothes. (Courtesy of TASS via www.Stavka.org.uk)

million men (more than a million dead, and the rest prisoners of war). This was 80 per cent of the total strength of the ground forces at the time of the outbreak of the war, and would amount to nearly 60 per cent of the military losses suffered by the Soviet Union in the whole four years of war. Armoured vehicle losses were close to 20,000 – about six times larger than the total size of the attacking German armour force. Some units fought with tenacity and incredible bravery, like the garrison of the Brest fortress; but many others folded up without a serious fight and surrendered. The criminally abusive treatment meted out by the Communist Party did little to engender loyalty to the Soviet state amongst the rank and file of Soviet soldiers.

Yet the Red Army managed to hold on. There were many fine young officers, too junior to have attracted Stalin's malevolent attention. Within a few months Russian attitudes began to harden. The fighting was no longer viewed as a defence of the Party, but a defence of the Russian homeland. Not surprisingly, the war is known as the Great Patriotic War to Soviet citizens. Reserves were called up, and by the end of 1941 the Red Army had been rebuilt to a strength equal to about half the divisions available at the outset of the war. The German Wehrmacht had finally overstretched its capabilities, and in bitter fighting on the approaches to Moscow it was finally stopped. Young officers were catapulted into regimental and divisional commands far beyond their experience. Many proved incapable, and as often as not died on the battlefield with their men. Many others learned the art of command under the most appalling of circumstances and helped lead the Red Army to victory after four bloody years of war.

The Germans retained the strategic initiative the following summer, ranging deep into the Ukraine and Caucasus in a drive for the Soviet oilfields. The summer of 1942 was very costly for the Red Army, with several catastrophic encirclements all too reminiscent of the debacles of 1941. But the Soviets were gradually learning their lessons. In the summer of 1942 they began deploying large armoured formations, the tank and mechanized corps. At first these were handled amateurishly. Experience and tactical skill in modern warfare came at a horrible price. But the skills were learned, as displayed most dramatically at Stalingrad in the winter of 1942–43. Stalingrad represented the high-water mark of the German invasion. Although it is often called the turning point of the war in the East, the Germans in fact retained the strategic initiative until the summer of 1943; it was the battle of the Kursk salient in June–July 1943 that marked the real turning point. Not only was the German assault decisively smashed,

A PM-10 Maxim machine-gun crew hammer out rounds. The riveted fabric belts were issued to the crew, who had to load the belt with loose cartridges. Empty belts were never discarded. Note that the Sokolov mount's shield and barrel jacket have been whitewashed. (From the fonds of the RGAKFD in Krasnogorsk via www.Stavka.org.uk)

but Soviet forces went over to the offensive on a strategic level, and would never again be seriously checked by the Germans.

Western views of the Great Patriotic War tend to be coloured by clichés and myths popularized by German generals in their books from the 1950s. The Red Army is sometimes seen as a great, plodding force relying on mass rather than tactical skill. At the small-unit level, the Red Army had its challenges; Soviet infantry platoons and companies were generally far more poorly trained than their German counterparts. Nevertheless, the gap in tactical skill between the Germans and Soviets narrowed as the war dragged on. The Germans were hard pressed to fill out their units, and by 1943–44, their own small-unit training declined. At higher command levels the Soviets began outpacing the Germans by the end of 1943. In the operational arts, the Soviet generals managed to bluff, baffle and overwhelm their German opponents. The debacle in Belorussia in the summer of 1944, which saw the complete rout of the German Army Group Centre, was the best evidence of the growing skill of the Red Army's commanders.

ORGANIZATION OF THE SOVIET ARMY FORCES

The Red Army (excluding the Air Force) comprised 19 branches from March 1936, growing to 21 branches by December 1941. These were divided into eight groups – six combat arms, services, and specialist officers – as follows:

(1) Infantry. The largest arm, it comprised rifle regiments ('Rifles' had formerly designated elite Tsarist infantry), mechanized battalions, motorized rifle ('Motor Rifle') regiments/battalions (1939), mountain rifle regiments and machine-gun battalions.

(2) Cavalry. An obsolescent branch since 1914, mounted troops were nevertheless still effective in open steppe country against infantry. It comprised cavalry regiments, Cossack regiments (from 23 April 1936) and mountain cavalry regiments.

(3) Armoured troops. These comprised tank regiments/battalions/companies, reconnaissance battalions/companies and (from 1940) motorcycle regiments.

(4) Artillery. This provided infantry support with super-heavy artillery regiments, heavy artillery regiments/battalions, field artillery regiments, howitzer regiments, rocket-launcher regiments/battalions, mortar battalions, anti-aircraft battalions and horse artillery battalions.

(5) Technical troops. These included engineer battalions/companies, electrical engineer maintenance battalions, ordnance battalions, pontoon engineer battalions (for bridging), construction engineer and road maintenance engineer ('Sapper') battalions/companies, railway engineer battalions, signal battalions/companies, motor transport battalions/companies and military transport and railway troops (31 August 1936).

This private (1/2) at the war's beginning wears the summer weight 1936 field uniform with 1941 distinctions, i.e., subdued collar tabs. He also wears the Kaska-36 helmet and old-style short marching shoes with puttees. The 1936 field equipment, of which little survived the first year of the war, includes a modern-style backpack, bedroll containing his greatcoat and shelter-cape, ration bag beneath the pack, two-pocket cartridge pouches, entrenching tool, water bottle, and gas-mask carrier. He is armed with the 7.62mm Mosin-Nagant M1891/30 rifle with the bayonet reversed in the carrying position. Also shown: a bakelite identification tube (3); a pointed type entrenching tool with carrier (4); an aluminium water bottle and carrier (5); a cartridge bandoleer holding 14 five-round clips (one pictured – 6). Later versions had cloth rather than leather securing tabs. Each of the rifle cartridge pouch pockets held two clips (7). The simple old-style cook pot (8) served as a multi-use cooking and eating utensil; low-topped laced marching boots (9); puttees worn with the low boots (10); BS gas mask and carrier (11). The horn-like projection between the eyes allowed a finger to be poked in to wipe fogged eyepieces, and scratch the nose. The air-filter is the T-5. (Howard Gerrard © Osprey Publishing)

(6) Chemical Troops. These comprised flamethrower battalions and anti-gas chemical companies.

(7) Services. These included the Supply and Administration Service, the Medical Service, providing medical battalions and field hospitals and the Veterinary Service, with veterinary hospitals.

(8) Specialist officers. Those who could be attached to units of any arm were technical officers, legal officers and bandmasters. Commissars ensured that unit commanders obeyed the Communist Party line.

MILITARY DISTRICTS

From the top down, the Red Army's command structure was first organized according to military districts. A military district (*Voenny Okrug* or VO) comprised a number of field armies, corps, divisions and other units. It was usually commanded by a *komandarm*, an army commander, from 13 July 1940 typically a *general-maior* (major-general). There were 18 military districts before June 1941, but four – Baltic Special, Orel, Kharkov and Odessa, all under enemy occupation – had been disbanded by September 1941. In time of war, military districts were converted into operational commands known as fronts, and five were transformed right away: Belorussian Special (became Western Front), Kalinin (Kalinin), Kiev Special (South-Western), Leningrad (Northern) and Transcaucasian (Transcaucasian). This left nine districts: Arkhangelsk, Moscow, North Caucasus, Central Asia, Ural, Volga, Siberian, Transbaikal and Far Eastern. As the Axis forces retreated, Steppe Military District was formed on 9 July 1943 from Central Asia District. Kharkov District was re-formed in September 1943, Kiev and Belorussian in October 1943. Of the four larger-scale commands known as Strategic Directions, which had been abolished in August–September 1941, the South-Western was re-formed in November 1941 under Marshal Timoshenko, to confront the Axis advance to the Caucasus, but was abolished again in May 1942. The Far Eastern Strategic Direction was activated 9 August–3 September 1945 for the Manchurian campaign, forming the 1st and 2nd Far Eastern and Transbaikal Fronts under Marshal of the Soviet Union Alexander Vasilevsky, former Chief of the General Staff.

FRONTS

In wartime a military district, which was essentially an administrative unit, became an operational army group called a front, typically with two to five armies plus corps and smaller units, including a strong air force contingent, under a *komandarm* or a *komdiv* (division commander). The Belorussian and Ukrainian Fronts were raised for the occupation of eastern Poland (September–October 1939); thereafter fronts – such as North-Western Front, formed for the Winter War with Finland (November 1939–March 1940) – were permanent wartime formations, remaining in being until 2 September 1945. To confront the Axis invasion of June 1941, eight military districts in Belorussia, the Ukraine, the Baltic, Transcaucasia and European Russia had formed 13 fronts by December 1941.

The number of fronts increased to 20 in late 1943, although most had undergone a second 'formation' or several redesignations. Stavka also retained a General Headquarters (GHQ) Strategic Reserve (RVGK) for emergency deployment. In October 1943, several fronts were reorganized as numbered 'Baltic', 'Belorussian' and 'Ukrainian' Fronts, to give the propaganda impression that these nations were liberating their own territories without Russian assistance. The fronts can be divided into five operational theatres:

It is often claimed that Red Army troops could not perform any other jobs but their own. Even though they may not have been initially trained on other platoon weapons, they often used them in the field. Here a section commander familiarizes his men with the 7.62mm DP machine gun. (Courtesy of the Central Museum of the Armed Forces, Moscow via www.Stavka.org.uk)

(1)   Northern. Six fronts: one (Karelian) fighting in the Arctic and Karelia, five (Leningrad, North-Western, Volkhov, Kalinin/1st Baltic, later Baltic/2nd Baltic) defending Leningrad and threatening the Baltic States.

(2)   Central. Three fronts defending Moscow and its flanks: Western, Central/Belorussian (formerly Southern Theatre) and Bryansk.

(3)   Southern. The critical theatre, with six fronts defending Stalingrad and its flanks: Voronezh/1st Ukrainian, Reserve/Steppe/2ndUkrainian, South-Western/3rd Ukrainian, Southern/4th Ukrainian, South-Eastern/Stalingrad/Southern (reassigned to Central Theatre in February 1943) and Stalingrad/Don/Central.

(4)   Caucasus. Three fronts, defending the Caucasus: Caucasus/Crimean/North Caucasus, North Caucasus and Transcaucasus.

(5)   Far Eastern. Two fronts, defending the Soviet Far East from a possible Japanese attack, and providing reinforcements for the West: Transbaikal and Far Eastern.

During 1944 the frontline narrowed as the Red Army advanced westwards, and so the field armies were concentrated into 14 fronts, further reducing in May 1945 to nine plus a cavalry-mechanized group, plus three fronts for Manchuria.

ARMIES

The basic strategic formation was the *armiya* (field army), commanded by a *komandarm*. This would initially have been a major-general, but by 1942 might also be a *general-leitenant* (lieutenant-general). Each military district raised up to five armies, to defend the home district or transfer to other districts under threat. Sixty armies (designated by numbers Third–Sixty-First, and Coastal) were in existence in September 1939–December 1941. The M41 army – in other words, the 1941-pattern structure – usually comprised army headquarters (HQ) troops including three regiments (replacement, construction engineer, and signals), and 12–14 battalions (two reconnaissance, security, two engineer, road maintenance engineer, ordnance, two to four motor transport, chemical, flamethrower and penal), plus one to three corps. After July 1943, army-level artillery included mixed artillery brigades, and anti-aircraft, anti-tank, mortar, rocket-launcher, and self-propelled artillery regiments, and armies also had independent tank regiments. From 1943, engineers were formed into assault engineer-sapper brigades from Front HQ or GHQ Reserve, for special demolition, bridging or assault missions.

Troops of the Lithuanian 16th Klaipeda Red Banner Rifle Division. This was one of the few national formations raised and one of even fewer with a distinctive unit insignia. (From the fonds of the RGAKFD in Krasnogorsk via www.Stavka.org.uk)

An assault engineer-sapper brigade comprised four to five engineer sapper battalions, plus flamethrower, motorized engineer, reconnaissance, and light transport companies. Also at army level, 62 *aerosani* (armoured snowmobile) battalions were formed in January 1942 for action on frozen ground and lakes, but by December 1943 these had been reduced to 57.

Twenty elite armies were formed as 'Guards', 'shock' or 'tank' armies, usually in GHQ Reserve to spearhead assaults. The Guards Army was established in August 1942, with up to 12 infantry divisions and tank corps, many of them already Guards formations. Ten armies had been redesignated as Guards armies by April 1943. The Shock Army, introduced in November 1941, had extra tank units; by December 1942, five armies had re-formed as First–Fifth Shock Armies. The Tank Army was established on 25 May 1942, and First–Fifth Tank Armies had formed by July 1942. Each had two tank corps and two rifle divisions (the latter replaced in September 1942 by a mechanized or cavalry corps), and by April 1943 had nine supporting artillery regiments: two anti-tank, two anti-aircraft, two mortar, two self-propelled, and one rocket-launcher. The veteran First Cavalry Army remained on the Far Eastern Front. The First–Tenth Construction Engineer Armies were allocated (up to three to a front) to build defensive works, but by October 1942 all had disbanded. The Reserve Army was formed by Stavka as an extra strategic reserve; its First–Tenth Armies were formed April–July 1942, but soon re-formed as field armies.

By 1942 there were 71 armies, later redesignated 'combined-arms' armies', many of which had been re-formed several times. However, in 1943 seven armies and in 1944 six armies were permanently disbanded, and their personnel redeployed to other armies or rear area garrisons. A further five armies were redesignated Guards armies. Thus by May 1945 there were 53 combined-arms armies. A combined-arms army comprised an army HQ with up to 14 specialist battalions, with anti-aircraft divisions/regiments, artillery divisions/brigades/regiments, self-propelled artillery regiments/ battalions, anti-tank or tank-destroyer brigades/regiments, rocket-launcher regiments, mortar and signal regiments, an assault engineer-sapper brigade, tank brigades/regiments, a tank or mechanized corps, and three to four rifle corps, the number and strength of these units varying widely.

CORPS

At the outbreak of the war there were 109 corps in the Red Army: one special, three territorial rifle, five tank, seven cavalry, 31 mechanized, and 62 rifle. A field army required three rifle corps; but due to the massive mobilization in June 1941, the shortage of qualified generals after the Great Purge, and the speed of the Axis advance, in fact only about 62 (numbered 1–62) of the 180-odd corps HQs required were actually formed. Consequently, Stavka abolished corps HQs on 15 July 1941, leaving each hard-pressed army commander to control nine rifle and other divisions directly. The unwieldy absence of any intermediate echelon between a field army HQ and its divisions, however, led to their reintroduction in 1942; 200 corps were formed – almost double the 1941 number.

Corps and divisions underwent rapid reorganization in 1942–43 as the Red Army contained the Axis threat and then re-equipped for counter-attacks, but from January 1944 the situation had stabilized. A total of 244 corps were operational: one cavalry, six mechanized, seven Guards cavalry, eight Guards mechanized, nine breakthrough artillery, 12 Guards tank, 25 tank, 41 Guards rifle and 135 rifle.

The Rifle Corps was ordered in early 1942 but was not common until 1943. The 26,500-strong M42 (1942-pattern) Rifle Corps typically had four units of corps HQ troops (engineer, machine-gun and medical battalions and a reconnaissance company), a field artillery regiment and two to three rifle divisions. Some 36 Guards rifle corps were formed (numbered 1–36), as new or converted rifle or airborne formations, often assigned to Guards and shock armies. A Guards rifle corps contained at least one Guards rifle division.

Tank corps were reintroduced from 31 March 1942. The 5,603-man M42 Tank Corps had no HQ troops, just two tank brigades (40 tanks each) and a three-battalion motor rifle brigade. This organization proved weak, and by December 1942 a tank corps had six main corps HQ units – a reconnaissance battalion with motorcycle and armoured-car companies, a rocket-launcher battalion and four companies (mining engineer, fuel transport, two maintenance) – plus three 1,038-man M42 tank brigades (53 tanks each), and a 4,653-man motor rifle brigade. The M43 Tank Brigade, introduced November 1943, had brigade HQ troops including a motorized sub-machine gun battalion and anti-aircraft machine gun and supply companies, plus three tank battalions (21 tanks each).

In all, 31 tank corps were formed, numbered 1–31. However, the Tank Corps was too small to challenge the German Panzerdivision, and from September 1942 the more powerful 15,581-strong M42 Mechanized Corps was formed. This had 175 tanks with substantial infantry support. Corps HQ troops included three regiments (self-propelled artillery, anti-aircraft and anti-tank), five battalions (rocket-launcher, motorcycle, engineer and

With a lack of infantry armoured fighting vehicles in its inventory, the Soviet Army frequently transported troops into battle riding on the outside of tanks. Such a position was appallingly vulnerable to sweeps of German machine-gun fire. (Courtesy of the Central Museum of the Armed Forces, Moscow via www.Stavka.org.uk)

maintenance) and two companies (mining engineer, fuel transport), and the corps comprised one motor rifle and three mechanized brigades. The M43 Mechanized Corps, introduced 1 January 1943, had 15,018 personnel but 204 tanks. Corps HQ troops now included a mortar regiment, a mixed 25-gun self-propelled artillery regiment (expanded August 1943 to three regiments), an anti-tank battalion (abolished August 1943), and a reserve tank battalion with 20 tanks.

Nineteen cavalry corps (numbered 1–19) were formed between December 1941 and February 1943, but by August 1943 all except 15th Cavalry Corps – under Fourth Army HQ in Transcaucasia – had been disbanded or redesignated as Guards. A Guards cavalry corps followed the M42 organization but with three Guards cavalry divisions. Seven Guards corps had formed between November 1941 and February 1943 (numbered 1–7), including 4th Kuban Cossack Corps and 5th Don Cossack Corps. By late 1944 there were nine breakthrough artillery corps (numbered 2–10), assigned as front or army HQ troops to control breakthrough artillery and artillery divisions. A breakthrough artillery corps usually comprised three rocket-launcher brigades and three breakthrough artillery divisions. Anti-Air Defence (PVO) controlled 79 M43 anti-aircraft divisions, each division having only 1,973 men, supported by barrage balloon divisions, each division containing a number of balloon detachments.

DIVISIONS

During this period 679 divisions of all types were operational, usually under a major-general or *polkovnik* (colonel); many underwent second and third formations as they were destroyed in action. The division reflected the general composition of the land army, being classified as rifle (infantry), tank, motorized, cavalry and artillery, plus some specialist entities such as breakthrough artillery divisions and Guards mortar divisions. The individual composition of each type of division, across the entire period of World War II, is a complex topic, the tables of organization and equipment changing as the Soviet Union adjusted both to scything losses, materiel and manpower expansions and to tactical adjustments as the Red Army moved from the defensive to the offensive position. We will see this evolving reality by narrowing our focus to the Soviet rifle divisions. These were the backbone of the Red Army, hence we shall explore in some detail the life and experience of the individual soldier within this branch of service, and the smaller regiment, company, platoon and section structures that defined

Opposite: A Red Army artillery crew man an M1937 152mm howitzer on the Eastern Front. Soviet use of artillery was heavy but could be tactically unimaginative, and mainly focused on enemy frontline positions rather than the more valuable rear areas. (Courtesy of the Central Museum of the Armed Forces, Moscow via www.Stavka.org.uk)

his organizational parameters. Before doing so, we should note, however, some of the other types of troops who eventually brought victory in the Great Patriotic War.

CAVALRY

The Red Army used cavalry forces more extensively than any other army during World War II. The Soviet cavalry forces had been substantially trimmed back after 1939, many of the old cavalry units forming the basis for new tank formations. The retention of this colourful and heroic branch was due to its prominent role in the Civil War, and to the personal sentiments of many of Stalin's old cavalry cronies like Budenny and Voroshilov. At the outset of the war there were nine cavalry divisions and four mountain cavalry divisions. They did not play a prominent role in the summer fighting; in August 1941 their establishment was considerably reduced from a theoretical strength of 9,240 men to a new light cavalry division with only 3,000 men. Rather than disappearing, Soviet cavalry divisions expanded in number. By the end of 1941 they reached 82 divisions. However, it should be

Red Army cavalry on the charge. As an offensive instrument, horse-mounted cavalry were quickly abandoned after the catastrophes of combat in 1940–41, but they had a continued utility as reconnaissance troops. (Courtesy of the Central Museum of the Armed Forces, Moscow via www.Stavka.org.uk)

noted that these formations were so small that they were really equivalent to brigades. They were normally formed into corps with two or three divisions, these cavalry corps being closer to a true division in strength.

The sudden expansion of the cavalry was due to the severe weakness of the Red Army in modern mechanized forces. The cavalry branch was used primarily as mounted infantry, and for scouting. In the wild Russian terrain, and in bad weather conditions, cavalry were usually more mobile than motorized formations on trucks. Indeed, the Soviets successfully used cavalry units alongside tank units in curious mobile attack groups. Even the Germans realized the utility of cavalry under the conditions of the Eastern Front, and expanded their mounted forces after their experiences in the winter of 1941/42.

The year 1942 was the heyday of the Red Army cavalry. In part this was because Russian cavalry had traditionally come from the southern lands, where much of the 1942 fighting took place. Many national cavalry divisions were formed from Central Asian troops.

The decline of Soviet cavalry was due to the revitalization in the summer of 1942 of the Soviet mechanized formations which took over the burden of mobile operations. By the summer of 1943 the cavalry had been trimmed back to 27 divisions. Cavalry continued to serve right through to the end of the war, however. During Operation *Bagration* in Belorussia in the summer of 1944, the 3rd Guards Mechanized Corps was linked up with the 3rd Guards Cavalry Corps to form a special Horse Mechanized Group (KMG) which was used with considerable success in the wooded areas of the western USSR. One of the most famous cavalry operations of the war came in August 1945, with the attacks of the KMG in the short war with Japan in Manchuria.

TANK AND MECHANIZED FORCES

Although the tank and mechanized forces of the Red Army amounted to only a tenth of the army's strength, they had a disproportionate influence on its eventual victory. The mechanized forces in 1941 were massive: numbering 29 mechanized corps, each with two tank divisions and one motor rifle division, they were far larger than the Panzer units of the invading Wehrmacht. Indeed, the Germans had only about 3,500 tanks against about 28,000 Soviet armoured vehicles. But the Soviet mechanized force of 1941 was a paper tiger; by December 1941, the Soviets had only about 2,000 tanks left to confront the Germans in European Russia.

Soviet ISU-22 tank destroyers on the offensive. The vehicle was armed with an A019S 122mm gun, and alongside the SU-152 and ISU-125 was capable of destroying the heaviest German battlefield armour at long ranges. (From the fonds of the RGAKFD in Krasnogorsk via www.Stavka.org.uk)

The Soviet tank force in 1941 was made up primarily of T-26 infantry tanks and BT cavalry tanks. These tanks have often been excessively disparaged. In fact, they were capable designs – a bit light on armour, but well armed with a 45mm gun. They were certainly comparable to the German PzKpfw II, which still made up a significant part of the Panzer force. Their main problem lay not in their design, but in their state of repair. The massive build-up of the Red Army in the 1930s reflected an obsession with numbers. Soviet factories churned out large quantities of tanks and armoured cars; but many were defective, and the factories largely ignored the mundane question of spare parts. As a result, by 1941 44 per cent were broken down and in need of rebuilding, and 26 per cent needed significant repair. Soviet tank units left a stream of broken-down tanks behind them as they retreated.

The Soviet tank force was in the process of rebuilding with a new generation of excellent new designs, including the T-34 medium tank and the KV heavy tank. The T-34 was a revolutionary design and a major advance in tank technology. The T-34 and KV gave the Germans a real shock in 1941; however, they had no decisive impact on the fighting, for two reasons. To begin with, both vehicles were very new and had serious outstanding technical issues. They had been rushed into production and suffered from mechanical problems with their engines and transmissions, which led to excessive breakdowns. Second, Soviet mechanized tactics were immature, especially when facing an experienced tank force like the German *Panzerwaffe*.

In the late summer of 1941, as we have seen, the Red Army abandoned all large armoured formations, abolishing the mechanized corps and disbanding most of the surviving tank divisions. The Soviet commanders did not have the experience, skill or equipment to handle these enormous units. Instead, they went back to basics. The new formations were tank brigades, roughly equivalent to a (Western) battalion of tanks with a motor rifle company added to round it off. By the summer of 1942 the Soviets had gained enough confidence in the use of armour that they began forming larger armoured units again. The first use of the new formations in the summer of 1942 was very discouraging, and several of the new units were virtually wiped out by the veteran German Panzer force. But the Soviets gained invaluable experience, and by the winter of 1942 the tank and mechanized corps were finally replacing the cavalry as the Red Army's fast, mobile force. The record of tank and mechanized corps in the savage winter fighting around Stalingrad in January 1943 showed that the Soviet tank force had finally come of age.

More than 84,000 T-34s of all variants were produced between 1937 and the late 1950s. The vehicle offered excellent mobility, speed, decent armoured protection and a gun respected by the German armoured counterparts. The T-34/85, with its high-velocity 85mm gun, was arguably the finest all-round tank of World War II. (From the fonds of the RGAKFD in Krasnogorsk via www.Stavka.org.uk)

The T-34 had finally had the bugs wrung out of it and was proving a very capable design. The KV tank, in many respects, was a disappointment; though it was very well armoured, its gun was the same as that used on the T-34, but its mobility was not as convincing. Soviet tank battalions at the beginning of 1942 were mixed, fielding a company of KVs, a company of T-34s and a company of light tanks. This mixture proved impractical, and as the year dragged on the Soviets gradually developed homogenous tank brigades based around the T-34 alone. KV heavy tanks were relegated to independent tank regiments for infantry support, as their slow speed made them unsuitable for use in T-34 formations.

Soviet tactical shortcomings stemmed from two main areas of difficulty: training and vehicle design. Soviet tank training, like most Soviet training during the war, was constrained by the enormous demand for manpower. The average Red Army tanker received considerably less training than his German counterpart. German tankers were very critical of Soviet driver training, for example. Soviet tanks often drove along the crest of hills or along predictable routes since this made driving easier; they did not make use of terrain to hide their vehicles from enemy fire.

A unit of Soviet tankers receive their orders during a training exercise, with their T-34 tanks waiting behind them. (Courtesy of the Central Museum of the Armed Forces, Moscow via www.Stavka.org.uk)

Also important were deficiencies in Soviet tank design. Soviet tanks during the war focused on the big three: armour, mobility and firepower. Soviet tanks were usually on an equal footing with German tanks when judged by these criteria. Their main shortcomings were in crew management. In the early years of the war, the T-34 and KV used an archaic crew configuration with the commander doubling as loader. This distracted him from his main tasks of locating targets and directing the tank. German tanks used three-man turret crews, leaving the commander free to command. The Soviet tanks also suffered from extremely poor commanders' stations. German tank commanders generally operated with their head outside, scanning the horizon. Soviet tanks were poorly suited to this, and on early versions of the T-34 and KV it was virtually impossible for the commander to operate in this fashion. That the Soviets appreciated these deficiencies is evident in the tanks that began to appear in 1943, like the T-34/85, and IS-2. However, the Soviets continued to build the wretched little T-60 and T-70 into 1943, largely because the automobile plants that manufactured them were incapable of building the larger T-34. In 1943 they switched to the SU-76 assault gun, which became a staple of the infantry formations.

The summer campaign of 1943 saw the largest armoured confrontation of the war in the area around Kursk–Orel. On a tactical level, Soviet tank units still had many lessons to learn from the Germans; but on an operational level the Soviet commanders were very adept in the use of mobile forces, and the Germans finally lost strategic initiative on the Eastern Front. By 1943 the quality gap between the Soviet and German tank crews had narrowed greatly. German training began to slip down to the Soviet level.

The German adoption of the Panther as their new main battle tank in 1943 forced the Soviets to switch the balance of their tank programmes in 1944–45. The Soviets had become very dissatisfied with heavy tanks due to problems with the KV and had allowed heavy tanks to fade away by the summer of 1943; but with the appearance of the Panther, they were forced to reinvigorate their heavy tank units. They responded with the IS-2 Stalin. Although called a 'heavy' tank by the Soviets, it was in fact in the same size and weight class as the Panther. After 1943 the new, upgunned T-34/85 made up the bulk of the Soviet tank force, but heavy armour like the IS-2 (and its tank destroyer cousins the IS-C-122 and ISU-152) made up a larger percentage of the Red Army mechanized force than ever before.

AIR ASSAULT FORCE

The Red Army was the first European army to experiment with airborne forces on a large scale. Soviet paratroopers were used in the war with Finland, and during the occupation of Romanian Bessarabia in 1940. At the outset of the war in 1941, there were five airborne Airborne Assault Troops (VDV) corps in Europe and a brigade in the Far East. Soviet airborne operations during World War II were hampered by the lack of transport aircraft. The Luftwaffe shot up most of the TB-3 heavy transport aircraft in June 1941, and the VDV units had to make do with transports obtained from the civilian Aeroflot. As a result, the airborne corps were used mainly as elite infantry during the 1941 fighting.

The first major airborne operations of the war began in January 1942, but a combination of weather and lack of airlift doomed them to failure. The largest of these operations was an attempt to drop the 4th Airborne Corps into the Vyazma area: it was a fiasco. To airlift the corps in a single jump would have required 600 aircraft; they had 22. The air drops began on 27 January and were not completed until 23 February, in very rough winter conditions. The corps was badly scattered, and ended up fighting its way back to Soviet lines in isolated groups until June 1942. As a result of the lack of aircraft in 1942, the remaining airborne corps were first converted to Guards rifle divisions, only to be reconverted back to Guards airborne divisions beginning in September 1942. Most remained in service as infantry units in spite of their titles. The last major airborne drop in the European theatre took place in September 1943 when the 1st, 3rd and 5th Guards Airborne Brigades were dropped over the Dnieper River to secure a bridgehead. It was a bloody failure. The Soviets conducted a number of small-scale drops using naval infantry and improvised army units, but in general Soviet air assault operations in the Great Patriotic War were failures.

ARTILLERY

Soviet artillery was the killing arm of the Red Army in World War II. Soviet sources claim that it accounted for 60–80 per cent of enemy casualties. Although the artillery was very important in the fighting, it lost the decisive impact it had possessed in World War I, largely due to the decisive contribution of armoured vehicles and the more mobile nature of the war. Soviet artillery had long been the favourite combat branch of the Russian Army; it attracted many of the most skilled weapons designers and talented officers.

At the outset of the war, rifle divisions were equipped with two artillery regiments with 76mm, 122mm and 152mm guns and howitzers. The heavy losses of equipment in 1941 led to major cuts in divisional artillery; this was reduced to one regiment with a battalion of 76mm guns (like the ZIS-3) and another with 122mm howitzers. In addition, each rifle regiment had a battery of short-barrelled 76mm regimental guns. Guns above 122mm howitzers were retained in front- and army-level units. Rifle divisions came to depend very heavily on mortars to supplement their tubed artillery.

Divisional artillery expanded later in the war, mostly in terms of quantity of tubes. The Soviets tended to concentrate their growing artillery force in units such as the High Command Reserve (RVGK). At the outset of the war this force amounted to only about 8 per cent of the artillery, but by the war's end it amounted to 35 per cent. The new RVGK included artillery divisions, and in 1943, special artillery breakthrough corps. The RVGK also controlled smaller regiments equipped with special large-calibre weapons. These units were centrally controlled and allotted to armies and fronts depending on the importance of their missions.

The Soviets favoured the multiple rocket launcher – the legendary Katyusha or 'Little Kate' – to a greater extent than most other armies. Katyushas were well suited to the Russian predilection for massed firepower. They could deliver a very heavy concentration of fire in a very short space of time compared to conventional tubed artillery. Their elementary construction also appealed to the Soviets. Conventional artillery requires

A ripple of *Katyusha* rockets splits apart the night on the Eastern Front. There was little accuracy in each of the rockets, but together they had a devastating compound effect as an area weapon. (Courtesy of the Central Museum of the Armed Forces, Moscow via www.Stavka.org.uk)

elaborate machine tools to manufacture and rifle the barrel; Katyusha launchers used simple rails that can be built by a small machine shop. The Katyushas were officially called 'Guards' mortars' in the Red Army during the war; by the war's end, there were seven Guards mortar divisions compared with 30 regular artillery divisions.

German artillery officers were impressed by the volume of Soviet artillery fire, but not by the conduct of fire. They felt that Soviet artillery was too predictable, and too often favoured area bombardment over precisely targeted strikes. The Germans also found that in the first years of the war the Soviets largely concentrated on targets along the immediate front, often ignoring important targets in the deep rear. However, the Germans conceded that Soviet tactics improved greatly as the war went on. If the German artillery officers were sometimes contemptuous of their opponents, the same was not true of the German infantry. To German frontline troops, Soviet artillery was a much feared and respected arm. The situation grew worse for them in the later years of the war as Soviet artillery increased in volume. During operations in 1941–42 Soviet artillery strength was seldom higher than 70–80 guns and mortars per kilometre in a major attack sector. By the summer of 1944 it had risen to 220 guns and mortars per kilometre of front where a major attack was taking place. By the time of the Berlin operation, it was often up to 375 guns and mortars on a kilometre of front – producing a truly earth-shaking barrage.

The Soviets never developed a mechanized artillery force during the war, favouring conventional towed artillery. Self-propelled guns like the SU-85 and SU-100 were designed as tank destroyers. Heavy assault guns like the ISU-122 and ISU-152 were direct-fire weapons, usually manned by tank troops, and not intended for the artillery's traditional indirect-fire role. The ubiquitous SU-76 assault gun was used mainly for direct-fire support of the infantry, though it was capable of being used for indirect fire.

NAVAL INFANTRY

The Soviet Navy, especially the surface fleet, saw very little action after the initial fighting in the summer of 1941. The Baltic Fleet was largely bottled up in Leningrad. The Black Sea Fleet, although more active, was often confined to port by German air power. As a result, the navy became a reserve of idle personnel. It traditionally had naval infantry brigades attached to the fleets which could be committed to land combat. In October 1941, 25 new naval infantry brigades were formed, which fought alongside Red Army formations, and ten more were added later. They were most heavily committed on the Leningrad Front, but also took part in the defence of Moscow, and were very active in the fighting in 1942 along the Black Sea. Besides these regular formations, many fleets formed improvised battalions and small units during the course of the war. Naval infantry took part in over a hundred small-scale amphibious landings, mainly in the Black Sea area.

A young Red Army soldier mans an anti-aircraft gun on the Eastern Front. Anti-aircraft troops became an integral element of combined-arms formations in the Red Army, with entire anti-aircraft divisions by 1942. (From the fonds of the RGAKFD in Krasnogorsk via www.Stavka.org.uk)

NKVD SECURITY FORCES

Aside from combat units of the Red Army, Soviet state security forces fielded a large number of combat units during the war. In 1941, the NKVD was responsible for the Border Troops who patrolled along the frontier, and these took a very active part in the initial fighting of June 1941. The war also saw a major expansion in the NKVD internal troops. These units were organized like rifle or cavalry divisions and were intended to maintain internal order in the Soviet Union.

At the beginning of the war the NKVD formed 15 rifle divisions. At times of crisis, these units were committed to the front like regular rifle divisions. Indeed, the NKVD formed some of them into Spetsnaz (special purpose) armies, and one of these was used during the breakthroughs in the Crimea in 1944. However, this was not their primary role. They were intended to stiffen the resistance of the Red Army, and during major operations were often formed into 'blocking detachments' that collected

A conference of the officers of a rifle regiment. The officer standing next to the regimental commander, with a satchel slung over his back, is probably the deputy commander for political affairs – *politruk*. The *politruk* wore no insignia to identify him as such. (From the fonds of the RGAKFD in Krasnogorsk via www.Stavka.org.uk)

stragglers and prevented retreats. Their other role was as *istrebitel* or 'hunter' units, tracking down anti-Soviet partisan groups, and carrying out punitive expeditions against ethnic groups suspected of collaborating with the Germans.

The NKVD Special Troops were expanded in the final years of the war, eventually totalling 53 divisions and 28 brigades, not counting the Border Troops. This was equal to about a tenth of the total number of regular Red Army rifle divisions. These units were used in the prolonged partisan wars in the Ukraine and the Baltic republics, conflicts that lasted until the early 1950s. They were also involved in the wholesale deportations of suspected ethnic groups in 1943–45. In some respects, the NKVD formations resembled the German Waffen-SS in terms of independence from the normal military structure. However, the NKVD troops were used mainly for internal security and repression, and were not heavily enough armed for frontline combat. Unlike the Waffen-SS, they had no major armoured or mechanized NKVD formations.

AIR FORCE

The Red Army Air Force was established as the Workers' and Peasants' Red Military Air Fleet (RKKVF) on 28 January 1918. Subsequently it underwent a series of cosmetic redesignations: to RKKA Air Force (RKKA-VSRKKA) in 1935, RKKA Military Air Force (RKKA–VVS-RKKA) in 1936 and Red Army Military Air Force (VVS-KA) in September 1939. Russian sources refer to it simply as the VVS.

The VVS was a combat arm of the Red Army, commanded by the head of the Air Force Main Directorate at the People's Commissariat of Defence. The VVS suffered particularly badly from Stalin's purges, and many senior commanders were executed by the NKVD in 1941 for perceived military failures.

The main air force branches at the beginning of the war were as follows:

(1) Air Force. This comprised all elements except those listed below, including fighter, ground-attack, bomber and night-bomber air regiments; airborne (paratroop) brigades; and airfield guard battalions.
(2) Services. The supply and administration, medical, and veterinary services were also available to the VVS.
(3) Specialist officers. The VVS had its own technical, legal and political officers and bandmasters.

The Ilyushin Il-2 Shturmovik was one of the most successful aircraft in the Soviet Air Force. It was a formidable ground-attack platform, being equipped with two 23mm cannon, two 7.62mm machine guns, one 12.7mm machine gun (rear facing) and up to 600kg of external ordnance. (Courtesy of the Central Museum of the Armed Forces, Moscow via www.Stavka.org.uk)

In April 1939 the air division began to replace the air brigade as the principal tactical flying formation. Between five and eight air divisions were allocated to each of the 13 existing military districts, the two Independent Red Banner armies (First and Second), and the three special purpose air armies (AON 1–3) formed from 1936 for strategic operations.

Unsatisfactory VVS performance during the Winter War against Finland led to a reorganization into four principal groupings. The AONs were disbanded from 29 April 1940, and that November were largely re-formed under the single designation Long Range Bomber Air Force with five air corps. In early 1941 the Anti-Air Defence (PVO) formed PVO Zones, one per military district, to co-ordinate fighter air divisions, anti-aircraft and searchlight batteries, and balloon barrage defences. The Frontal Aviation supported the army fronts with 61 air divisions, while 95 Army Aviation Corps squadrons carried out reconnaissance missions for the field armies. The Aeroflot Civil Air Fleet had formed air detachments in June 1940 to transport troops to the Baltic and Bessarabia, and in June 1941 these formed VVS transport air regiments.

The highest tactical formation was the air corps, with two or three air divisions. In June 1941 there were 79 air divisions – about 40 per cent fighters, 30 per cent ground-attack, 20 per cent bombers, 7 per cent night bombers, and 3 per cent mixed – mostly bearing 200-series numbers. An air division contained four to six air regiments; a fighter or ground attack air regiment comprised a two-aircraft HQ flight and four 15-aircraft squadrons, totalling 62 aircraft. A bomber air regiment also had 62 aircraft, divided into a two-aircraft HQ flight and five 12-aircraft squadrons; but a heavy bomber air regiment had 40 aircraft in four ten-aircraft squadrons. In 1941 some VVS personnel formed infantry-style airfield guard battalions.

About 1,000 VVS volunteers served with the Republican Air Force in the Spanish Civil War, 1936–39. Some 450 pilots of the Soviet Volunteer Group of the Chinese Nationalist Air Force flew against the Japanese in October 1937–April 1941, and aircraft of the First and Second Independent Red Banner Armies fought them over Khalkin-Gol in 1939. VVS units faced minimal opposition in eastern Poland. Nevertheless, the occupation force that entered the Baltic States on 28 September 1939, under former VVS commander Alexander Loktionov, contained a large air contingent: two air brigades plus nine more air regiments. The VVS absorbed the Estonian, Latvian and Lithuanian air forces after June 1940. Although facing a Finnish air force with only about 145 aircraft, during the Winter War the VVS units lost 700–900 aircraft, mostly bombers, and in often atrocious weather conditions Soviet fighters were unable to defeat the Finnish and foreign volunteer (mostly Swedish) pilots.

The Soviet fighter arm eventually gained air supremacy over the Luftwaffe on the Eastern Front, on account of its evolving superiority in tactics plus its dominance in sheer numbers over the overstretched German Air Force. (Courtesy of the Central Museum of the Armed Forces, Moscow via www.Stavka.org.uk)

In June–July 1941, therefore, it is not surprising that the Luftwaffe rapidly achieved air supremacy over the ill-prepared and poorly equipped VVS, which, in spite of individual bravery, had lost 7,500 aircraft by September 1941. The VVS reasserted itself from 30 September during the battle for Moscow, however, when aircraft of 6th PVO Air Corps, the Stavka Reserve Air Corps and Frontal Aviation fought desperately. Despite suffering huge losses, they achieved local air superiority in winter conditions, helping to halt the German advance in December 1941.

- The VVS-KA was renamed Red Army Aviation (AKA) in 1942. It was commanded from 17 March 1943 by Alexander Novikov, a gifted strategist, who reformed the AKA into a formidable fighting machine. General Novikov completed the definitive reorganization of the air force into five sections (plus the paratroopers) on 11 April 1942:
- The Long Range Bomber Air Force was redesignated Long Range Aviation in March 1942. Under direct Stavka command, this comprised seven bomber air divisions, expanding to 16 in May 1943. However, the priority enjoyed by tactical over strategic bombing hampered the development of this force.
- Frontal Aviation and Army Aviation were reorganized from 5 May 1942 into 17 air armies numbered in sequence, developed from the ten air strike groups (UAGs) that Novikov had formed to defend Leningrad in 1941. An air army had anything from 150 to 1,000 aircraft, usually in five air divisions, plus air regiments and squadrons. However, First Air Army eventually comprised 13 divisions. One or two air armies were assigned to each front.
- The GHQ Reserve, comprising 13 air corps, each with 120–270 aircraft, could be deployed to reinforce the air armies.
- The interceptor Air Defence Fighter Aviation (PVO – IA-PVO) provided fighter cover for important cities including Moscow (with 40 fighter air regiments in 1942), Leningrad and Stalingrad.
- The echelon below the air army was the numbered air corps, designated either bomber, fighter, mixed or ground-attack. The next level was the air division, designated as bomber or fighter. Within the division was the Air Regiment, either bomber (BAP), long-range bomber, fighter, artillery-spotter, reconnaissance, medical evacuation, mixed, ground-attack or transport – many transport regiments were manned by Civil Air Fleet personnel. An air regiment comprised four 15-aircraft

squadrons. The tactical groupings were the two-aircraft Para, four-aircraft flight, and the group with six to eight aircraft.

By 1943 the VVS/AKA had generally taken the offensive over all sectors of the front, and a new generation of increasingly experienced pilots and leaders had replaced the catastrophic losses of 1941. The strength of the Luftwaffe on the Eastern Front was significantly reduced by the withdrawal of fighter units to defend the Reich from the Allied bombing offensive, and after the battle of Kursk in July 1943 the VVS/AKA gained permanent air superiority.

From January 1944, indeed, the AKA maintained air superiority over all its theatres of operations, supporting Soviet strategic offensives. It faced a Luftwaffe badly weakened by transfers to the west to oppose the Anglo-American strategic bombing offensive and, from June 1944, the Normandy landings and subsequent operations in north-west Europe. The AKA remained a tactical force, although Eighteenth Air Army (ex-ADD) mounted a limited bombing offensive over eastern Germany in 1945.

THE SOVIET RIFLEMAN

The Soviets referred to their infantry branch as Rifle Forces, reflecting an old Russian tradition that viewed *streltsy* (riflemen) as more elite than mere *pekhoty* (infantry). The Rifle Forces were the largest single element of the

A wash platform has been built on a stream bank to prevent the water from being muddied. Field living conditions were spartan to say the least, even when in training. (Courtesy of the Central Museum of the Armed Forces, Moscow via www.Stavka.org.uk)

Red Army during the war, amounting to 75 per cent of its line divisions. At the outbreak of the war the Red Army had 303 divisions, of which 88 were in the process of formation and not entirely combat ready. There were four principal types of rifle division at the time: the basic rifle divisions (178), mountain rifle divisions (18), motor rifle divisions for the Mechanized Corps (31) and independent motor rifle divisions (two).

In the summer of 1941, the rifle division was in a state of reorganization after the debacle in Finland. Under the new April 1941 orders, each division numbered 14,483 men based around three infantry regiments. Fire support came from two artillery regiments, an anti-tank and an anti-aircraft battalion. Tank support was very modest – only 16 light tanks – as most of the tanks were being hoarded in the new Mechanized Corps. The June 1941 invasion caught the Red Army in the middle of the reorganization, and most infantry formations were based on older tables. The summer 1941 fighting was horribly costly, with over 100 rifle divisions destroyed.

The war led to the immediate call-up of all 23 to 36-year-old males, the 18 to 22-year-olds having already been inducted before the outbreak of war. By July 1941 some 5.3 million Soviets were under arms. The Red Army of 1941 was primarily Slavic: Russian, Ukrainian or Belorussian. The Red Army did not recruit extensively from Central Asia, the Caucasus or the Far East even though the non-Slavic minorities represented over a quarter of the Soviet population. The problem was mainly one of assimilating the non-Russian-speaking groups into the army. The exceptions to this were the mountain rifle divisions, which typically recruited Georgians and other peoples from the Caucasus, and cavalry divisions. This recruitment policy would change as the war dragged on.

Some idea of the horrendous losses suffered by the Red Army during this period can be gained from the fact that the Soviets raised 400 new divisions between the summer of 1941 and December 1941, but only had 80 divisions ready to field against the Germans at the end of that period. A total of 124 rifle divisions were erased from the records due to heavy losses, and some new formations were built around the skeletal remains of old divisions, sometimes with only a few hundred survivors.

The enormous casualties suffered by the Red Army in the summer of 1941 led to a drastic reorganization of the rifle divisions. The motor rifle divisions, intended to complement the tank divisions in the Mechanized Corps, had never been entirely formed. Many were wiped out, and the handful that survived until December 1941 were motorized in name only.

They mostly disappeared through attrition. One independent motorized division, the 1st Moscow Motor Rifle Division, was kept in service largely due to its fine performance. The basic rifle divisions were subjected to another reorganization in July 1941, mainly owing to the loss of equipment in the great encirclement battles. The pressing need for new formations led to their dilution in strength. A total of 286 new rifle divisions were formed between the outbreak of war and December 1941. Divisional strength fell from 14,483 to 10,859 men. The heaviest cut came in artillery, with divisional firepower suffering greatly as a result. Indeed, it was not until the winter of 1944–45 that Soviet rifle divisions began to be built up to pre-war levels in terms of available artillery support, relying instead on mortars.

The quality of Soviet infantry fell very rapidly. Training was minimal. Of the 286 new divisions, 24 were people's volunteer divisions, which were nothing more than elderly civilian volunteers with small arms. A further 22 divisions were formed by absorbing troops from other branches of the service, often with no infantry training. Nevertheless, they accomplished their purpose. By the winter of 1941–42 the front had been stabilized, and the Germans had been beaten back from the gates of Leningrad and Moscow.

The Slavic ethnic groups suffered most heavily from the enormous manpower losses of 1941–42. In addition, the German occupation of the

WOMEN IN THE RED ARMY

To cope with the enormous losses of 1941–42, the Red Army also increased its intake of Russian women. Women had traditionally been recruited as doctors and medics, and at first filled non-combat support positions in rear areas. However, the situation became so bad that women were eventually allowed into the combat arms. Women were used in anti-aircraft units; there are the celebrated cases of three combat air regiments with women crews. Women were also recruited as snipers, although they were not generally assigned to normal infantry units. In the last year of the war, the ranks of tankers had become so depleted that women who worked at the tank plants, and who were familiar with driving and repairing tanks, were recruited as drivers. Many proved so able that they eventually rose to the command of their tank units. A total of 76 Russian women were awarded the highest Soviet military distinction, the 'Hero of the Soviet Union'. A third of these went to aircrew (27), and a third to partisans or resistance fighters (21). Eight women snipers, two scouts, one tanker and 12 medics also won the award, many posthumously. By the end of the war, about 10 per cent of the personnel of the Soviet Armed Forces were women, mainly Russians.

western USSR covered much of the Ukraine and most of Belorussia. As a result, the Soviets were obliged to recruit more heavily amongst the ethnic minorities of the Caucasus, Central Asia and the Far East. During the war the Red Army formed at least 42 'national' divisions and over 20 national brigades, composed of Lithuanians, Uzbeks, Armenians and other ethnic

Women were employed as *rukovodstvy* (traffic controllers), an important job from both a logistical and a combat viewpoint, especially in an age of mobile warfare. This soldier wears the grey felt winter boots, effective at protecting against frostbite but only suited for use in heavy snow conditions. (From the fonds of the RGAKFD in Krasnogorsk via www.Stavka.org.uk)

groups, generally commanded by Russian officers. The Baltic units served a political as well as military purpose, being intended to show local acceptance of Soviet rule after the annexation of the Baltic republics in 1940. In the Transcaucasus, the reasons were primarily military, due to the fighting in the region in 1942. Details of these national divisions are unclear, since some were regular rifle divisions that happened to be raised in the regions, while others were specifically earmarked as ethnic formations.

The Soviets also formed several allied armies in 1943. The Polish People's Army (LWP) was the largest of these, formed mainly from ex-prisoners of war and deportees. The LWP grew quite sizeable in 1944–45, when Poland was wrested from German control. For example, during the Berlin fighting Polish units made up nearly a tenth of the forces involved. A Czechoslovak and a Yugoslav army were also formed, but they were very small owing to a lack of manpower. After the fall of Romania and Bulgaria, these armies were allied to the Red Army, but they remained equipped and organized as before the switch in allegiance.

EQUIPMENT

Distribution of Soviet infantry weapons depended on the type of infantry unit. The normal rifle company during the middle of the war had three rifle platoons and a machine-gun platoon, with a total of three heavy Maxim water-cooled machine guns, nine DP light machine guns, 85 rifles or carbines, 12 sub-machine guns (SMGs) and eight pistols. Officially, an infantry squad of nine men was armed with one SMG (for the *serzhant* – sergeant – who led the squad), a DP squad machine gun, and seven rifles. Thus, in 1943, the normal Soviet rifle unit was actually not much different from its German equivalent, with very few SMGs compared to rifles. Where the Soviets tended to concentrate their SMGs was in the motor rifle units attached to tank and mechanized corps, or to independent tank brigades. A motor rifle company would have nine DP section machine guns, 27 rifles or carbines, 57 SMGs and five pistols. In a motor rifle section, the majority of the troops would be armed with automatic weapons.

The motor rifle units were the shock troops of the Rifle Forces. Despite their name, they had very few motor vehicles. They were usually carried into battle riding on tanks, a practice called *tankovy desant* by the Russians. The Soviet motor rifle units were the equivalent of German Panzer Grenadier units. Another factor affecting the distribution of infantry weapons was the matter of Guards' status. The 'Guards' distinction was another throw-back to Tsarist practice. Units that won Guards status due to their combat performance were entitled to higher pay, better clothing and a better selection of equipment. This often meant that Guards rifle divisions were closer to the official tables of organization as far as equipment was concerned when compared to less distinguished rifle units. The distribution of weapons changed with time. At the beginning of the war Red Army rifle units had few if any SMGs. Officially, by the end of the war, even regular motor rifle units had a mixture of about one-third SMGs and two-thirds rifles and carbines. However, few divisions in combat actually reached these levels.

One of the major drawbacks in Soviet infantry tactics was the lack of attention paid to infantry mechanization. The Red Army was the only major European army not to adopt an armoured infantry carrier during the war. As mentioned earlier, Soviet motor rifle troops usually went into action riding the tanks themselves – a risky substitute for infantry vehicles. German officers who served in Russia during the war singled out the lack of Soviet mechanized infantry as one of the main tactical failures of the Red Army during the war. The reasons for this appear to have more to do with production constraints than with tactical doctrine. The Soviets were hard pressed to maintain tank production sufficient to replace combat attrition for most of the war. Production of armoured infantry vehicles would have cut into tank production, or some other vital aspect of weapons production. The Soviets viewed them as an unaffordable luxury during the war, though they began an extensive programme of infantry mechanization after final victory.

The war on the Eastern Front was characterized by the heavy use of tank forces; and it was infantry units that were often victimized by tanks. The Soviets were much more backward in developing effective anti-tank weapons than any of the major European armies. In 1941 they began adding anti-tank rifle units to their formations; a rifle battalion received an anti-tank rifle platoon with six PTRD or PTRS rifles, and a motor rifle regiment had an anti-tank rifle company added, usually with 24 rifles. These weapons were suitable against the lightly armoured tanks of 1941–42; but due to the rapid escalation in tank armour forced on the Germans by the T-34, by the end of 1942 these guns were fast becoming ineffective against the frontal armour of the Panzers. The Soviets failed to develop a rocket-propelled grenade, comparable to the German Panzerfaust or Panzerschreck, the American bazooka, or even a spigot projectile like the

British PIAT. The Soviet infantry were forced to rely on anti-tank grenades or anti-tank mines. This is all the more surprising, as the Soviets were very active in the development of rocket artillery like the Katyusha, and had

and by 1943 large numbers were issued. He is armed with a 7.62mm PPSh-41 with a 71-round drum. A spare drum is carried in a belt pouch along with a three-pocket grenade pouch. By 1944 35-round curved magazines were being issued for the PPSh-41 with a three-pocket pouch and they were also used with the PPS-43 (**2**). Grenade pouches were widely issued. At the war's beginning a one-pocket pouch was available, here with an F-1 fragmentation grenade (**3A**). A more practical three-pocket pouch was soon issued, here with an RG-42 fragmentation grenade (**3B**). The two-pocket pouch was specifically designed for the RGD-33 blast grenade, here with a slip-on fragmentation collar (**3C**). The ultra-simple backpack (**4**) was introduced in 1942 and was merely a bag with shoulder straps and a tie-cord. A hatchet with belt carrier (**5**) was issued to each section; the new type mess kit was based on the German model (**6**). (**7**) is an issue enamelled steel cup. Owing to aluminium shortages, glass bottles were issued with cork stoppers (**8**). As well as green they were issued in brown or clear glass. They could be carried in standard carriers or this insulated type. The BN gas mask had a mitre box allowing voice communication and had an improved TSh filter canister (**9**). The carrier was provided with two side pockets, one for an individual decontamination kit and the other

This corporal (**1**) in late 1943 wears the 1943 uniform on which rank was displayed on shoulder straps rather than collar tabs owing to the small standing collar. The SSh-40 helmet also saw wide issue by 1942. SMGs came into wider use from 1942 for spare eye lenses and anti-dim cream to prevent lens fogging. A reserve ammunition pouch was carried on the back centre of riflemen's belts, holding six five-round clips (**10**). (Howard Gerrard © Osprey Publishing) even worked on rocket anti-tank weapons before the war. However, the Red Army made extensive use of captured German Panzerfäuste, and there is some evidence that the Soviets began manufacturing a copy in 1944–45 as the RPG-1. Soviet rifle regiments had a battery of 45mm anti-tank guns, and they became adept at using these for anti-tank defence.

The elite of the Red Army rifle forces during the war were the *razvedchiki*, the scouts. The Red Army did not form very many special purpose units, relying instead on scout units; usually, each rifle regiment would receive a company of scouts, and each division would have a battalion. Scouts were drawn from the best troops in the division, and were usually given preference in equipment, food and clothing. One of the more obvious signs of their elite distinction was the camouflage coverall worn by scout troops.

THE CONSCRIPTION SYSTEM

'[The] defence of the Motherland is the sacred duty of every citizen of the USSR.' So declared the 1936 Constitution of the USSR. It further stated that 'universal military service is law' and 'military service in the Red Army of Workers and Peasants is an honourable duty'.

Military service was a fact of life for the physically and mentally fit in the 'workers' paradise' that was the USSR. Not only was it a constitutional duty for all citizens, but it was also clearly specified in the 1939 Law of Compulsory Military Service, which stated that all able-bodied males were eligible for conscription on reaching the age of 19. By 1939 the Soviet Union was already on a war footing. Only those enrolled in secondary or technical schools could have their service deferred. The same applied to the chronically ill. Such deferments were granted for 3–12 months, and could only be granted a maximum of three times. Those under arrest, deported to Siberia or deprived of their suffrage rights were exempt from conscription, as were those with serious physical defects. Certain categories of specialists were also exempt: these included skilled workers (especially those in remote rural areas), scientists, rural school teachers, relocated farmers (forced to work on collective farms) and essential factory workers and technicians. The mentally deficient were exempted and militia (police) records were checked for possible enemies of the state unworthy of bearing arms. Only on reaching the age of 50 were Russian men exempt from military service.

Prior to the war there were three forms of military service: active duty, extended leave (commanders) and furlough (NCOs and lower ranks), and reserve duty. Leave and furlough were granted to commanders and soldiers

who had completed active duty, or before completing five years' active duty if their services were not required. They were still on the rolls, but could return home and accept civilian employment, although they technically remained under military regulations and could be recalled immediately. Personnel placed on reserve duty had completed their active service or a combination of active duty and leave/furlough. Typically, a private would serve two years' active duty and three years on furlough, and then be assigned to the reserves until age 50. Sergeants served three years' active duty and two years' furlough. A soldier could extend his active service in five-year intervals and could be retained on active duty two months beyond his release date. Of course, in times of war service was extended beyond any peacetime limits – deferments could be cancelled, the age of reservists was increased to 60, and all reservists were eligible for mobilization. Volunteers were also accepted and large numbers of idealistic young men signed up prior to and in the first couple of months of the war, especially from the

A platoon commander reads excerpts from a newspaper to his SVT-40 rifle-armed men. Such readings were a standard means of keeping troops informed, building morale and reinforcing belief and belonging. Many soldiers were illiterate or could not read very well. (Courtesy of the Central Museum of the Armed Forces, Moscow via www.Stavka.org.uk)

Local civilians, joined by a soldier, perform a traditional dance for soldiers. Army dance and music troupes performed for soldiers and gave a great morale boost. (From the fonds of the RGAKFD in Krasnogorsk via www.Stavka.org.uk)

cities where conditions were cramped and shortages prevailed. A new Conscription Act was passed on 31 August 1941, and the conscription age was lowered to 18 for those without secondary education and 19 for those educated to that level.

The average soldier had no inkling of the vast bureaucratic system that called him to military service. The system was purely statistical, based on the numbers and categories of troops needed by the field forces. Conscription was administered by over 20 military districts, each of which could in theory raise an army. These districts were divided between *oblasty* (regions), the primary administrative sub-division of the USSR, and they in turn were further sub-divided into *raiony* (counties). It was from the *raion* military commissar that men received their draft notifications. Each *raion* was given quotas and the numbers of specialists necessary. The better-qualified men were often assigned to the NKVD, the vast internal security organization, while the Red Army often had to make do with sub-standard recruits. Studies showed that many conscripts, especially from rural areas, had a vocabulary of just 500–2,000 words. With the German invasion the system soon fell apart, especially in the more populous west, as Soviet territory was occupied and the government fell into turmoil. Huge numbers of potential soldiers were lost to the occupation. Those that fled east were eventually conscripted within the Red Army. They were under no administrative system, however, as their home records were lost. The NKVD rounded up undocumented men and turned them over to the Red Army. The difficult situation and lack of time prevented any more organized system from developing. The situation was so desperate that soon after the invasion ten divisions were raised in Siberian gulags using 130,000 convicts.

As the war progressed, former German-occupied areas were liberated and the inhabitants became liable for conscription. However, there was widespread political distrust of these *zapadniki* ('westerners') owing to their having been under German control. Many of the territories, the western Ukraine and the Baltic States for example, had only been absorbed into the USSR just prior to the war and the inhabitants, while glad to be relieved of German occupation, were by no means enthralled to see the return of Soviet domination. The NKVD screened potential army recruits and agents made enquiries as to their demonstrated loyalties to the Motherland during the occupation. Even partisans were screened. Those deemed politically unreliable were 're-educated' or simply sent to the gulags instead of reporting for active duty with the Red Army.

THE TYPICAL RED ARMY RECRUIT

In a country as vast as the USSR, with its melting pot of ethnicities, there was no typical Red Army conscript or recruit. A *Krasnoarmeyets* (lit. 'Red Army Man') could be from a large city, town, village, or a remote rural area. He might have been uneducated or, if he had just graduated from school, most likely had never held a job. If not conscripted out of school he might have worked in a factory or shop, as a labourer, in the service industry or in any number of other jobs. Many were agricultural workers. Forestry, mining, petroleum and transportation were other major industries.

Numerous conscripts were raised on *kollektivnye khoziaistvi* (collective farms) – *kolkhoz* for short. The *kolkhoz* was a state-owned agricultural co-operative where peasants, typically in units of 75 families, under the direction of Party-approved plans and 'elected' leadership, were paid wages based on the quantity and quality of their work contribution and the success of their harvest. Each family could 'own' a small plot of land for gardening, which remained part of the *kolkhoz*, and a few head of livestock. Forced collectivization was implemented between 1929 and 1937, and while

An officer reads instructions during a guard mount. The double-breasted greatcoats were made of shoddy wool, as can be seen in the appearance of these soldiers' coats. Some officers wore lined black or dark-brown leather jackets as here. (From the fonds of the RGAKFD in Krasnogorsk via www.Stavka.org.uk)

resisted in some areas, particularly the Ukraine, it was welcomed by many serfs. Previously much of the land was owned by *kulaky*, 'wealthy' serfs who owned farms, sawmills, dairies and so forth, or privately owned motorized machinery, and may have rented out land. Collectivization destroyed the *kulaky* and redistributed the land. The former *kolkhoznik* soldier was particularly reliant on the cradle-to-grave benefits given by the Soviet state.

Conscription-age soldiers had been born in the early and mid 1920s. They knew nothing of a pre-communist Russia. They had been raised on a steady diet of state propaganda, dictates and ever-changing regulations. News, information and history were controlled by the government – their view of the outside world was a result of what the state told them, namely that they lived in a nation in danger of 'capitalist encirclement', with enemies on all sides. The reality was that the 'worker's paradise' was below the European average in education, health care, standard of living, agricultural and industrial production, everything except for quantity of military hardware. There were shortages of everything. The country was run by a bloated, centralized bureaucracy pouring scarce resources into a lumbering military machine, acting under fear of external enemies and of a secret police searching for enemies within.

BECOMING A RED ARMY RIFLEMAN

Prior to the war, mass conscription was conducted over two or three months at the beginning of the year. Call-up notices mailed out by the district military commissariat directed conscripts and reservists to report to an assembly point, often a local school. Typically they walked to the assembly point with a cardboard suitcase or bag containing a set of spare clothes and underwear, toilet articles, tobacco and maybe socks, as many had been told they would be issued less desirable footwraps. They were given a quick physical examination and transported by train to mobilization reception centres operated by the military districts. It was the first train ride for many of the recruits. Many reported in drunk from farewell celebrations and this was indeed encouraged, as they were easier to manage while sleeping it off on the train.

At the military district reception centre, the conscripts turned in their civilian clothes to be mailed home and underwent another physical; heads were shaved, and they were given a *banya* (steam bath) to rid them of lice. Uniforms, typically ill fitting, were issued. The issue was one or two uniforms, two sets of long underwear, cap, belt, boots, greatcoat and footwraps. Care and cleaning of his uniform was the soldier's responsibility, except for the underwear – this was exchanged every ten days, usually longer in practice, for a washed set that had been worn by someone else. It was often said that the only two things that fitted were the boots and footwraps. One of the first things the recruits learned from a sergeant or recalled reservist was how to apply footwraps to minimize creases. Their first ten days were spent in quarantine from other troops.

Riflemen (Specialty Code 133) would be issued most of their individual equipment, but probably not a weapon – there were too few firearms and they had to be shared during training. Besides cartridge pouches, a water bottle, shelter-cape, ration bag and cooking pot, the conscript might be issued a canvas field clothing bag. He might not be issued an entrenching tool and gas mask until assigned to a combat unit. The recruit would possibly also be issued with an identity tube. This was a 19mm-diameter, 63mm-long eight-sided black Bakelite tube with a screw-on cap. Later in the war they were made of black-painted wood. The tube contained a long narrow form on which 19 entries served as a personal record with information such as name, date of birth, unit number (sequential serial numbers were not assigned), parents' names and address, date of conscription/enlistment, promotions, wounds, etc. The tube was carried in a pocket. Soldiers were also issued a Red Army Pass, a tan or red booklet containing basic personal data to be carried at all times.

PRE-CONSCRIPTION TRAINING

In theory students received a degree of pre-military training while still at school. As early as first grade, instruction began with physical training and motivational indoctrination one hour a week, which increased to ten hours by tenth grade. A two-week pre-military summer camp was attended in eighth and ninth grades. Training continued through tenth grade and upon graduation students received a 'Maturity Certificate' stating their eligibility for military service. In secondary (eighth–tenth grade) and vocational schools, instruction was provided in basic military skills thought sufficient to prepare boys to function as members of a platoon.

This instruction included physical fitness, drill, military sports, skiing, marksmanship, chemical defence, scouting, sentry and messenger duties, section (squad) attack and defence, actions against tanks, first aid, military orientation and history. Girls were taught military skills, but they were not expected to become frontline soldiers and so the training was focused on other key roles, such as medics or telegraphers. The average boy may or may not have been enthused about pre-military training. Instruction was provided by reserve officers and sergeants and its quality and completeness varied. Much of the instruction was by lecture only, with limited hands-on training owing to scarce equipment and training facilities. In rural areas it may have been non-existent. In cities and large towns it was more effective,

The 1936 uniform had a stand-and-fall collar, normally with collar tabs. The centre man is armed with a 7.62mm PPSh-41 SMG; note the 71-round drum magazine pouch on his belt. The man to the left has an F-1 'lemon' fragmentation grenade on his belt. (Courtesy of the Central Museum of the Armed Forces, Moscow via www.Stavka.org.uk)

especially if there was a military base nearby from which instructors and equipment might be borrowed.

Youths could also join the OSOAVIAKHIM (Union of Societies of Assistance to Defence and Aviation and Chemical Defence of the USSR) at 14. This organization provided military-related training in shooting, radio operation, driving, chemical defence, parachuting, glider-flying and other skills. Hundreds of thousands made parachute jumps, as parachuting became a national craze. The OSOAVIAKHIM offered a diversion for youths; there was little else to do and it was paid for by the government. The organization claimed 13 million members in 1941. While the quality of pre-military instruction in both schools and the OSOAVIAKHIM may have been patchy, it did help the mobilization effort and provided some degree of preparation. The USSR was able to field large numbers of parachute units, radio operators (with a basic knowledge of Morse code), qualified vehicle drivers and experienced shooters.

CONSCRIPTION TRAINING

In peacetime, training would last six months to a year, but during the war it was reduced to weeks, based on whatever time was available. Training conditions were difficult for instructors and troops. Weapons, ammunition, technical equipment, ranges and simple training aids were in short supply. Many of the instructors were unskilled and not always familiar with their subjects. Some instructors were reservists and not conversant with the newer weapons and tactics.

The training day began with reveille between 0500 and 0600hrs. The recruits dressed and cleaned up to rush though a quick breakfast. Training lasted 10–12 hours six days a week. Sunday was off, but far from a free day – quarters were cleaned, any weapons and equipment were maintained and there were lessons to study. There were short hourly breaks throughout the day and an hour for lunch. Dinner was eaten after training was completed. In the evenings boots and equipment were cleaned and prepared for the next day. The study of manuals might be required or there could be political indoctrination lectures, films and discussions.

In the first days of training the military regulations were read to the recruits and motivational/propaganda talks given. Training was unimaginative for the most part, although the few combat veterans (most recent veterans were at the front) would present more practical instruction, especially in small-unit tactics. Instruction was repetitive and often learned

THE MILITARY OATH

Recruits took the Military Oath of the Red Army after they demonstrated an understanding of the regulations regarding discipline and of the oath's significance, but not later than two months after assignment to a unit. This was scheduled for a Sunday and regarded as a unit holiday, with the entire unit paraded in full uniform and colours. Each man swore the oath individually and signed the document, and the date was entered in his Red Army Pass. The oath ran as follows:

I, _____, a citizen of the Union of the Soviet Socialist Republics, entering into the ranks of the Red Army of Workers and Peasants, take this oath and solemnly promise to be an honest, brave, disciplined, vigilant fighter, staunchly to protect military and state secrets, and unquestioningly to obey all military regulations and orders of commanders and superiors. I promise conscientiously to study military affairs, in every way to protect military and state property, and to my last breath to be faithful to the people, the Soviet Motherland, and the Workers-Peasants' Government.

I am always prepared on order of the Workers and Peasants' Government to rise to the defence of my Motherland, the Union of Soviet Socialist Republics; and as a fighting man of the Red Army of Workers and Peasants, I promise to defend it bravely, skilfully, with dignity and honour, sparing neither my blood nor my life itself for the achievement of total victory over our enemies. If by evil intent I should violate this, my solemn oath, then let the severe punishment of Soviet law and the total hatred and contempt of the working classes befall me.

only by rote and unthinking reception. This system was complicated by the limited vocabulary of many recruits, the complicated Russian military vocabulary and poor, or lack of, comprehension of Russian by some troops. Much of the instruction was presented by lecture, often merely read from the manual. The recruits sat on the ground, weather permitting. There were few if any classrooms available. In the snow or rain, the troops would stand to attention in formation as the lecture was presented. On hot days when the troops began to nod off, they would also be stood to attention.

Much time was first spent on the drill field, learning how to march in formation, conduct facing movements and drill with the rifle (often with sticks as substitutes). The recruits learned to move as a unit and to understand the importance of paying attention to commands. It was here that non-Russian speakers acquired the words of command, often by mimicking the actions of others, reinforced by shouts, punches and kicks. They also dug, with their little entrenching tools, fighting positions, trenches, drainage ditches and dugout shelters. Exposure to the weather and hard work conditioned them mentally and physically. Time permitting, in the winter they might receive ski and snowshoe training, although this was more often done within units.

TACTICAL LESSONS AND TRAINING MANUALS

The Red Army's 1936 infantry tactics manual was simplistic and straightforward. The November 1942 manual, incorporating lessons learned, remained uncomplicated, and the following discussion of tactics is based on the 1942 manual. The manual's simplicity was just as well,

Two officers, one seated in the centre (captain) and the other standing to the right rear (senior lieutenant), chat with their soldiers. The shaven-headed man to the right is a sergeant-major. They wear the 1936 uniform and collar rank insignia. (From the fonds of the RGAKFD in Krasnogorsk via www.Stavka.org.uk)

considering the inexperience of leaders and troops. Small-unit movement and battle formations, and the layout of defensive positions, were simply described and kept to a minimum of variants that were relatively easy for inexperienced soldiers and commanders to visualize and comprehend. They were also easy to control and shift from one formation to another. The basic principles of these formations, tactics and organization applied to all echelons up through the regiment.

The infantry manual spelled out the responsibilities of a soldier. In the West, military manuals served as guidelines to be modified as the situation warranted. In the Red Army, manuals had the force of law and infractions of the manual were punishable offences. According to the manual, every soldier must:

- carry out without disagreement, precisely and quickly all orders and instructions of his commander
- learn his combat mission and that of his section and platoon

Snipers climb a riverbank as they search for good firing positions. Snipers operated in pairs, covering the same sector from nearby positions or one firing and the other spotting. They are armed with specially selected 7.62mm Mosin-Nagant M1891/30 *snaiperskayiye* (sniper rifles) with turn-down bolt handles and telescope mounts, here with the 4× PE. (From the fonds of the RGAKFD in Krasnogorsk via www.Stavka.org.uk)

- possess complete knowledge of his weapons, maintain his mastery, and their permanent readiness
- know his place in the battle formation from which he can carry out the commands and instructions of his commander, maintain constant co-ordination with his commander and neighbouring soldiers
- strive for mutual aid
- constantly support his comrades with fire, bayonet, grenades, entrenching tool and by personal example
- protect and cover the commander in battle
- in battle shoot carefully and accurately, report to the commander when he has expended half his ammunition so that it can be replenished
- remove ammunition and grenades from the dead and wounded, and collect ammunition found on the battlefield
- bring ammunition whenever returning from the rear
- at all halts dig in and camouflage
- continuously observe the battlefield, neighbouring units and the sky, and report all observations to the commander
- if the commander becomes a casualty, take command of the section and continue the battle
- if separated from his section, join the next section and continue the battle
- if wounded, bandage himself and continue the battle; he is allowed to go to the aid station only with approval of the commander and must take with him his weapon and cartridge belt (magazines). If he cannot go on, he crawls to cover with his weapon and awaits a medic.

Soldiers were further admonished that 'It is forbidden to leave the battlefield to escort the wounded' and 'Every soldier must hate the enemy, maintain military secrecy, be vigilant, unmask spies and saboteurs, and relentlessly act against traitors to the Motherland.' Furthermore, 'Nothing, including the threat of death, allows a soldier of the Red Army to surrender or in any way reveal a military secret.' Just about anything to do with the military was secret in the security-paranoid USSR.

WEAPONS TRAINING

Weapons training was often limited owing to arms and ammunition shortages. Firing ranges were not always available. Operator training and maintenance was conducted with a few shared weapons. 'Dry firing' – without ammunition

– to learn weapon operation, sighting and firing positions was conducted. Many soldiers were fortunate to fire just three to five rounds before combat. When issued a weapon, they usually went into combat without firing it or zeroing its sight. As with learning tactics and how to survive on the battlefield, those living through their first battles became proficient with their weapons and often understood how to operate all of those in their unit.

More care was given to machine-gun training, but, again, too often only a few guns were available and the operators might not fire any live rounds during the instruction phase. Anti-tank riflemen received more careful guidance, oriented to choosing firing positions and targeting vulnerable points on tanks. Mortar training was frequently poor because of the scarcity of ammunition and the average conscript's difficulty in understanding the complexities of indirect, unobserved fire and the mortar's intricate sight. Even officers had difficulty learning the weapon's complexities in their rushed training. Crews did gain proficiency in combat, however, making the mortar a valuable weapon.

Other training provided to rifle troops was typical of any other army: bayonet, fire against aircraft, actions against tanks, scouting, observing and reporting information, duties in outposts, messenger duties, chemical defence, guard duty, field sanitation, first aid, camouflage, field fortifications and breaching obstacles. Land navigation and map reading were something only sergeants and commanders were taught.

A PM-10 Maxim is hand-carried forward at a more rapid rate than it could be dragged on its wheels over the rough ground. Removing the shield significantly reduced its weight. Examples are found with both fluted and smooth barrel jackets, the latter being of earlier production. The ammunition held a 250-round belt. (From the fonds of the RGAKFD in Krasnogorsk via www.Stavka.org.uk)

MOVEMENT AND FORMATION TRAINING

Training in section and platoon movement and assault formations began on an open field where the troops could see what was going on and where everyone was supposed to be. Then they moved to fields of high grass or scattered brush, and finally to a forest. Positions were well camouflaged. It is said that soldiers who had been peasants and or had lived in the country excelled at camouflage, making it appear natural and blending it into surrounding terrain. Soldiers from cities were less skilful. Obstacles and positions were often emplaced on reverse slopes to conceal them from ground observation and direct fire, although this location silhouetted an attacking soldier against the sky as he crested the high ground. Positions were also emplaced within forests and villages rather than on the edges. Decoy positions were common.

The Soviet soldier was renowned for withholding fire until the Germans were at close range. At the beginning of the war, Soviet doctrine called for weapons to engage the enemy at maximum range, but it was found more effective to 'ambush' him with a surprise burst from all weapons within optimum range from multiple directions. Reserve (alternate) firing positions were prepared for crew-served weapons, not only to occupy when the primary positions became untenable, but to mislead the enemy as to the location and numbers of weapons by constantly shifting positions. Supplementary positions were prepared to allow weapons to cover other sectors – flanks and rear.

Training was often cut short. Troops were needed at the front to organize new units or rebuild battered formations. Such events frequently occurred without warning. Troops would be ordered to return to their quarters, pack their gear and march to the nearest railroad station, sometimes without weapons. Weapons and ammunition would be issued at a railhead. There were actually incidents as depicted in the motion picture *Enemy at the Gates* (2001), when every other man was handed a rifle and a few clips, and the rest told to pick up weapons from the fallen.

Training units sent to the front in an emergency may have fought as units in some instances, with unfamiliar officers assigned directly from academies. Conversely, they might have been broken up into sub-units to replace other units destroyed in battle. The soldiers could also be assigned as individual replacements. More often, trained replacements were sent to the front in 'march units' as individual replacements to be assigned to engaged units, units in reserve, or units being reconstituted after prolonged action.

ORGANIZATION AND ATTACK FORMATIONS OF A RIFLE REGIMENT

The *vzvod* (rifle platoon) had a four-man headquarters and four nine-man *otdyeleniye* (rifle sections) for a total of 40 men. Previously 11-man sections had been fielded for a strength of 48 men. The platoon had two 'light' or Type A sections with one light machine gun apiece and two 'heavy' or Type B sections with two guns each. Both were the same strength, the number of riflemen being different. Owing to shortages, there might be only one machine gun per section. With losses, platoons typically fielded three or even just two sections and the remaining machine guns were more or less evenly allocated among 20–30 men. The section commander had a rifle, but by 1943 he more commonly had an SMG, and there might be two or three more SMGs assigned to each section, including to the assistant machine-gunner.

Each section fell in to the left of the section commander, a junior sergeant, who signalled this by standing at attention with his left arm outstretched horizontally to his side. The rest of the section fell in at arm intervals. In training they fell in by height, but in an organized fully trained section it was in a specific order according to duties from the left of the section commander: machine-gunner, assistant machine-gunner, second machine-gun crew if assigned, observer/guide and the riflemen.

The last man in the file, the 'closing man', was the most dependable rifleman, who brought up the rear, ensuring no one lagged behind. The observer/guide, a corporal, was the assistant section commander, aiding with control. The platoon would fall in with its two to four sections in parallel ranks. The platoon commander was centred in the front, the deputy platoon commander (sergeant) to the rear, and the two platoon messengers fell in at the end of sections with fewer men. The messengers may have relayed orders to section commanders, but their primary responsibility was to relay information to the company commander, who would send orders back with them or use his own messengers.

The basic section movement formation was the single-file column or 'chain'. The men were arranged in the same way as when they fell in, with the section commander at the head of the file. There were no wedge (inverted 'V'), echeloned or more complex movement formations. The column was easy to control, was relatively fast moving – each man did not have to break his own trail as in dispersed formations, something especially useful in dense vegetation or deep snow – was the quietest at night and in thick vegetation for the same reason and helped keep men from becoming

Opposite: Scouts cautiously search a peasant's cabin. The Germans might leave a few rearguards behind to harass, but the real danger was booby-traps. This PPS-40 SMG-armed soldier has an RGD-33 blast grenade at the ready. (From the fonds of the RGAKFD in Krasnogorsk via www.Stavka.org.uk)

separated. The only variant of the column was the skirmish column with the men positioned at extended intervals, up to eight paces depending on visibility, rather than one or two paces. There was only one attack formation, the skirmish line. Moving in a column, the section commander ordered 'Halt', and the men assumed the prone position. The section commander would then order, 'By the centre skirmish line', or 'Skirmish line to the left/ right'. 'By the centre' meant the machine-gun crew moved to the right of the section commander and the observer/guide to the left. If there was a second machine-gun crew it would move to the left and the observer/guide to its left. The assistant gunner was always to the gunner's right. Riflemen would then alternate moving to the right and left after the observer/guide until all were on line. This would be accomplished all at once at the run and required only seconds – a soldier did not wait for the man in front to move before moving himself. 'Skirmish line to the left/right' saw the men swinging out to the left or right of the section commander, remaining in their same order. 'Skirmish line to the left' resulted in the section commander being on the right end of the line and the left end for 'skirmish line right'. The interval between individuals was six to eight paces. Platoons moved and attacked in the same formations. A platoon skirmish line occupied a front of about 100m with four sections on line.

The only complex platoon formation was the platoon rhomboid (diamond) with one section forward, two some distance to the rear and separated by almost 100m, and one to the rear with the platoon command

Unit officers share vodka and black bread after a briefing, a common practice. The officer to the left wears the *shuba* sheepskin coat. All wear the popular *shapka-ushanka*. (From the fonds of the RGAKFD in Krasnogorsk via www.Stavka.org.uk)

group forward of the rear section and roughly between the flanking sections. This formation allowed sections to be manoeuvred to outflank an enemy position or respond to an enemy surprise attack.

The key difference between Soviet section and platoon tactics and those of the Germans (and Western Allies) was that there was no fire and manoeuvre or leap-frogging of sections whereby one unit covered those advancing. Sections and platoons assaulted as a body. Other platoons might provide covering fire along with supporting fire from crew-served weapons, but the assault platoons simply advanced as one. Platoons and sections could advance at a walk or run, move in short bounds from cover to cover or low-crawl depending on the situation, enemy fire and available cover. This manner of movement was specified when the attack order was given. The section commander and observer/guide ensured the men were generally aligned, but the line was not expected to be perfectly dressed – it could be staggered. If enemy fire was heavy and concealment existed, the unit infiltrated or 'seeped' into the enemy position.

When the platoon had closed in and was able to make its final assault rush, the troops were ordered to ensure that weapons were fully loaded and grenades prepared. On the order, *Na shturm, marshch!* (Assault, march!), they rose as a body and advanced at a run without bunching up or halting. Within 40–50m of the enemy positions they shouted the Russian battle cry, a deep drawn out *Urra!*, pronounced 'oo-rah', which translates as 'Hurrah!' and is thought to come from the Turkish word for 'kill'. They fired on the move and, when within range of enemy positions, threw grenades. They closed in rapidly for *blizhny boi* (close combat) with point-blank fire, bayonets, weapon butts, entrenching tools and fists.

Once the objective was seized the troops mopped up, ensuring dugouts and fighting positions were cleared. Communications trenches, gullies and other routes leading into the positions were secured and covered, and also exploited to continue the advance into the enemy's flanks and rear. The troops were to align themselves with only the most advanced men and be prepared to repel enemy counter-attacks.

APPEARANCE

The average Slav was 1.7m tall, as were most of the USSR's ethnic minorities. There were blonde, brown and red heads, but by far most had black hair and brown eyes. One contemporary description described 'Great Russians' as 'possessing eyes ranging from dark to light, fair to dark complexion, greater than average stature, moderate brachycephaly [short-headedness], and well-proportioned and well-developed limbs.' Hair was generally kept clipped very short all around. Even if worn an inch or so long on the top, the sides were clipped. This was for sanitation reasons – it made hair less vulnerable to head lice and easier to wash. Short-trimmed moustaches were seen, but were quite rare. Long moustaches were common among Cossacks.

Red Army uniforms were simple and functional, with little in the way of insignia. The insignia system was dictated by the 1935 *Prikaz* 176 regulations (traditional rank titles were not reintroduced until this year), and general ranks were restored in May 1940. Previously, position titles were used. The new rank titles and insignia were based on those of the Russian Empire, although they underwent some modifications. In an effort to improve morale, in 1943 new regulations were issued, *Prikaz* 25, which re-established traditional insignia and honorific titles, providing for other insignia and new uniform components. Gold braid was even requested through Lend-Lease, but rejected by the United States.

There was no unit identification, only branch of service devices and coloured piping worn on rank shoulder straps and collar tabs. The infantry used raspberry piping, but had no branch insignia as other branches did. Loyalty was to the Party and state, not to a unit. Personal awards for valour, merit and service were increased and worn on the uniform, even in combat.

Even before the 1943 reforms, the Soviet soldier wore traditional Russian-style *zashchitny tsvet* uniforms of light olive-brown or olive-drab. Photographs, however, depict soldiers wearing uniforms ranging across tans, browns, greens and greys, all within the same unit and with mismatched tunics and trousers. From 1944 uniforms were a darker olive-green shade. Different models of uniform were sometimes worn within the same unit. Newly raised units and units sent to the rear for rebuilding would be outfitted with new uniform issues. Soldiers considered their uniforms to be comfortable and often of better quality than their civilian clothes.

Headgear included the *pilotka* (side cap), the distinctive overseas-type field cap, often worn jauntily canted down to the right ear. It bore an olive-green star with a raised hammer and sickle, but could be replaced by an enamelled red star bearing a gold hammer and sickle. Officers were issued a *shlem* or *budionovka* (peaked cap), a round service cap with a black visor. The cap band, with a red enamelled metal star, and the crown edge piping were in the branch colour.

The olive-drab steel helmet was to be worn in combat, sometimes with a solid or outlined red star painted on the front. They might be whitewashed in winter or white cloth covers were fabricated. Steel helmets offered no protection from the cold and could even cause frostbite on the tops of ears – soldiers sometimes removed the liner so it could be worn over the fur cap. Commanders often had problems enforcing the wear of helmets as soldiers considered helmets unmanly and so fines and penalties had to be imposed. In the early days, helmets were not available to many units and some still lacked them in 1945.

The 1936 uniform consisted of the *gymnastyorka* (tunic) based on the traditional peasant's blouse. The loose-fitting pullover had a front opening extending halfway down the chest. Its patch-type breast pockets had buttoned flaps and it had a stand-and-fall collar, usually worn buttoned closed. Collar and front opening buttons were concealed.

Olive-green metal rank insignia were worn on elongated collar tabs that were the same colour as the uniform. Officers usually had branch-colour piped tabs. The olive-green pocket flap buttons were exposed, but might be replaced by brass buttons, especially on officers' tunics. The 1943 field uniform was similar to the 1936, but had a more traditional standing collar, and rank was displayed on shoulder straps. A white tack-stitched collar liner was used, but often disappeared during field duty. It had three front-opening and two collar buttons, olive-green or brass. The breast pockets were concealed, but with single-buttoned flaps. Rank was displayed on the

Sergeants receive decorations. Their shoulder-strap rank stripes and edge piping are in the rifle troops' raspberry red. Medals and orders suspended from ribbons were generally worn on the left breast and badges on the right, but there were exceptions. (From the fonds of the RGAKFD in Krasnogorsk via www.Stavka.org.uk)

shoulder straps. The *sharovari* (trousers) were semi-breeches, loose-fitting around the thighs and tight at the ankles with tie tapes. The field uniform was cotton for summer wear, which faded considerably, and wool for winter. Late in the war the United States provided high-quality uniforms through Lend-Lease.

Black leather ankle-high boots were standard issue for the summer months. These were worn with tan or olive-drab puttees. In the winter high-top black leather marching boots – termed *govnodavy* (shit-tramper) – were issued. In reality, either boot might be worn in any season. Marching boots were issued a size larger so two or more layers of footwraps could protect the feet. Boots would also be lined with newspaper, straw or cloth in the winter. *Portyanki* (footwraps) – cotton or wool rectangles – were traditional and preferred by many old soldiers. They cost less than socks and did not wear out as fast. Footwrap cloth was issued in bolts and soldiers cut the wraps to size. Officers were sometimes issued socks and socks might be sent by a soldier's family. German footwear was commonly looted.

The brownish-grey wool *shinel* (greatcoat) completed the uniform; its traditional colour was effective camouflage in winter woods against brownish-grey tree trunks and mist, although some were olive-drab. It

Snowsuit-clad troops pass through a burned village. Both sides habitually burned buildings when retreating to deny the other side their shelter from the cold. Note that bayonets are not carried fixed, counter to normal practice. (From the fonds of the RGAKFD in Krasnogorsk via www.Stavka.org.uk)

was carried in all but the hottest summer months. The Soviet soldier was not issued blankets or sleeping bags; his greatcoat was meant to suffice. Of course, commandeered civilian and captured German blankets were valued.

The *plasch palatka* (shelter-cape) was a roughly triangular-shaped waterproof multi-use item. A tape and button at the base of the hood fastened around the neck and held the cape in place when worn over the shoulders. On the lower centre of the back was a wooden toggle to which the lower corner grommet was attached to keep it off the ground. The grommets were leather-reinforced. As a shelter, the shelter-cape could be rigged as a lean-to or ground-cloth, or the soldier could roll up in it. Two could be laced together with a cord through the grommets, but the ends were open. A cramped six-man tent could be rigged with two laced-together capes on either side and one on each end. As a bedroll it was rolled in a U-shape with the greatcoat inside and the ends secured by a leather strap or cord. Shelter-capes were usually light olive-green, grey-green or dark tan. The similar officer's *plasch nikidka* could not be used as a shelter-half; it had arm slits in the sides, an adjustable neck tape, and buttons to hold the hood in place when not used.

The brutal Russian winter demanded protective clothing. Even though the Red Army was intimately familiar with the winter, in the early stages of the war it was not always well prepared, often due to production shortfalls. It was, for example, impossible to produce sufficient clothing for issue in the winter of 1941/42. The invasion took the logistics system by surprise and it was unable to issue standard uniforms and equipment to the rapidly expanding army and prepare for the winter, which imposed itself less than five months after the Germans attacked. Cold weather clothing was inadequate during the Winter War in Finland and changes were only just being implemented.

The old-type bluntly pointed *budionovka* or *vki* (wool cap) had a fold-up woollen ear and neck flap and a small visor. It had proved ineffective in Finland's severe cold, but was still being issued. The 1940 *shapka-ushanka* (fur cap) had a fur-lined brownish-grey wool crown, fold-up visor, and ear flaps that tied over the top when not needed. The visor and ear flaps were fur-covered and known as 'fish fur caps', as the artificial fur bore no resemblance to that of any animal.

The winter uniform consisted of a *telogreika* (padded jacket) and *vatnie sharovari* (padded trousers) worn over the wool winter field uniform. They were sewn with vertical tubes filled with cotton batting. The *telogreika* lacked breast pockets, had a full-length front opening secured by loops and toggles or buttons, and could have a short standing collar or an earlier stand-and-fall-type. Other issue winter clothing included a *polushubok* (sheepskin jacket), *shuba* (sheepskin coat) and *sakui* (sealskin coveralls). There were shortages throughout the war and much use was made of civilian and German winter clothing. White cotton and wool long *portyanki* (underwear) were issued along with the knitted wool *sviter* (sweater), *rukavitsa* (mittens) and knitted, canvas and leather *perchatka* (gloves) with fur lining. Women knitted millions of scarves and socks and these were distributed to troops by the Party. For very cold weather, high-top compressed grey felt boots – *valenki* – were issued and proved popular, but soaked through and disintegrated in the spring snowmelt. Civilian equivalents were often commandeered. During the rainy spring and autumn, high-topped *kirozovy sapogi* – waterproof canvas boots with leather soles – were sometimes issued. In the early days of the war it was not uncommon for troops to go into combat wearing civilian clothes, Western-style business suits with waistcoats, and workers' uniforms with round caps. Gulag convicts went into combat wearing their black uniforms.

WEAPONS

Soviet infantry weapons were known for their simplicity, ruggedness and general reliability. The average soldier had very little in the way of technical knowledge. Factory workers and farmhands used only simple tools, often manual. Equipment operators were taught to operate one type of machine or were responsible for one function on an assembly line. Therefore, weapons needed to be simple to operate and maintain. Reliability was essential, not only for the obvious reason – effective function in combat – but also to endure the climate extremes and the poor logistics that could not be counted on to provide spare parts and repairs. The Soviet soldier would not hesitate to criticize an ineffective weapon, which he would call a *pukalka* (wind-emitter).

It was not until the 1890s that Russia began developing its own weapons, and foreign-designed weapons or weapons borrowing foreign influence were still in use in the Great Patriotic War. Most infantry weapons at the war's beginning were adequate and by 1943 numerous new and more effective weapons were being fielded. For most soldiers the rifle was the most complex piece of machinery they had ever dealt with – for a farmhand experienced in handling picks, shovels, hoes and sickles, the bolt-action Mosin-Nagant 7.62mm M1891/30 rifle was advanced technology. The

M1891/30 remained the standard infantry rifle through the war and was known to soldiers as the *vintovka Mosina* (Mosin rifle) or by an old term, *trechlineynaja* (three-line). (The term was based on an old system of measurement in which 'one-line' equalled 2.5mm. 'Three-line' equalled 7.62mm or .30-cal.) For the era it was a comparatively long rifle, being 1,232mm long, 127mm longer than the German Kar 98k carbine. While rugged and reliable, its bolt was overly complex and required good cleaning. The rifleman also considered his weapon heavy at 3.97kg – with its web sling and bayonet another half a kilo was added.

The 432mm-long M1891 cruciform *shtik* (spike bayonet) had a locking socket that fitted around the foresight. It also had a screwdriver-type flat tip and could be used as such. The bayonet was habitually carried fixed to the rifle and seldom were scabbards issued. (Prior to and early in the war, bayonet scabbards were issued to some units. These were simple tubular leather or canvas sheaths.) When the soldier was in rear areas, travelling in trucks or trains, or inside restricted fortifications, the bayonet was reversed with the blade running down the fore-end. It was usually a tight fit and difficult to remove and attach. On early production rifles, the fitting often loosened.

Advancing rifle troops halt for a meal break. An M1944 carbine can be seen on the simple backpack in the lower centre. On the parapet of an old trench are numerous sub-machine guns. (From the fonds of the RGAKFD in Krasnogorsk via www.Stavka.org.uk)

A sharpshooter has obviously been successful in downing a German. The Red Army was comprised of soldiers representing scores of ethnic groups. They wear the baggy camouflage suit with dull black splotches on an olive-drab backing. (Courtesy of the Central Museum of the Armed Forces, Moscow via www.Stavka.org.uk)

The Mosin's shooting qualities were reasonable. The rear sight was graduated from 100–2,000m and was ill suited for a fine degree of accuracy, but its realistic combat range was about 400m. The bolt action was fairly smooth and quick to operate, but the safety was stiff. It was operated by rotating the knob on the end of the bolt to the right to lock it on safe. If wet and then frozen, it could be difficult to unlock – soldiers were taught to urinate on it for an immediate thaw-out. The rifle's internal magazine was loaded with a five-round charging clip, which was inserted into slots in the rear of the receiver and the rounds pushed down into the magazine with the thumb. When the bolt was closed, a round would be chambered, but the rounds could be depressed into the magazine with the thumb and the bolt closed over the round. A charger was not necessary, as rounds could be inserted individually into the magazine. A rifleman could crack off eight to ten aimed rounds a minute with reloading.

Two carbine versions of the Mosin were issued to engineers, artillerymen, cavalrymen, signalmen and other auxiliary troops. By 1943 they were also being issued to some infantry units fighting in cities, notably Stalingrad, to provide a more manageable weapon in confined spaces. The M1938 was only 1,016mm long, weighed 3.46kg, and had a rear sight graduated for only 100–1,000m. A bayonet could not be fitted as it was of little use to cavalrymen and support troops. The M1944 was identical, but had a permanently attached 311mm-long folding spike bayonet, which folded along the right side. Prototypes of this carbine were issued in Stalingrad in late 1943. The carbines were noted for their hard recoil owing to their short barrels.

The USSR was one of the first nations to adopt a semi-automatic rifle on a large scale. Early efforts were too flimsy, complex and expensive. This was especially true of the Tokarev 7.62mm SVT-38 rifle. It was dropped in 1940, although it was pressed into service after the German invasion. The SVT-40 was a bit more robust, but still considered too fragile for general combat use. Prior to the war, a few units were fully armed with the SVT-40, but they were destroyed in combat and the remaining rifles distributed piecemeal to Mosin-armed units. They may have been given to selected soldiers or sergeants.

The SVT-40 was 1,221mm long, making it almost as long as the Mosin, because it had a muzzle break. It weighed 3.9kg without its detachable ten-round magazine. It had a conventional 241mm blade bayonet with a metal scabbard. A man armed with an SVT-40 usually carried one spare magazine in a leather pouch and routinely reloaded the magazine in the rifle using two five-round charger clips. A good shooter could fire and reload about 40 rounds per minute (rpm), if he had four ten-round magazines. If he had to reload with chargers he might get off 20–25rpm. Firepower was not significantly increased, with just a few SVTs distributed to a rifle platoon.

A key weapon of the rifle section was its one or two 7.62mm Degtyarev DP light machine guns adopted in 1928. The bipod-mounted DP could be fired from the ground or from the underarm or hip position when advancing. It was provided with a 47-round pan magazine, resulting in its being called the '*proigryvatel*' (record-player). It weighed 11.95kg loaded and was 1,270mm long. It could hammer out 500–600rpm. The DP was about the same weight, length and bulk as the 7.92mm MG34, the German squad automatic weapon, but the MG34 was a belt-fed weapon with a quick-change barrel, was more rugged and put out 800–900rpm. Fired in short bursts, the DP had a practical rate of fire of about 80rpm, but

A Guards private carries two German weapons, a Panzerfaust 60 and an Eihgr.38 'egg grenade'. The Panzerfaust was considered a valuable capture and widely used because the Red Army fielded no comparable light, portable, one-man anti-tank weapon. The soldier wears the Guards badge on his right breast and the Order of Glory on his left. The orange-and-black-striped decoration was the most common valour award. The Medal for Victory over Germany used the same ribbon, but with a round medal. (From the fonds of the RGAKFD in Krasnogorsk via www.Stavka.org.uk)

was considered a bit fragile and its operating spring was coiled around the under-barrel operating rod, which resulted in the spring heating up and distorting, causing malfunctions. The DP was redesigned and the DPM was fielded in 1944. The recoil spring was relocated to a tubular housing protruding from the rear of the receiver, the safety lever was improved, a pistol grip added and the bipod fitting strengthened and redesigned so the gun could be set up on uneven ground. To make up for shortages, DT tank machine guns were adapted to infantry use. The DT had a ratchet-type telescoping steel butt stock, pistol grip, and 60-round pan magazine. In the infantry role a bipod was attached to the firing port adapter ring and iron sights added. The DT was widely used in the infantry role and reported to be popular due to the magazine capacity. (The magazines were not interchangeable between the DP/DPM and DT/DTM.) The DTM, incorporating similar improvements to the DPM, was also modified to an infantry machine gun.

The fighting in 1941 forced the Soviets to examine the equipment needs of the Rifle Forces. Soviet infantry equipment was based on both tactical needs and the restricted abilities of Soviet industry to provide equipment. One of the most obvious differences between the Red Army and the Wehrmacht was the relative balance of rifles to sub-machine guns (SMGs). During the war the Soviet Union manufactured 18.3 million rifles and SMGs of which 6.1 million (34 per cent) were SMGs. In contrast, the Germans manufactured 11.6 million rifles and SMGs, of which only 1.2 million (11 per cent) were SMGs. Indeed, by the end of the war, the popular image of the Red Army soldier was the 7.62mm PPSh-41. Also known as the *peh-peh-shah* or *balalaika*, the PPSh-41 was a rugged and reliable weapon, being only 842mm long, but heavy at 5.45kg with a loaded 71-round drum magazine. The underpowered pistol round was its major deficiency; another was the magazine, which was heavy, slow and difficult to load, expensive, easily damaged and rattled. In 1944 a more reliable curved 35-round magazine issued with the PPS-43 (see below) became available for the PPSh-41 and reduced the loaded weight to 4.2kg. Its rate of fire was unnecessarily high at 700–900rpm. The PPSh-41 required an exceedingly heavy 9–11kg trigger pull. A less frequently used sub-machine gun was the PPS-43. It was largely made of stampings and had a folding steel stock: with the stock extended the gun was 831mm long, folded it was 616mm long. It weighed 3.62kg with its loaded 35-round magazine and fired at a more practical 650rpm.

Soviet preference for this type of infantry weapon stemmed from two causes. On the one hand, the PPSh-41 and its close relatives (particularly the later PPS-43) were cheaper and easier to manufacture than normal rifles, which required longer rifled barrels and precise machining. The PPSh-41 used pistol ammunition, which was also cheaper than rifle ammunition as it consumed less propellant and brass. The other reason was related to training. Rifle fire, to be effective, requires training and practice – commodities that were in short supply in Russia during the war. In contrast, the PPSh-41 required little marksmanship training, and was ideally suited to close-range skirmishing. German SMGs like the MP40 were precision-crafted weapons. They were usually given to section leaders or troops with special requirements; they were never issued as lavishly as the Soviet SMGs, and many German infantrymen prized captured Soviet SMGs over the standard German 98k rifle. (It might also be noted that Russian troops, especially scouts, prized captured German MP38s and MP 40s for their compactness and light weight.)

Rifle troops clad in the padded winter uniform. The man to the left is armed with a 7.62mm SVT-40 semi-automatic rifle. The others have various German weapons. The man in the centre with the black cap has a 7.92mm Kar 98k carbine and the second from the left a World War I Kar 98a carbine. (Courtesy of the Central Museum of the Armed Forces, Moscow via www.Stavka.org.uk)

Handguns were mainly issued to officers, but many company officers armed themselves with SMGs. Most weapons crewmen were issued carbines or SMGs. It was common for the gunner himself to be armed with only his primary weapon, especially if this was a machine gun. The Tokarev 7.62mm TT-33 was a compact pistol with an eight-round magazine and weighed 0.8kg. Wide use was also made of the obsolete Nagant 7.62mm M1895 double-action revolver. It had a unique means of sealing the gap between the cylinder and barrel. The mouth of the cartridge case protruded slightly beyond the cylinder (the bullet was completely recessed in the case). When cocked, the cylinder cammed forward and the end of the case was set into the barrel. This system increased the velocity and range of the otherwise underpowered round. As the gun was of small calibre, the cylinder had seven chambers. The revolver weighed 0.75kg.

Hand grenades were widely used and included the F-1 fragmentation (known as the *limonka* – lemon), RG-42 fragmentation and RGD-33 blast grenades, the latter with a slip-on fragmentation sleeve. *Ruchnaya Protivotankovoye Granata* (hand anti-tank grenade) types included the RPG-40, RPG-43 and RPG-6. Large numbers of German 3kg magnetic hollow-charge hand mines were also used. These represented such a threat that the Germans were forced to apply 'anti-magnetic' plaster on their tanks and assault guns for protection from a hand-delivered weapon of their own making. What the Russians called a *butylka s goryuchej smesyu* (lit. 'bottle with flammable mixture') was seldom referred to as a *Molotov-kokteil* (Molotov cocktail) as it was not 'politically correct' to make light of their leaders' names. Besides the usual Molotov cocktails made in the field with rag wicks, in 1940 the Soviets provided two 'incendiary liquid kits' to ensure more reliable ignition: No. 1 and the KS. These consisted of a sulphuric acid-based compound in two long paper-covered tubes attached to gasoline-filled vodka or cognac bottles by two rubber bands. When the bottles shattered upon impact the sulphuric acid reacted with and ignited the gasoline. Another method, when incendiary kits were not available, was to tie or tape a rag wad to the neck of a plugged bottle. The rag wad was soaked with gasoline from another bottle, lit and the bottle thrown to ignite when shattered. This technique prevented the leakage problem. Other than the anti-tank hand grenades and mostly ineffective anti-tank rifle grenades, there were no anti-tank weapons available to the rifle company.

Two types of 14.5mm anti-tank rifles were often attached from battalion and regimental levels. Both bipod-mounted rifles were heavy and long, but could be broken down into two sections. The Degtyarov PTRD-41 was a single-shot bolt-action rifle, 1,999mm long and weighing 17kg. The Simonov PTRS-41 was semi-automatic with a five-round magazine and saw less service – it was expensive and complex. The 14.5mm armour-piercing incendiary round could penetrate 20mm of armour at 100m. Soon obsolete, the anti-tank rifles nevertheless remained in use, with tactics emphasizing side and rear attack as well as use against light armoured fighting vehicles (AFVs), especially if used in large numbers. Some Lend-Lease anti-tank weapons were provided by the United States and Britain: 2.36in M1 bazookas, 0.55in Boys anti-tank rifles, and PIAT Mk 1 anti-tank projectors.

Each unit from section upwards possessed its own fire-support weapons. There were also additional supporting weapons at each echelon from company up that could be attached to selected subordinate units to augment their firepower, and/or were retained under the parent unit's control to allow the commander to reinforce or influence the combat capabilities of a sub-unit. The regiment especially was provided with a generous number

A dismounted cavalry unit serving as infantry. Cossacks and some other cavalrymen traditionally wore dark-blue breeches. At least six cavalry divisions (numbered 15 and 116 Don; 12, 13 and 50 Kuban; and 53 Terek) were recruited from the Cossack communities, and all attained Guards status by 1942. (Courtesy of TASS via www.Stavka.org.uk)

of supporting weapons and rear service sub-units, more so than any other nation's infantry regiment. Rifle companies were provided with two, sometimes three, 50mm *Rotney Minomyot* (mortars): the RM-38, RM-39, RM-40 or RM-41. The first three were of the conventional Brandt design used by most countries, but each model was soon replaced owing to cost and manufacturing time. The RM-39 was also too heavy compared to the others. The RM-41 dispensed with the bipod to provide an even simpler weapon on a large baseplate. Except for the 17kg RM-39, the mortars weighed 9–12.1kg and had an 800m range. They all fired the same high-explosive round, which was little more effective than a hand grenade. All models remained in use, but production ceased in early 1942, and they were withdrawn from service in 1944. Remaining rounds were converted to hand grenades.

The spigot-type RM rifle grenade launcher firing the VGD-30 fragmentation and RPG-40 anti-tank grenades was used until phased out in 1943. The VPGS-41 rod-type anti-tank rifle grenade, which did not require a launcher, was merely inserted in the rifle; it was withdrawn in 1942. It had poor penetration and short range, and repeated firing damaged the rifle. Another infantry weapon that was quickly withdrawn was the 37mm 'spade mortar'. The hinged blade served as a base plate and a monopod was stowed in the barrel. It had only a 250m range, its tiny bomb was ineffective, and it made a poor shovel.

Use was made of captured German arms, especially after the USSR went on the offensive in 1943. Soldiers sought 9mm Luger P08 and Walther P38 pistols, 9mm MP40 machine pistols, MG34 and MG42 machine guns, hand grenades, hand mines and the Panzerfaust, which they called a *Faust*. This anti-tank projector was especially valuable owing to the lack of comparable Soviet light, portable anti-tank weapons. Coloured pyrotechnic flares were fired from a compact 26.5mm signal pistol, and this could fire captured German signal cartridges.

PERSONAL EQUIPMENT

The rifleman's equipment was simple and functional. At the beginning of the war the equipment was of generally good quality. Because of the massive losses, the sudden shortage of materials and the demands of mass production, simplified designs began to be fielded.

The 1936 equipment was of modern design and well made. The backpack was of the rucksack type with two small flap-closed pockets. The securing straps for the main compartment and the pouch flaps were made of leather.

Straps were provided on the bottom to fasten a small pouch carrying pegs, pole sections and guy rope to make the shelter-cape into a two-man tent when paired with another man's. The shoulder straps and back were padded. Inside the main compartment were carried a change of underwear, footwraps, rations, small cooking pot and maybe a cup.

The toilet kit and rifle cleaning kit were carried in the external pockets. The greatcoat and shelter-cape were carried in a horseshoe roll strapped to the pack. If the pack was not used the greatcoat and shelter-cape were carried as a bedroll over the left shoulder and the ends strapped or tied together at the right hip. Small essential items were carried in the roll.

A dark-brown leather belt was issued. On either side of the belt's front was a leather two-pocket rifle cartridge pouch, each pocket holding two five-round charger clips for a total of 40 rounds. A canvas reserve cartridge pouch was on the belt's back, holding six five-round clips. A cloth bandoleer might be issued for 14 more clips to carry a *boyekomplekt* (full complement) of ammunition. In place of the reserve cartridge pouch, a ration bag was often carried. The entrenching tool and water bottle (which held just under 1 litre) were attached over the right hip. The cover was a simple bag, sometimes with a drawstring, with a buttoned cloth strap to secure the water bottle. The gas mask was carried on the left side suspended by a strap over the right shoulder. By 1942 gas masks were mostly turned in as unnecessary, but maintained in depots. *Bolshaya sapyornaya lopata* (entrenching tools) had either a pointed or square blade. The carrier was square-shaped with the flap secured by a leather strap and buckle or a cloth strap and button. Some men carried a small hatchet inside a canvas carrier.

Much of the early-issue equipment was lost during the defensive battles of 1941 and their mass loss of troops. Its production ceased and to replace it extremely simple and low-quality equipment was issued. Coarse canvas and thin webbing were used and shoddy leather or artificial substitutes were introduced, such as rubber-impregnated canvas. Fabric colours varied and were sometimes mixed in the same item. Most items were dark-tan or light olive-drab. The new belt was 38mm wide canvas reinforced by a 19mm leather strip. Fittings and fasteners were cheap metal, plastic buttons, wooden toggles and loops, or tie-tapes. Leather cartridge pouches were still issued, but also artificial leather and canvas. One- to three-pocket canvas hand grenade pouches were also issued along with special pouches for other weapons' magazines. Often soldiers were not issued complete sets of equipment, making do with what was available.

The 1941 *veshhevoi meshok* (simple backpack) was a canvas sack with a drawstring top closure, and was actually a revived World War I design. A U-shaped shoulder strap was attached to the bottom of the pack and the 'top' of the 'U' was simply knotted around the puckered top closure in such a manner as to adjust the strap's length to the wearer. A buckled chest strap held the shoulder straps in place. Basically the same items found in the 1936 pack were carried. The shelter-cape tent items, ration bag and reserve cartridge pouch were seldom issued. Glass water bottles with cork stoppers were often substituted for metal. Often not even a pack was issued. Everything was carried in an over-the-shoulder bedroll of the greatcoat and shelter-cape which could also be carried with the simple backpack. There were instances where soldiers went into combat without a single item of equipment, carrying their ammunition in trouser pockets.

Personal items were spartan. A *perevgzochnii paket* (wound dressing packet) was carried in a tunic pocket; it was a light grey cloth with red markings. A soldier would be fortunate to have a small towel and toothbrush. Toothpaste and powder were almost unheard of luxuries, and often soap was just as rare. Usually a stick with a chewed end sufficed for a toothbrush, birch being particularly good for this. The soldier might have a comb, pocket mirror and straight razor, often shared within his section. Someone in the section had a sewing kit, a little folding five-pocket canvas pouch with needles, thread, thimble and buttons. Such items might be carried in a small cloth bags or simply rolled up in a towel. Cigarette lighters were made from 12.7mm cartridge cases by soldering on a flint igniter wheel. Commercial lighters were used but scarce, as were common wooden matches. Not every soldier was issued with weapons cleaning gear, but a few sets were carried by a section. A two-compartment tin container held oil and solvent. A tan cloth envelope-like pouch with tie tapes held a bore guide, dual-purpose tool (screwdriver and firing pin protrusion gauge), cleaning rod handle and cleaning jag.

The pre-war mess kit was similar to the German version, but more commonly issued was a small cook pot with a pail handle. An enamelled plate and cup were carried by most troops, along with a spoon. Recruits were directed to bring a spoon, which they tucked into a boot, when reporting for duty. A small utility or hunting knife was frequently carried, more as a tool than a weapon. Popular types were the *finka* and Finnish *puukko*; each had a short, broad blade with a leather sheath fully enclosing the knife up to its pommel.

Officers were issued a quality brown leather belt with an open-faced rectangular buckle and shoulder strap, haversack, leather-trimmed canvas map case, 6×30 B-1 binoculars, wrist compass, wristwatch and a brown leather pistol or revolver holster.

CONDITIONS OF SERVICE

The degree of discipline, state of quarters, quality and abundance of food, sanitation conditions, standard of training and the availability of equipment and training facilities varied greatly due to the size of the Red Army and the desperate wartime situation. A soldier from one unit might report that he received quality food during training while another said he nearly starved, receiving mostly spoiled food while the good food was sold on by the cooks.

Quarters could be any structure that would serve the purpose. One unit might be quartered in heated barracks with two-tier bunks, mattresses and pillows. Often only two- and three-tier plank sleeping platforms were provided. The soldiers might be issued two sheets, a pillow case, and a brown cotton blanket. Mattresses and pillows were usually stuffed with

In the defence a rifle platoon dug one-man fighting holes, but if the position was occupied long enough these were connected by trenches. Here troops move down the trench to reinforce another sector. They wear the old Kaska-36 helmet. (From the fonds of the RGAKFD in Krasnogorsk via www.Stavka.org.uk)

straw by the soldiers themselves. Quarters were cramped, as the mass influx of troops did not allow the regulation space per person; other troops slept outdoors on straw on the ground with a thin blanket. Tents were sometimes available, usually with straw on the floor, or even cots. Soldiers might also be quartered in village houses and barns, in which case they were often fed by civilians. Peasant log cabins – an *izba* – were often draughty and lice-infested. Families might be turned out or remain to feed the troops. In the rear areas troops might be quartered in public buildings, offices and business establishments, schools, warehouses or any other available shelter.

Latrines with running water were inadequate or inoperable, making latrine pits necessary. Kitchen facilities were often poorly maintained and unsanitary. Garbage was infrequently disposed of. In general, sanitation was poor, resulting in boils, diarrhoea, stomach disorders, tuberculosis and a variety of other disorders. Troops were to visit a *banya* (bathhouse) every ten days and exchange underwear. In practice it might only be once or twice a month.

A cook mixes a concoction, probably for the unit's officers, as enlisted men's food was prepared in large batches while officers received special rations. (Courtesy of the Central Museum of the Armed Forces, Moscow via www.Stavka.org.uk)

FOOD

Red Army rations were frequently dismal. Food shortages were serious during the early defeats and retreats. The early loss of the Ukraine, the USSR's bread basket, caused serious shortages and worsened just a few months later with the onset of winter. Often villagers, voluntarily or under orders, provided food, which was known as 'grandmother's rations' and typically consisted of boiled chickens and potatoes. But an army with thousands of troops could not live off the land, especially during mobile warfare. There were instances of only bread and butter for breakfast and for dinner a small wash tub of boiled beetroots was eaten communally. There was no lunch at such times of shortage. Soldiers seldom had money to purchase food locally, as it had been driven to exorbitantly high prices. Conditions did improve somewhat after 1943, but there were always shortages.

Armies and fronts possessed rear service organizations, which foraged and purchased food, harvested crops and raised livestock. Butter, grains and vegetables were purchased locally by the army rations and fodder division. Divisions possessed flour mills to grind grain, and livestock were delivered on the hoof to regimental kitchens. Captured German food stocks were valued. As in all armies, the rear service troops were unpopular and were referred to as *krysa* (rats) or *tylovaya krysa* (rear rats) by the frontline riflemen. Much of the field ration was bread, canned meats and fresh and preserved vegetables. Dried peas were issued in packaged blocks. Black rye bread was baked in regimental bakeries. Tinned meats included *tushonka* (stewed pork or beef – very greasy) and tinned herring and other fish such as *kilka* and *bichki* (cooked in tomato sauce when available). Spam (canned lunch meat) was provided through Lend-Lease by the United States and called *vtoroy front myaso* (second-front meat). Stalin credited it with saving the Red Army. Another Lend-Lease food was *Rosevelt yaitsa* (Roosevelt

Troops eat their meal from the standard mess kit, a simple pot, in a well-constructed trench. Porridge and soups were typical fare. (Courtesy of the Central Museum of the Armed Forces, Moscow via www.Stavka.org.uk)

eggs) – powdered eggs. Salted herring and *moskovskaya* (summer sausage) supplemented meat rations. Grits, macaroni and vermicelli (thin spaghetti) were issued along with cooking oil and *salo* (pork back fat).

Two of the most common dishes were *shchi* and *kasha*, resulting in a soldier's slogan – *Shchi i kasha, pisha nasha* ('Shchi and kasha, that's our fare'). The Russian soldier was already familiar with them. *Shchi* is cabbage soup made with meat broth, although water frequently replaced the broth. Potatoes, carrots and onions might be added, though seldom did they grace the dish on the frontline. *Kasha* was a roasted buckwheat groats porridge boiled in water and salt. *Kasha* might be considered a breakfast food, but like *shchi*, might have been served as any meal's main course. *Kasha* made with millet was known as 'shrapnel' owing to hard uncooked grains. Boiled potatoes and potato soup (*kartofel' sup*) were also served along with *borsch* (beet soup with carrots and onions).

A rare treat was *kissel*, stewed fruit thickened with cornflour. The standard beverage was *chai* (hot sugared tea), often brewed in a liberated charcoal-fired samovar. Real Russian tea is brewed in a small amount of water to make a concentrate. This is poured into a glass to which boiling water and sugar are added. Beer, cognac and vodka were also issued. The *Narkom 100-gramm* (People's Commissariat of Defence 100-gram) described the supposed daily issue of vodka. Soldiers had a reputation for drinking anything. Vodka was a drug of sorts and there is truth to the stories of units being deliberately intoxicated before driven to attack.

The Soviet soldier's ration included tobacco and cigarette papers. *Makhorka* was a poor, cheap, finely chopped tobacco. Soldiers rolled their own cigarettes using *makhorka* and whatever paper they could find, usually newspaper. Before the war, no Western-style cigarettes were produced; there were only *papirosi*, paper tubes with the front one-third

A recalled reservist lights up a *makhorka* cigarette. They were traditionally rolled in a 'fat' manner in whatever paper was available. Some soldiers developed a fondness for them and continued to smoke them after the war. (Courtesy of the Central Museum of the Armed Forces, Moscow via www.Stavka.org.uk)

filled with tobacco. Officers were issued better commercial cigarettes such as the Kazbek brand. Field exchanges were available down to division-level where soldiers could buy toiletry items, paper and pencils, etc. There were also canteens serving tea and snacks, and barber shops.

Meals were prepared by company or battalion field kitchens such as the PK-43 mobile kitchen. If at all possible, a hot breakfast and dinner were served. Hard biscuits, sausage or bacon or canned meat, and tea would be provided for lunch and on operations that took the soldiers away from the kitchens. Alternatively, if supplies were short they might receive only a *soldat buterbrod* (soldiers' sandwich), a single slice of black bread.

MEDICAL CARE

Medical care was marginal. Each higher echelon was responsible for evacuating casualties from their subordinate units; for example, the battalion sent two litter teams to each company. Ideally, two doctors operated the battalion aid station. Individuals in platoons were trained as medics as a secondary duty. Dressings, instruments and procedures were usually inadequate and outdated. Sulpha drugs and other antibiotics were

Regimental and divisional bakeries produced black bread, a main staple, here to be delivered to frontline units by a *pulk* sled drawn by a sturdy Bashkir pony. (Courtesy of the Central Museum of the Armed Forces, Moscow via www.Stavka.org.uk)

scarce and morphine almost unheard of. Illness was a major problem and most Russians had not received preventive inoculations as in Western countries. Peasant remedies were often the soldiers' only resort. Particular problems were encountered with typhus, pneumonia, dysentery, meningitis, tuberculosis, diphtheria and malaria. Frostbite and trench foot caused massive casualties. Lice were also a serious problem. Periodic lice checks were to be made, called a 'Form 20'. The visits to the *banya* served to rid the troops of lice and their uniforms were supposed to be laundered and steamed, but this was impossible during prolonged field duty. Troops spent a lot of time picking lice out from uniforms. One method of lice removal was to bury the uniform with a collar tip poking out of the cold ground and burn emerging lice with a cigarette.

PUNISHMENT

The Red Army legal system was complex, with no single regulation codifying all crimes and misdemeanours and under the control of no single agency. The type of punishment, its extent, and on what rank categories it could be imposed depended on the command echelon. For example, a section commander or assistant platoon commander could warn, privately reprimand, reprimand in ranks, delay discharge by one week or assign one day's extra fatigue to his men. A company commander could reprimand all subordinates, reprimand soldiers in ranks, delay discharge six weeks for soldiers and four for sergeants, assign extra fatigues to soldiers for eight days and sergeants for four, arrest soldiers for ten days and sergeants for five, hold a Comrade's Court of soldiers and sergeants, forbid leave or confine to

PAY

Soldiers were paid once a month, but often they never saw the money unless in the rear. All or part of the pay could be allotted to next-of-kin, but this was sometimes impossible owing to massive civilian displacements and casualties. Often pay was held and at some future time the soldier would receive back pay. Soldiers were, however, exempt from taxes. The 1943 base pay was 600 rubles (600R) for a private, 1,000R for a corporal, 2,000R for a junior sergeant and 3,000R for a sergeant. There were categories of special pay, including field pay to combat troops, Guards units, anti-tank, and tank troops (50 per cent base pay), jump pay for paratroopers (25R per jump), and bonuses for the award of certain decorations. Allotments were also paid to fathers over 60; mothers over 55; invalided parents, wives, and children; and children under 16.

quarters for three days. By regulation the only crimes for which the death penalty and confiscation of property were allowed were desertion by both enlisted men and officers and absence without leave by officers. In reality, officers and enlisted men were also executed for cowardliness, retreating or ordering retreat without authority, aiding the enemy and spying.

The disciplinary system included encouragements and awards bestowed on men who conducted themselves conscientiously and assiduously in their duties. They might be given expressions of gratitude in the ranks or in orders of the day, granted extra off-duty time, be presented with valuable gifts or monetary awards or have any disciplinary penalties withdrawn. Units also received decorations and honorific titles for battles as a means of improving morale.

ENTERTAINMENT

The importance of entertainment was recognized as a means of improving troop morale and a further method for disseminating propaganda and improving motivation. Co-ordinated by political officers known as

A rifle company marches through a liberated German city. Loot is evident, and includes a guitar. This platoon's three sections appear to comprise six or seven men each. The assistant platoon commander brings up the rear. (Courtesy of the Central Museum of the Armed Forces, Moscow via www.Stavka.org.uk)

A captain of sappers is grateful for the delivery of a food parcel from home, regardless of its condition. He displays the old-style rank and branch insignia on a blue-piped black collar tab, which was replaced by shoulder straps in 1943. (Courtesy of the Central Museum of the Armed Forces, Moscow via www.Stavka.org.uk)

politruki, motion pictures were shown on outdoor screens. These were not purely propaganda movies; even selected American films were shown. Military-organized musical, dance and singing troupes also conducted tours, all emphasizing Russian culture and traditions. The *balalaika*, a small string instrument, was revived as the Russian national instrument, with the government encouraging its use and forming *balalaika* orchestras.

Sex was an issue handled almost prudishly by the Soviet government. Basically, it did not exist. The official policy was that the focus of men was to fight the war and work the factories or fields, while women maintained the home and raised children, whose source was never explained. The reality was that women worked in industry and agriculture and even the armed forces alongside men. With the civilian population mobilized, there was no idyllic home awaiting soldiers such as was touted in propaganda.

The Red Army did not provide field brothels. In the rear areas unofficial brothels emerged, but they were not widespread. As far as can be determined the Red Army was the only World War II army that did not issue condoms, resulting in increased venereal disease, for which there were severe penalties. Rapes occurred on an epidemic scale once the Red Army entered Germany. However, this had little to do with sex; it was the basest form of revenge and humiliation the soldiers could inflict on the Germans. There were instances where rapists were executed, but these were exceptions to the norm, which was to condone and even encourage such practices.

It was common for commanders and occasionally soldiers to 'adopt' *pokhodno-polevy zheny* (field marching wives) or PPZh – a play on the designation for the PPSh-41 SMG. Officers would sometimes enter these camp followers on unit rosters and assign them duty positions for rationing purposes.

A chauvinistic attitude existed towards female soldiers, with all suspected of having sold or traded themselves for sexual favours. After the war, it was said of women wearing decorations *za boevye zaslugi* ('for military service') that the decorations actually meant *za polevya zaslugi* ('for sexual service').

ON CAMPAIGN

It is often said the Soviet soldier was immune to discomfort, pain and cold. He could endure endless suffering and hunger owing to his previous harsh civilian life. He could march endlessly without sleep and food and would keep going under the most hopeless and brutal conditions. Russians, however, are humans like anyone else. They kept going because they had no choice. Army commanders and military councils were directed by Stalin to:

(1) in all circumstances remove from office commanders and commissars who allowed their troops to retreat without authorization by the army command and send them to the Military Councils of the fronts for court-martial

(2) form three to five well-armed *zagradotryady* [Guards (barrage) units], deploy them in the rear of unstable divisions, and oblige them to execute panic-mongers and cowards on site in case of panic and chaotic retreat, thus giving faithful soldiers a chance to do their duty before the Motherland

(3) form five to ten penal companies where soldiers and sergeants who have broken discipline due to cowardice or instability should be sent. These units should be deployed in the most difficult sectors, thus giving these soldiers an opportunity to redeem their crimes against the Motherland by blood. [They performed mine clearance, sometimes by simply being herded through the minefield, and other tasks included obstacle emplacement or breaching under fire, recovering bodies, etc.]

No officer had the authority to call for the withdrawal of his unit. That could only come from higher headquarters. The barrage units, formed of reliable combat veterans, did not hesitate to shoot down retreating soldiers. They themselves were exempt from direct combat, unless they faltered.

BIVOUAC

Soviet fighting positions were just that and no consideration was given to living in them. Small circular or rectangular one-man foxholes were the usual rifleman's position. The Germans called this a 'Russian hole'. Soldiers often dug shallow, full-body-length slit trenches for protection from shelling and bombing. Slit trenches were often dug as sleeping shelters.

Sleeping in the open was a frequent requirement. There are numerous accounts of soldiers sleeping in their greatcoats; no blankets or sleeping bags were issued. There was more to it than just bundling up in a coat, however. Soldiers slept in pairs. A bed of pine or fir boughs, piled leaves or evergreen needles, straw or cut grass was laid and covered with a shelter-cape. (The soldiers might dig a pit in the snow or a double-wide slit trench as the bed's foundation.) The bed was essential for protection from wet or cold ground, mud, or snow. Two soldiers lay down on their sides, spooned front-to-back with knees curled. They placed one greatcoat over their legs with its shoulders over their feet and the hem came up to their shoulders. Their booted feet were tucked up in the coat's shoulders. The second coat was placed with its shoulders over their heads, which were protected by caps and wrapped scarves. Its hem reached down past their knees. They sometimes had the luxury of wrapping up in a liberated blanket or two. This whole arrangement would be covered by the second shelter-cape. Warm on one side and cold on the other, they would periodically turn to their other side in unison. Such accommodations, however, were inadequate for below-freezing conditions.

FIGHTING AGAINST THE ELEMENTS

The weather conditions were brutal or at least difficult throughout the USSR. The Russian winter, *General Moróz* (General Frost), was an enemy to both sides and certainly in some areas the Red Army was no more prepared than the Germans. In the north the first snows appeared in mid September and about five weeks later in the south. Temperatures plunged to -29°C and even as low as -51°C. Vehicles could not move in the snow; draught horses, on which artillery and supply columns relied, died *en masse*; troops suffered every form of extreme cold-weather injury and illness; weapons failed to function; shells and grenades were smothered in the snow; and landmines froze solid. Spring emerged in April and May and with it came massive snowmelt and rains. Sucking, sticky mud pulled off high-topped boots and added so much weight to the feet that it became painful and difficult to walk. If laboriously scraped off it would build back in a dozen steps. Trucks and even tanks became mired. More tanks were bogged down in the mud and abandoned than were lost to enemy fire. The short summer was hot, dry and dusty. With the equally short autumn came massive, flooding rains and the *rasputitsa* (big mud), which was even worse than the spring mud.

* * *

The Red Army ultimately brought victory in the Great Patriotic War, but at a cost that staggers the imagination. By the end of the conflict in 1945, military casualties were an estimated 22 million, including eight million dead. (The total Soviet death toll, including civilians, is anywhere up to around 25 million.) Lessons had certainly been learned, at all levels of command and organization, although life in Stalin's continuing shadow meant that the degree to which these lessons were openly discussed and assimilated was variable. Nevertheless, as the Soviet Army went into the post-war era, it was apparent that the new army had to look and operate quite differently from the army of World War II.

The spring rains and snowmelt and the ceaseless autumn rains turned roads into rivers of mud. Here the rains have just begun. The road will soon be churned into a knee-deep quagmire. (Courtesy of the Central Museum of the Armed Forces, Moscow via www.Stavka.org.uk)

These BMP-Is are fitted with the Sagger ATGW missile atop their hull, to give them tank-killing capability. Note also the infantryman armed with an RPG-7; Sagger and RPG teams frequently worked together, complementing each other in terms of range capability. (Cody/AirSeaLand)

CHAPTER 3

COLD WAR ARMY

IN THE INTERVAL BETWEEN WORLD Wars I and II, Stalin and his principal military leaders, Voroshilov, Budenny and Tukhachevsky, had been obsessed with their military experiences and what they chose to call the lessons of the Civil War. For none of them had seen any real fighting against the Central Powers. After 1945, however, Stalin and his military staffs lived and relived the battles of the Great Patriotic War, and for many years appeared to disregard the possible effect of atomic or nuclear weapons on the development of armed forces. Meanwhile, every effort was made to mechanize them completely, for the greater part of the Red Army in 1945 had still relied on horse-drawn transport and guns. The mass production of new tanks, armoured personnel carriers (APCs) and radio was also given great priority, so that by the mid 1950s the Soviet Army began to take on the new image of a heavily armoured and motorized force. In the event, almost by accident rather than far-sighted design, the Soviet Union had developed ground forces suitable for both nuclear and non-nuclear war.

Having neglected infantry mechanization during World War II, the Soviet Armed Forces did not make the same mistake during the Cold War. Here we see a true combined-arms exercise during the 1970s, the infantry accompanied by a BTR-60 APC and an Mi-24 Hind attack helicopter. (Cody/AirSeaLand)

BACKGROUND TO THE COLD WAR

As with the other combatants of World War II, in the immediate aftermath of the conflict, the Soviet Army underwent a massive programme of demobilization, the manpower dropping from a peak of about 13 million to around 2.8 million by 1948. Yet even as militarization appeared to de-escalate, a new potential conflict was emerging between the communist East and capitalist West, as the post-war map of Europe was redrawn along ideological lines. Over the years following the end of World War II, the Soviet Union consolidated its hold on the countries of Eastern Europe, while the US exerted a countervailing influence, seeking to halt the spread of communism globally, in 1949 entering into a military alliance (the North Atlantic Treaty Organization) with other Western anti-communist powers.

The 'Cold War', so called because there was never directly military conflict between the major powers involved, was characterized by the race to develop ever more powerful weapons technology, and resulted in a series of proxy conflicts and crises around the world. These reached a peak in the period 1948–53. In 1948, the Soviet Union began a blockade of West Berlin, the first serious crisis of the Cold War, but ultimately unsuccessful in its aims of compelling the adoption of Soviet currency. The following year, the victory of the communist side in the Chinese Civil War expanded the tension to a global scale and in 1950, the communist North Korea, supported by Soviet arms and equipment, invaded the capitalist South, opposed by direct military intervention from the US in a war which lasted for three years. Although the death of Stalin in 1953 led to a relaxing of tensions for while, the Cold War was to continue until the final years of the Soviet Union as the two giants competed for dominance not just in Europe and Asia, but in Latin America, Africa and even space.

The mushroom clouds of atomic, then nuclear, weaponry were also radically reshaping strategic realities. In 1953 the USSR fired a nuclear device (an atomic device had been detonated in 1949) and, four years later, launched its first intercontinental ballistic missile (ICBM). Shortly after 1957, the first tactical and field strategic missiles began to appear with the ground forces. The Soviet Union was now a nuclear power in the fullest sense of the word, able to threaten directly its most distant of ideological opponents, the United States.

MODERNIZATION

Following Stalin's death on 5 March 1953, the Ministry of Defence, under Nikolai Bulganin, replaced the Ministries of War and of the Navy, with Vasilevsky as the First Deputy and Zhukov as the Second Deputy and Commander of the Ground Forces. Leonid Govorov, an artillery officer, remained as Commander of the Air Defences. Two years later the collective leadership began to break up, Nikita Khrushchev emerging as the dominant figure with Bulganin as the titular premier. Zhukov became Minister for Defence. Before the end of 1956, however, Khrushchev had begun to find the arrogant and loud-mouthed Zhukov both an inconvenience and an embarrassment, particularly as he may have relied on Zhukov's support during his struggle for power. Zhukov was removed from all his offices, being replaced as Minister for Defence by Rodion Malinovsky. Andrei Grechko became the Commander of the Ground Forces.

By 1957 the Soviet Army had become completely modernized, backed by a strong fighter, bomber, ground-attack, air transport and helicopter force. It was still a conscript army, the recruit being called up at the age of 19 and serving for three years before being discharged to the reserve. Yet the military command system, introduced by Trotsky as a temporary measure and bitterly attacked by Stalin at the time, had apparently stood the test of the years, for it remained in 1957 very much as Trotsky and Lenin had designed it. In addition, the Soviet Army, in common with all the armed forces, contained as part of its permanent organization organs of the secret police, known before the war as the NKVD and subsequently as the KGB (Committee for State Security). The commissar remained an integral and vigilant presence within the ranks of the armed forces.

The year 1957 began a period of continued reorganization for the Soviet Army and the other armed forces in the Soviet Union, as it began forming a fifth arm, the Strategic Rocket Force, ultimately (from 1959) separate from the air, air defence, ground and naval forces. Khrushchev, aware that the USSR did not have the economic or military muscle at that stage to confront the West conventionally, placed much of his defence focus on strategic and tactical nuclear weaponry, at the expense of regular ground forces. This emphasis continued until he 'resigned' from office in 1964, from which point the Soviet Army began its inexorable climb to strategic greatness once again, peaking with some 166 divisions in the 1980s. The Soviet Navy also surged in both the numbers of vessels and its international

reach; Soviet submarines and surface vessels steadily began criss-crossing the world's oceans and loitering in tense waters off foreign coasts.

During the 1960s and 1970s, the Soviet conventional military doctrine was refined. The doctrine was heavily based on the possibilities brought about by the mass mechanization of the army, a development spurred by the painful lessons of the Great Patriotic War. Vehicles such as the BTR/BRDM family of amphibious armoured personnel carriers and BMP (an amphibious infantry fighting vehicle) gave the motor rifle units and formations full armoured mobility; airborne forces could draw upon the airportable BMD (airborne amphibious infantry fighting vehicle). Many of these vehicles were equipped with the emerging types of anti-tank guided weapons (ATGWs), such as the 3M6 Shmel (NATO name: AT-1 Snapper), 9M14 Malyutka (AT-3 Sagger) and the 3M11 Fleyta (AT-2 Swatter), making them respected participants on the armoured battlefield. The tank divisions and regiments received fresh generations of main battle tanks (MBTs), vehicles such as the T-54/55, T-62, T-64 and T-72, all with advanced long-range gunnery, superior armour and often the ability to operate in nuclear, biological and chemical (NBC) environments. Even at the level of the humble infantry, there were equipment transformations. From the late 1940s, each Soviet rifleman was equipped with Kalashnikov's AK assault rifle, a true revolution in standard-issue infantry firepower, while the new generations of shoulder-

PT-76 tanks of the Soviet Naval Infantry float and drive ashore during a beach assault exercise. The vessel from which they emerge is a Polnocny-class landing ship; the largest variant of this type could carry four main battle tanks or 12 BMP-2 APCs. (Cody/AirSeaLand) launched anti-tank weapons – the RPG-2 and RPG-7 in particular – plus dismounted versions of the Sagger missile, meant that the infantry had greater tank-killing capability than ever before. Ground forces also acquired major equipment for airmobile operations, via helicopters such as the Mil Mi-6 and Mil Mi-8, plus from 1977 additional close air support from the Mil M-24 'Hind' tactical multi-role helicopter. All these conventional resources were backed not only by the power protection of the nuclear-tipped Soviet Air Force, but also by the threat of the ICBMs.

From a strategic point of view, what was known as the 'Cold War' was characterized by two main priorities for the conventional Soviet forces. The first was to maintain a heavy guardian presence in Eastern Europe, both to protect against a possible incursion by NATO forces into communist territories, and, conversely, to make a rapid drive across Central Europe as part of an offensive campaign. The overwhelming thinking underlining the second of these options was *mass*, a Soviet onslaught overwhelming the technologically advanced NATO forces with sheer volume of armoured vehicles and troops, aiming at a baseline 3:1 superiority over the enemy. By the second half of the 1970s, the Soviet forces were on their way to achieving this intimidation in numbers. Total Soviet/Warsaw Pact forces deployed in the eastern USSR and Eastern Europe were 150 divisions, 27,000 tanks, 9,000 artillery pieces and 1.24 million men, against potential Western European NATO opposition of 45 divisions, 11,000 tanks, 6,000 artillery pieces and 1.2 million men. Yet the Soviets ultimately recognized that they were unlikely ever to have mass sufficient to overwhelm NATO across a broad front; hence its tactical focus was largely on fast localized encirclements or encounter battles along narrow axes of advance, achieving through surprise and channelled force what numbers alone could not provide.

The second element of Soviet strategic thinking was its involvement in the multiplicity of 'proxy wars' fought around the world during the 1950s–1970s, especially in the decolonizing territories of Africa, the Middle East, South America and South-East Asia. It was in these conflicts, and especially in the Arab–Israeli wars and in Vietnam, that Soviet equipment and tactics were given 'live' combat testing. The results were not always encouraging for the Soviet leadership. In the Arab–Israeli wars, for example, a modernized Israeli Defense Forces (IDF), armed primarily with US and European weaponry and fighting through Western decentralized command structures, seemed consistently to dominate Soviet-armed and influenced Arab forces, with some exceptions, such as Egypt's confident first few days of the Yom

Soviet troops embark on a train shortly after the end of World War II, destined for home. In the aftermath of the conflict, literally millions of Red Army soldiers would be demobilized, moving from the profound experience of war into an uncertain civilian life. (Cody/AirSeaLand)

Kippur War in 1973. Although Soviet troops themselves rarely entered combat during these localized conflicts, the level of their involvement in training and supply meant that the Soviets did achieve some measure of combat experience before the Soviet Union plunged into its major struggle in Afghanistan in 1979, the subject of our next chapter.

In the remainder of this chapter, we will profile the Soviet Armed Forces as they were constituted in the mid 1980s, when they were at the height of their power. Such was the scale of the Soviet military at this time that few people except informed experts could see some of the faultlines running through the military system, cracks in the surface that reflected those running through a weakening Soviet Union.

THE SOVIET ARMED FORCES

The Soviet Armed Forces (VS-SSSR) – they formally shed the title of Workers' and Peasants' Red Army (RKKA) in 1946 – consisted of five services, plus a variety of associated organizations:

- Strategic Rocket Force (RVSN)
- Ground Forces (SV)
- Air Forces (VVS)
- Air Defence Forces (PVO)
- Naval Forces (VMF).

As a matter of tradition, the first four services constituted the Sovietskaya Armiya (Soviet Army) even though all these services were administratively independent. One of the few visible manifestations of this tradition lay in uniforms, with the services of the Soviet Army following one uniform dress code, and the Soviet Navy following another. Besides these services, the Ministry of Defence also controlled about a dozen separate branches called Special Troops, which included engineer, chemical, signal, road-building, railroad building, automotive, construction and billeting, civil defence, rear services, inspectorate, armaments and cadres troops.

The Soviet Armed Forces also included two security formations: the Border Troops (GB) and the Interior Army (VV). These two forces were under the control of the Council of Ministers, the highest state ruling body for the Soviet Armed Forces, but they did not come under the control of the Ministry of Defence. The Border Troops were the KGB's military force for guarding the frontiers of the USSR. The KGB had other military units which were used to guard state officials and certain facilities, such as nuclear weapon storage areas. The Interior Army was the military wing of the MVD (Ministry of Internal Affairs, the state security service responsible for internal security), which also controlled the regional and local police (Militia). Interior Army troops were used to guard prison camps (gulags), certain storehouses and government facilities and large ammunition dumps. Most cities had a small interior army detachment to bolster local police in the event of trouble, and the Interior Army was also used on military bases to patrol weapon and ammunition storage areas and to prevent mutinies.

THE STRATEGIC ROCKET FORCE

The Strategic Rocket Force (RVSN) was considered the primary service of the Soviet Armed Forces. It was formed in 1959 as an independent service, previously having been under the control of the Artillery branch of the Ground Forces. The RVSN was the service responsible for Soviet intermediate range and intercontinental range ballistic missiles, manning the missile silos scattered across the USSR. Unlike its American counterpart, the Strategic Air Command (SAC), the RVSN did not control Soviet intercontinental strategic bombers.

The RVSN exuded an air of privilege. It had first pick of all conscripts. In view of the type of equipment it operated and developed, the RVSN received the cream of the crop from secondary schools and higher educational facilities. Its personnel appeared to contain a higher percentage of Russians than any other service, since it was felt that these troops were, by and large, better educated and more loyal. Although about 10 per cent of RVSN troops were from the national minorities, these personnel were used in support roles – e.g. as cooks and construction troops – and not in technical or security positions. Recruits had to have a clean political record.

Posting to the RVSN had its advantages and its drawbacks. On the one hand, the greater technical skills warranted higher average ranks and higher pay. Food and lodging at the RVSN facilities were a good deal better than at many other military bases. On the other hand, most RVSN bases were out in the hinterlands, with little opportunity for recreational activities off base. Furthermore, service in the RVSN significantly limited the chances of later obtaining visas to travel abroad.

THE GROUND FORCES

The Ground Forces (SV) were the largest single service in the Soviet Armed Forces. The Ground Forces had five principal branches: the Motor Rifle Troops, Tank Troops, Rocket and Artillery Troops, Army

During a May Day parade, a formation of ASU-85 self-propelled guns rolls through Moscow. The ASU-85 was designed specifically for airborne deployment; at a total weight of 15.5 tonnes the vehicle was capable of being transported inside fixed-wing transport aircraft and also carried as a slung load beneath heavy-lift helicopters. (Cody/AirSeaLand)

Air Defence Troops and Army Aviation Troops. About 70 per cent of all Soviet conscripts ended up in the Ground Forces. The Ground Forces did not rank particularly high in priority as far as recruitment was concerned. The more technically oriented services such as the RVSN, Air Forces, PVO and Navy tended to draw away many of the better-educated recruits, and the security requirements of the other services siphoned off a disproportionate percentage of the more reliable Slavic national groups. The Soviet Army, like the Tsarist Army before it, therefore preferred to draw more heavily on Russian conscripts for its combat and technical units. This was particularly due to language problems, especially in the non-Slavic minority groups, and also, as mentioned above, to Russian perceptions of the loyalty of other ethnic groups. Inevitably, however, the Ground Forces received a significant number of recruits from the minorities, particularly from Central Asia: non-Slavic troops probably constituted about 30 per cent of the recruits in the Ground Forces. Soviet policy was to ensure that these troops did not constitute a majority in any combat unit of significant size (probably battalion level). The Ground Forces attempted to select troops from towns and cities where there was a greater chance that the recruit would have picked up some Russian in school. As in previous times, there was no remedial language training in the Soviet Armed Forces of the post-World War II period; if you didn't speak Russian when you entered the service, you would learn it on the job.

The combat organization of the Ground Forces was primarily built around two basic types of division: the motor rifle division and the tank division. In 1986 there were a total of 142 motor rifle divisions and five tank divisions, according to US sources. However, it should be noted that not all Soviet units were kept at full strength during peacetime. NATO intelligence generally categorized Soviet Ground Forces divisions as Category 1, Category 2 and Category 3. A Category 1 division was at a wartime readiness level, with 75–100 per cent of its troops and equipment at hand. A Category 2 division was deployable in about 10–30 days and had 50–75 per cent of its troops at hand, and about 90 per cent of its equipment. A Category 3, or cadre, division was deployable in about 60 days by fleshing it out with reservists, and had only 10–35 per cent of its troops and 35–50 per cent of its equipment at hand.

Category 1 divisions usually had the prime equipment (such as T-64, T-72 or T-80 tanks), while Category 2 divisions had older equipment (like

T-62 or T-55 tanks), and Category 3 divisions scraped the bottom of the barrel for equipment and troops. About a third of all divisions were at each of these levels. The different categories of divisions were not evenly divided geographically: divisions in the Groups of Forces deployed in Central Europe were uniformly Category 1, as were most divisions in the western Soviet military districts. Divisions in the interior of the USSR were usually of the poorest quality, while units facing China were about 15 per cent Category 1 and 35 per cent Category 2.

THE AIRBORNE ASSAULT TROOPS

The Airborne Assault Troops (VDV) were a semi-autonomous element of the Soviet Army, with traditional links to both the Air Forces and the Ground Forces. The VDV was the primary strategic reserve force of the Soviet High Command, and could be expected to receive particularly challenging tasks in the event of war.

The VDV numbered seven divisions, and played a particularly prominent role in Soviet actions outside the USSR after 1945, such as the seizure of Prague in the 1968 Czechoslovakia invasion, and the 1979 invasion of Afghanistan. For this reason, the VDV enjoyed preferential treatment in the selection of recruits. While the VDV did not have the priority afforded the Strategic Rocket Force, there was only limited friction between the recruiting requirements of these services, since they were each looking for a different type of recruit: the VDV placed more stress on athletic skills compared to the Strategic Rocket Forces' search for recruits with higher academic skills. The VDV's main recruiting grounds were the parachute clubs of DOSAAF (see below).

THE AIR FORCES

The Air Forces (VVS) were the third most senior service of the Soviet Armed Forces. The VVS had (and still has today) three main elements: Frontal Aviation, Long Range Aviation and Transport Aviation; these roughly corresponded to Strategic Air Command, Tactical Air Command and Military Airlift Command in the US Air Force. Frontal Aviation was the largest force, and contained all tactical combat aircraft such as fighters, ground-attack aircraft and military helicopters. Long-Range Aviation was the strategic nuclear attack force, and was equipped with intercontinental bombers, as well as supporting aircraft such as aerial tankers. The Transport Aviation branch included all large, fixed-wing transport aircraft.

1) Sergeant, VDV, summer field dress (camouflaged). This paratrooper carries the RPO launcher, which can fire either high-explosive or incendiary rounds.
2) Motor Rifleman, summer field dress (camouflaged). The most common camouflage uniform: the KLMK, in grass green with angular sand splotches.
3) Motor Rifleman, summer field dress (camouflaged). In the mid 1980s this new, two-piece version of the KLMK was introduced, in a coarse sacking material treated to reduce infrared visibility. This RPG gunner carries the new RPG-16. (Ronald Volstad © Osprey Publishing)

The Air Forces required a technically talented pool of recruits, and were allotted a level of priority somewhat less than the Strategic Rocket Force, but considerably more than the Ground Forces. The Air Forces could pre-select some recruits for specialized positions, especially pilots, from the aspiring ranks of young trainees in the DOSAAF sailplane and aviation clubs. These clubs could also serve as a recruitment ground for other specialized skills, such as mechanics. As in the case of the Strategic Rocket Force, the Air Forces preferred, and tended to receive, a larger percentage of Slavic recruits. Not surprisingly, service in the Air Forces was popular, and the life of military pilots was glamorized in the Soviet press. The service tour for many specialists in the Air Forces was longer than for conscripts into the Ground Forces, but the pay was better, living conditions more comfortable and the food more palatable.

THE AIR DEFENCE FORCES

The Air Defence Forces (PVO) were formed in 1947 by breaking off the air defence artillery units from the Ground Forces. The PVO was the subject of continuing changes from 1981, heavily affecting its basic organization. By the second half of the 1980s, there were four or five major branches of the PVO. Interceptor Aviation (IA-PVO) controlled air defence interceptor regiments, equipped with aircraft like the MiG-25 and Su-15. This element of the PVO was the most heavily affected by structural changes: while IA-PVO had previously controlled all interceptors, the changes in the early 1980s meant that it only controlled interceptor units in the interior military districts. Interceptors in the border regions were turned over to the Frontal Aviation branch of the Air Forces.

The largest element of the PVO was the Zenith Missile Forces (ZRV), which controlled surface-to-air missile (SAM) forces. The ZRV was primarily responsible for fixed air defence sites in the USSR and abroad, using such systems as the S-75 (SA-2 Guideline), S-125 (SA-3 Goa) and S-200 (SA-5 Gammon). The ZRV was also administratively responsible for the mobile air defence missile units in the Ground Forces, such as the units equipped with the ZRK Kub (SA-6 Gainful), ZRK Strela 1 (SA-9 Gaskin), ZRK Krug (SA-4 Ganef) and others. The ZRV operated the schools at which the Ground Forces air defence officers were trained, and apparently administered the design and development of the Ground Forces air defence weapons. However, these mobile air defence units were under Ground Forces tactical control.

The Radio-Technical Troops (RTV) branch encompassed the radar and other electronic sites associated with the PVO. This branch controlled the radar sites used to survey the Soviet frontier, and trained the troops who manned the radars associated with the ZRV's air defence missile regiments.

The most enigmatic elements of the PVO were the Space Defence (PKO) and Anti-missile Defence (PRO) branches. The Anti-missile Defence branch manned and operated the anti-ballistic missile sites around Moscow, equipped with the UR-96 (ABMI Galosh) and ABM-3 Gazelle missile systems. The PKO was responsible for space defence, which included anti-missile (ASAT) efforts as well as the Soviet equivalent of the US Strategic Defense Initiative (SDI, 'Star Wars') programme. Little is known of either branch. The PVO shared a similar recruiting priority level with the Air Forces.

THE SPECIAL TROOPS

Special Troops is the term applied to the non-combat support elements of the Soviet Army. Some of these, such as the engineer troops and chemical defence troops, were highly trained, combat-capable units comparable to the normal Ground Forces units with which they served. These services were not unlike the Ground Forces in terms of recruiting practices.

The majority of the Special Troops, sometimes called Rear Forces (such as the road troops, railroad troops, and construction and billeting troops), received little or no combat training and had no immediate counterparts in most NATO armies. These support troops served in functions that would be performed by civil engineering and construction firms in most NATO countries. In the Soviet Union, however, there was a long tradition of army involvement in large construction projects (for example, Special Troops played a prominent role in the construction of the new Baikal–Amur Magistral rail line).

Furthermore, the support services provided a niche in which conscripts unwanted by the combat arms could serve out their two years of military service. The groups singled out for these roles were the least assimilated or most suspect of the national minorities, or conscripts who had criminal or political records. About half of the construction troops were Central Asians, especially those from rural backgrounds who had little or no knowledge of the Russian language; and another 20 per cent were from the Caucasus, such as Armenians and Georgians. They were assigned to menial tasks, and training was negligible. Other minorities, such as Jews, West Ukrainians and

Soviet mountain troops
conduct a training exercise.
The Soviet Army rejuvenated
its mountain infantry units
in the 1980s, presumably in
response to its demoralizing
experience in Afghanistan.
(Cody/AirSeaLand)

Balts, were disproportionately represented in the support services. Yet since
they were apt to be from urban backgrounds, could understand Russian and
were relatively well educated, many quickly found their way into the NCO
ranks or into other responsible posts. An officer in one of these *stroibaty*
(construction battalions) described the typical breakdown of labour in such a
unit: Russians would operate any specialized equipment such as construction
machinery; Ukrainians, Jews and other Europeans would be used to lay cable
in the building under construction; and the remaining troops would be used
to dig ditches or perform any other physical tasks.

WARSAW PACT

The full capability of the Soviet Armed Forces can only be understood if
placed in context of the wider Warsaw Pact military resources at Moscow's
disposal. The combined ground forces of the seven non-Soviet Warsaw Pact

(NSWP) countries came to total more than 775,000 active troops, rivalling the United States' 781,000-man active army. They also maintained almost two million ground forces reserves. These figures do not include the air forces, naval forces and the many internal security and border units.

The official designation of what is commonly referred to in both the East and West as the Warsaw Pact is the 'Agreement on Friendship, Co-ordination and Mutual Assistance'. The agreement was signed on 14 May 1955 in Warsaw by the USSR, Albania, Bulgaria, Czechoslovakia, German Democratic Republic (East Germany, DDR), Hungary, Poland and Romania. Shortly thereafter it was given the additional title of the 'Warsaw Pact' for sake of brevity. A period then took place where each of the signatories made bilateral treaties with each other, concluding in 1957. The DDR, Hungary, Poland and Romania each made additional agreements with the USSR permitting the stationing of Soviet troops in their countries. Even without the existence of the Warsaw Pact, the Soviet forces would have remained in these countries and would have been unimpaired by its dissolution due to the 1945 Potsdam Agreement signed by the Allies (US, UK, USSR and France).

The signing of the Warsaw Pact treaty was, in effect, the Soviet Bloc's reply to the admission of the Federal Republic of Germany (West Germany, BRD) into NATO ten days before the formal signing of the Warsaw Pact

Hungary, 1956 – Soviet tank-destroyers lie wrecked in the streets of Budapest. Although the Hungarian resistance was eventually overwhelmed by Soviet firepower, the Hungarian militias nonetheless managed to kill some 700 Soviet or regime troops and wipe out many armoured vehicles with Molotov cocktails and hand-held explosives. (Cody/AirSeaLand)

treaty. The actual purpose of the Warsaw Pact, which had been planned well in advance, was to act as a counter to NATO, in existence since August 1949. It was also to provide the machinery by which the USSR could formally control the Eastern European armed forces, transmit its foreign policy, and exercise political control. Economic, transportation and energy control was provided through another Soviet-dominated organization, the Council of Mutual Economic Aid (COMECON), of which all Warsaw Pact countries were members.

The pact was intended to remain in effect for 20 years. It would automatically be extended for another ten years if no member state

A Mil Mi-2 helicopter, fitted with extended downward-facing pipes to create a crude smoke screen for troops below, flies over a 122mm 2S1 Gvozdika self-propelled gun, while on exercises in Poland in the early 1970s. (Cody/ AirSeaLand)

announced its intent to withdraw within the one year required prior to the 20th anniversary. The 20-year period ended in 1975 with no such intent being declared. The next ten-year period ended in May 1985, and the Warsaw Pact agreement was extended another 20 years, but it was ultimately dissolved in 1991 with the collapse of the Soviet Union.

The Warsaw Pact was not without its problems, with most being provided by the 'brother' states. In 1956 the Hungarian Revolt broke out when the government demanded that the USSR withdraw its troops from Hungarian soil, and stated that it would withdraw from the Warsaw Pact to become a neutral country. The USSR brutally crushed the revolt and installed a new government, all the while using the Warsaw Pact as 'legal' justification. In 1958 Romania similarly withdrew from its agreement to permit the stationing of Soviet troops on its soil, and ceased to take part in Warsaw Pact exercises. Beginning in 1960, Albania ceased to take part in any Warsaw Pact activities, becoming formally inactive in 1962, and at that time beginning to adopt the ideology of communist China.

In 1965 the USSR attempted to establish a non-aggression pact between the Warsaw Pact and NATO, looking toward the dissolution of both

The 2S3 Akatsiya was a Soviet 152mm self-propelled gun that entered service in 1971 and is still in use today. It can fire two to three rounds per minute to a maximum range of 18.5km with conventional ammunition, or 24km with rocket-assisted projectiles. (Cody/AirSeaLand)

organizations. (The former Warsaw Pact countries would, of course, have remained under Soviet control, while the Western European countries would have been without central organization. The United States Armed Forces would certainly have been withdrawn, leaving the front door to the West wide open.) This effort failed. Czechoslovakia attempted in 1968 to form a 'socialist democracy', which was counter to the aims of the Warsaw Pact and COMECON. Soviet and other Warsaw Pact forces invaded the country later in the year in order to restore a pro-Soviet government and 'return an errant brother state to the fold'. Albania, already inactive in the Warsaw Pact as stated above, formally withdrew from the treaty in protest at the invasion.

SERVICE IN THE POST-WAR SOVIET ARMED FORCES

Having provided an overview of the post-1945 Soviet Armed Forces, we can explore the experience of those serving in them during the later years, particularly the tense stand-off years of the 1980s. As we will see, by focusing primarily on the infantry, there is some level of continuity with the service of those during the wartime years, minus the combat of course. For life in the Soviet military was, regardless of its era, typically spartan and with few luxuries or comforts, unless you belonged to one of the more elite formations.

PRE-SERVICE INDOCTRINATION

'Military service is the sacred obligation of Soviet citizens.' So read the 1936 Constitution of the USSR. For a young Soviet man, the chances were very great that he would be obliged to serve for at least two years in one branch or another of the Soviet Armed Forces. By the time they reached the conscription age of 18 years, most Soviet boys would already be far more familiar with military life than their counterparts in Western Europe or America. Soviet society was far more militarized than most other European societies, even compared with the other Warsaw Pact countries. The exploits of the Soviet Armed Forces during the Great Patriotic War were recounted daily on television and radio and in the print media. It was rare to find a bookstore without a shelf devoted to war stories, or to read a magazine aimed at young adults that did not contain such material. In some areas it became a Soviet tradition to lay flowers at a war memorial following wedding ceremonies. Members of the Young Pioneers, the state

These Soviet troops are all wearing the SSh-40 steel helmets, one of the signature uniform items of Cold War troops. The banner behind them, suggestive of where they are deployed, translates 'Carpathian teachings are excellent!' (Cody/AirSeaLand)

youth movement for pre-teenagers, served as guards of honour at local war memorials, bedecked in special uniforms and often carrying weapons.

This fixation on the war stemmed, in part, from the enormous human cost of the fighting – nearly one in ten Soviet citizens were killed between 1941 and 1945. Other countries, such as Poland and Yugoslavia, suffered similar or greater levels of human and physical loss without a consequent militarization of their societies. But in the Soviet Union the state's Marxist-Leninist ideology grew stale and unattractive to the young, and fostering a romantic image of past martial glories and national heroism served as an alternative, helping to create among the young a more traditional feeling of national loyalty than any promoted by appeals to a 'socialist internationalism'.

A less subtle approach to the militarization of the young was revealed by universal military training. The 1967 changes to the Soviet constitution included the addition of mandatory and universal pre-induction military training. There were two main agencies for sponsoring pre-induction military training: state youth movements, and the school system. The Young Pioneer movement was in some ways similar to the Boy Scouts and Girl Scouts in Britain and the United States, but it was state sponsored, and included a hefty dose of political and military indoctrination. Soviet children belonged first to the Octobrist youth group until the age of nine, when they could graduate to the Young Pioneers. Bright children, and those with sports skills or leadership qualities, were particularly pressured to join, since the Young Pioneers was one of the main avenues of later recruitment into the Communist Party. The Young Pioneer movement fostered martial tradition by ceremony, like the guard of honour duties mentioned above, and through proselytization.

1) Motor Rifleman, Honour Guard, summer parade dress. The most formal category of uniform worn by enlisted men. Note the winged national insignia on cap, peculiar to the parade dress. 2) Crewman, Armoured Force, summer everyday (off-duty) dress. Note the simpler national insignia on the cap, and trousers worn loose over shoes. 3) Motor Rifleman, summer work dress. The most common uniform of the enlisted man, work dress was usually of a cheaper material than field dress, and faded to a pale khaki. (Ronald Volstad © Osprey Publishing)

Books, comics and television programmes aimed at the Young Pioneers created a heroic image of military service. The Soviet government organised summer youth camps, both for members of the Young Pioneers, and for other young students, which usually included a military aspect. Many of the camps sponsored military training in the form of the *Zarnitsa* (Summer Lightning) war games. The camps were visited by local military personnel, together with a few armoured vehicles, and mock war games were performed, with the children brandishing unloaded rifles. These activities were understandably very popular among the small boys and often provided far more excitement than the unappealing and regimented activity otherwise offered by the summer camps. Young Pioneers, at the age of 14, transferred to the Komsomol, the Young Communists.

In the post-war era, the Komsomol movement became a very important element in state indoctrination for conscripts, since young men remained in the movement during their military duty. The Komsomol sponsored similar summer war games to those in the Young Pioneer summer camps, called *Orlyonok* (Eaglet). These exercises were closer to real military training, and involved squad, platoon and company drills as well as preliminary weapons training. The camps familiarized young students with Soviet Army equipment and basic drill. Although this may sound pretty dull, much of the training was conducted as sport: for example, classes to familiarize Komsomol members with military communications usually involved radio direction-finding contests with teams assigned to locate a hidden transmitter.

Besides the military training offered through youth groups, all Soviet students, both boys and girls, received military training at school during the ninth and tenth grades as a part of the NVP (basic military training) programme. NVP was introduced under the 1967 changes, when the basic duty term for conscript soldiers was reduced from three to two years. It was hoped that the schooling would act as a partial substitute for the year deleted from the draft duty. Even though girls were not drafted, their inclusion in the programme was presumably based on the assumption that they would be drafted in time of war, as they had been during World War II.

The actual level of military training, and its content, varied enormously from region to region. The situation was so bad prior to 1977 that new guidelines had to be laid down to formalize schooling requirements. The ideal facilities for a school included a military office where the classes could be conducted, a weapons room for storing training weapons, a firing range, a drill field, an obstacle course, a sentry post and an anti-radiation shelter.

By 1982 most schools had the military classroom and weapons storage room, but half of them lacked a firing range and only a quarter had the full training range. There were also problems in finding qualified teachers, known as *voenruki* Ideally, the *voenruk* was a reserve military officer with higher military training and some teaching skills. In some of the less developed areas, such as in Central Asia, former officers and reserve officers were in such a demand that *voenruks* had to be recruited from the ranks of reserve NCOs. However, most reserve NCOs in the USSR were not professional soldiers and had received very little higher military training or command experience during their brief two-year duty stint. Part of the problem was that many smaller schools did not have enough students to justify a full-time *voenruk*.

Soviet soldiers train with the AGS-17 automatic grenade launcher. This blowback-operated weapon fires 30×29mm grenades up to a maximum range of 1,700m at a cyclical rate of 400rpm. Note the 'CA' shoulder boards, identifying the Soviet Army. (Cody/AirSeaLand)

The NVP curriculum consisted of 70 hours of annual training for students in ninth and tenth grades. Young men who left school before reaching this age were given the same basic course at training points located in civilian factories. The basic curriculum included weapon training, tactical training, drill training, military topography, medical training, civil defence, technical training and first aid. It will be noted that boys received more training in weapons and drill, while girls were given more training in first aid. This was in part due to traditional sexual stereotyping in Soviet society; the majority of doctors were women.

Separate from the Komsomol and the school system was the DOSAAF (Voluntary Society for Co-operation with the Army, Air Force and Navy). DOSAAF was a governmental organization directed by the Ministry of Defence to support youth activities of interest to the Soviet Armed Forces. Probably the most familiar aspect of DOSAAF to Soviet young men was its sponsorship of sporting clubs. In the European sections of the USSR, DOSAAF sponsored three especially popular types of facility: flying clubs, sky-diving clubs and marksmanship/hunting clubs. The flying clubs provided pre-induction military training through classes on basic navigation, flying, instrument reading and communications. Club members were taught on sailplanes and military training aircraft ranging from primary trainers like the Yak-18 through to advanced trainers like the L-29 Delfin jet. The DOSAAF-sponsored flying clubs were the primary source of recruitment for pilots for the Soviet Air Forces and PVO. The sky-diving clubs used military-type aircraft, usually beginning with the An-2; these clubs were the primary source of recruitment for paratroopers of the VDV Airborne Assault Troops. (Paratroopers of the VDV wore their DOSAAF jump qualification badges when in the service.) The DOSAAF marksmanship clubs were intended to foster basic rifle and pistol skills, and the club members were familiarized with military as well as sporting weapons.

In more rural regions of the USSR, DOSAAF sponsored motoring clubs. Since there were so few private cars in the USSR, these clubs served to teach fundamental driving skills, as well as basic automotive repair. DOSAAF also sponsored more conventional sports clubs, as leadership in sports was regarded as a good indicator of leadership ability in the army. The national sports effort was also closely tied to the military, since professional sportsmen could retain their 'amateur' standing while on active duty.

Activity in DOSAAF was noted on the induction records of young men and affected their potential selection as NCO or officer candidates.

Every year, between January and March, all 17-year-old young men were required to register for conscription at their local *voenkomat* (military commissariat). This began the process of conscription. The local *voenkomat* set up a file on all potential conscripts with the aim of helping the services select new recruits. The files contained information on the recruit's educational achievements, leadership skills, family background, ethnic origins, educational plans, political background and special skills. All of these considerations were important, since each of the services had its own requirements as far as recruits were concerned.

CHOOSING A SERVICE

Unlike citizens of Western Europe or North America, young Soviets were given very little leeway in selecting the service they would serve in. (Though obviously an ambitious and astute young Soviet desiring a career in the Air Forces could unofficially help his chances by belonging to a DOSAAF aviation club, and a member of a DOSAAF parachuting club had a better than average chance of getting a posting to the VDV Airborne Assault Troops.)

Conscript levies took place twice a year in the Soviet Union, in April–May and after the harvest in October–November. Each year about 75 per cent of

Victorious Soviet troops parade with their PPSh-41 SMGs shortly after World War II. Within five years, the SMGs were on their way out, replaced (as were the Mosin-Nagant bolt-action rifles) by the new AK-47 assault rifle. (Cody/AirSeaLand)

all eligible 18-year-old men were drafted; the remainder received deferments. There were three principal types of deferment: on educational, health or hardship grounds. Educational deferments applied to young men accepted into certain institutes of higher learning, including universities and certain vocational training schools. These men would later be eligible for the annual draft, unless they joined an officers' training programme at their school. Health deferments applied both to young men with permanent disabilities and to those with temporary medical problems which made service in a given year impossible; those with temporary problems would be drafted later. Hardship deferments included men who were the sole support of elderly parents who could not support themselves, fathers of at least two children, and similar cases. Although some young men in each age-bracket escaped the first troop-levy, most were eventually brought under the colours. Only about 12 per cent of Soviet young men managed to escape military service altogether.

The new conscripts reported to the local *voenkomat* in their city or district for induction. Recruitment practices varied considerably. A central element in the procedure was the *pokupatel*, literally, a 'military buyer'. Several *pokupateli* would visit a particular military commissariat with papers entitling them to a given number of recruits; the papers outlined the number of troops, qualifications and ethnic backgrounds desired. The *pokupateli* represented either entire military districts or individual units.

On the basis of documents collected since the recruit first registered at the Military Commissariat at the age of 17, some pre-selection of recruits was done for special training. Recruits who showed special aptitude or leadership ability were singled out for NCO school. The Soviet Army did not rely on a professional NCO class as did most NATO armies. Indeed, only about 5 per cent of all NCOs were professionals, the remainder being conscripts. NCOs were recruited from the annual draftees and served a two-year term like the rest of the men from their age group. Many of the NCO candidates were selected at induction, but a portion were selected later on the basis of their performance during initial training. Special pre-selection was also made of candidates for officer school, aircrew training, the VDV airborne forces and other elite postings.

A common technique used by the *pokupateli* to 'buy' their troops was simply to load a given number of conscripts on to a train destined for a particular military district. During the course of the trip, the *pokupateli* would 'buy' the troops they needed for their unit or military district, and each recruit would be informed of the results. These train trips could be quite lengthy, since the Soviet Army had a policy of stationing troops away from their homes. In the case of many of the minority nationalities, there was a policy to station them completely outside their national republics.

The initial experiences of a Soviet conscript soldier varied. In some cases, the conscript was sent directly to his unit to undergo training. In other cases, he reported to a special unit at the military district for training, after which he would be transferred to his unit. Basic training for the ranks was four weeks for most – shorter than in most contemporary NATO armies, since there was the presumption that pre-induction training in school had already covered many matters. During the four-week 'quarantined' training period, the conscript was issued his uniforms and equipment, received medical treatment (mostly consisting of inoculations and examinations), and was given a rough-and-tumble basic military training. For about a third of the conscripts, life was somewhat different. These conscripts, selected at induction for NCO or specialist training, were sent to NCO or specialist schools, often located in special training divisions. These future NCOs received the same four-week quarantined period for basic training and induction, followed by five months of specialist training.

THE ANNUAL TRAINING CYCLE

In the Soviet Union, military life followed a seasonal pattern tied to the bi-annual induction of draftees. At any one time a quarter of the troops in

Soviet troops conduct a winter exercise, using a GAZ-69 four-wheel-drive light utility vehicle for mobility. More than 600,000 GAZ-69s had been built by the time the production run came to an end in 1972. (Cody/AirSeaLand)

tank and motor rifle divisions were new recruits and, likewise, twice a year a quarter of the army returned to civilian life in a mass exodus unmatched in most other European countries.

In October, while the inductees were in transit from their homes, the summer training period came to a close, and about a quarter of the troops prepared to leave military service. At this time the first batch of new junior officers arrived, fresh from the military academies, or from civilian universities where they were enlisted on officer training courses. In November the new crop of NCOs, inducted in the previous April–May draft, had completed their training in training divisions and arrived at their division in time to greet the new inductees. At this time, the conscripts also undertook their four weeks of basic training. November marked the end of one training year, and December the beginning of the next. The Minister for Defence made a major speech that outlined the special focus of the new year's training. In December, the first unit training began as part of the winter training schedule. Unit training started at platoon level and worked its way through company and battalion levels.

The winter training period ended in May. As in the previous November, that quarter of the troops who had completed their two-year active duty

The Soviet May Day parades, four of which were held between 1945 and 1990 (annually in Moscow since 1995), were an opportunity for the NATO alliance to view some of the latest kit and equipment in Soviet service. In this 1985 parade we see 2S3 Akatsiya self-propelled guns. (Cody/AirSeaLand)

obligation were released into the reserves. The NCOs who had been inducted in October–November had completed their six-month training and arrived at their divisions along with the new conscripts. The four-week basic training was completed in May, and in June the summer training period began.

GARRISON LIFE

The daily life of a Soviet conscript was heavily regimented, monotonous and sometimes brutal. Very little free time was allowed to new recruits, on the assumption that they would only get into some form of mischief. Idle time was filled with repetitive drills, or 'make-work' projects: there were always some rocks desperately in need of a coat of whitewash, or some trench which needed digging or filling – or both. The style of life in Soviet barracks was more traditional than was the case in most NATO countries, and would not have been unfamiliar to a European or American soldier of the nineteenth century.

Life in the barracks was stratified by seniority and ethnicity, and at the top of the heap were the senior sergeants. Usually, after two years of service, most conscripts would have risen to NCO rank; these sergeants wore a two-year duty stripe. Below them were soldiers from later drafts, with a year-and-a-half s seniority, a year's seniority or six-months' seniority. At the bottom of the heap were the new recruits, who did the filthiest jobs and were subjected to a certain amount of harassment, verbal and physical abuse by senior troops, as were non-Russian troops.

Conditions in the garrison were spartan by Western standards. Sanitary conditions in many garrisons were basic, and in the field they were worse; diseases such as hepatitis and dysentery were not uncommon in some areas, and were very serious under field conditions, for example in Afghanistan. Army food was bland, and often insufficient, and Soviet emigrés who served in the Ground Forces remember hunger as a universal feature of army life. But to draftees from the Soviet hinterlands, these conditions were not as unfamiliar or as harsh as they might seem to a Western European or American.

Most young Soviet recruits, especially Russians and Ukrainians, were patriotic in an old-fashioned way, and regarded their tour of duty as a normal obligation that must be endured. The patriotic sentiment was not necessarily shared by the ethnic minorities.

THE DAILY SCHEDULE

Reveille was at 0600hrs, followed by about 40 minutes to clean up, make up the bunk and do calisthenics. At 0650hrs, there was an inspection, or a lecture by the unit's *zampolit* (political officer) on 'world political highlights' – political indoctrination remained a major concern of the Soviet leadership. At 0725hrs, the unit went off to the mess for breakfast.

Usually breakfast was served family style, with each squad occupying a single table in the mess hall. NCOs and more senior soldiers from previous levies often took advantage of the newer recruits by taking larger portions of food. In the Soviet Army, as in Soviet society, benefits flowed from rank and seniority. The normal breakfast, which amounted to about a quarter of the food issued daily to troops, consisted of two slices of white bread, a slice of black bread, 20g of butter or margarine, 300g of either *kasha* (a grain porridge) or potatoes, and 50g of meat or fish. Meat, infrequently served, was often the unforgettable 'head cheese', which was a sausage made from some of the less desirable extremities of some hapless creature. Fish was more common, and was normally *selyodka*, a common type of Russian salted herring. This hearty if bland meal was washed down by several helpings of the ever popular *chai* (tea), sweetened with up to three cubes of sugar per breakfast issue.

Officers were fed separately, cafeteria style, and received a better selection of food, including dairy products, eggs and fruit. It was an invariable rule in the Soviet Army that the conscripts received the poorest grades of food, the NCOs a somewhat better selection (if only due to their own efforts in 'accepting' offerings from the conscripts) and the officers the best, though still depending somewhat on rank.

DAILY TRAINING

Daily training began at 0800hrs and lasted about six hours. The detail varied from branch to branch; as the most common types of units were the motor rifle regiments and tank regiments, these merit a more detailed examination.

Soviet training contained many of the elements common to all military training, stressing physical fitness, hardiness and unquestioning obedience to the instructions of superior officers. The Soviets had been heavily influenced by their experiences in World War II, when shortages of even the most basic supplies were endemic, and soldiers often had to forage for food. While peacetime conditions were not as severe as this, Soviet training

1) Motor Rifleman, summer field dress, fighting load. The fighting load consists of belt, load webbing, gas mask haversack, decontamination or medical kit (left of buckle), 6Kh4 bayonet and magazine pouch for AK-74. 2) Lieutenant, Motor Rifles, summer field dress. The field peaked cap is often worn instead of the issue helmet by officers as a distinguishing feature. 3) Motor Rifleman, summer field dress, existence load. The existence load differs from the fighting load in that additional clothing, food, mess implements, and a blanket are carried in the R-45 rucksack. (Ronald Volstad © Osprey Publishing)

Winter warfare continued to be a post-war focus of the Soviet military, especially with the possibility of fighting NATO forces in northern Europe. The soldiers here are using a GT-T tracked transport vehicle, designed in the 1950s as an all-terrain artillery tractor but also used for carrying troops and supplies. (Cody/AirSeaLand)

practices did not encourage reliance on extensive logistical support for their combat arm. Ammunition and fuel took priority, if necessary to the exclusion of all else.

This focus affected many areas which NATO troops would take for granted. Field sleeping practices are a good example. In nearly all northern NATO armies, troops were issued with a sleeping bag for cold weather field conditions. In the Soviet Union, sleeping arrangements had changed little since those experienced by the soldiers of World War II. When questioned about the seeming lack of sleeping bags in the Soviet Ground Forces, a number of emigré Soviet ex-servicemen expressed astonishment that anyone would even expect Soviet infantrymen to receive such luxuries. According to them, the usual practice was to send a foraging party into the woods to cut down boughs; in the steppes they substituted sheaves of oats, hay or other suitable material. These were laid on the ground or placed in a shallow entrenchment to form a primitive mattress, on which the soldier slept in his greatcoat. The only sleeping bags that these soldiers had ever seen were rare examples purchased privately by officers from sporting goods stores.

The same applied to load-carrying equipment. Soviet troops were not regularly issued with rucksacks except for certain specialized roles (such as the rocket grenade rucksacks for RPG-7 teams). Although military rucksacks did exist in both small and large sizes, they were relatively uncommon, and appear to have been reserved for specialized units such as mountain or airborne troops. What personal gear the troops needed was carried in their armoured personnel carrier.

The emphasis on hardiness was sometimes carried to extremes. It was very uncommon to see Soviet troops wearing glasses, for example. This was to some extent due to the notion that young men should not need glasses; they were therefore not issued them.

INFANTRY TRAINING AND WEAPONS

Weapons training was not dissimilar to that carried out in most armies. The Soviet Army did not, however, appear to provide as much live small-arms practice and basic rifle drill as most NATO armies, and seemed still to place greater emphasis on basic drill and parade practice. The comparative shortage of live firing time was partly because of the expense, and partly due to Soviet infantry tradition since World War II, which stressed massed fire, not precision marksmanship. The reliance of the World War II-Red Army on the SMG carried over to the AK family of assault rifles. Soviet infantrymen were trained in aimed fire, but field exercises also stressed firing from the hip while charging forward in conjunction with armoured troop carriers. It was felt that in the heat of battle, aimed fire from infantrymen was too much to be expected. What precision marksmanship was required could be provided by snipers, who were available in larger numbers in the Soviet Army than in NATO armies.

The basic tactical unit of the motor rifle formations was the squad or section (*otdyeleniye*). The infantry squad varied in size and composition from the 1960s, but gradually stabilized at a dismountable squad of seven to nine men, depending upon the type of mechanized vehicle in the unit. This total did not include the other two squad members, the vehicle driver and vehicle gunner, who generally remained in the BTR or BMP during combat. The exact composition of a squad depended on its position in the company. In a normal motor rifle platoon with three squads, the first, a nine-man dismountable squad, consisted of the platoon leader (a lieutenant), the squad leader (a sergeant), two squad machine-gunners (with PKMs), four riflemen (with AKMs or AK-74s), an additional rifleman with an SVD sniper rifle and an anti-tank grenadier with an RPG-7 or RPG-16.

The second squad was usually smaller with eight dismountable men, including a squad leader, one or two squad machine-gunners, an anti-tank grenadier, and four or five riflemen. The third squad was configured like the first, but had the platoon sergeant in lieu of the platoon lieutenant, and a Strela-2 air defence missile operator in place of the sniper.

The platoon leader (lieutenant) was normally authorized a pistol, but might also carry an AKSU carbine. The squad leaders were all sergeants, and carried an AKM or AK-74 rifle and 120 rounds of ammunition (a 30-round clip in the rifle, three magazines in the ammunition pouch). These squad leaders were normally conscript sergeants, often straight out of their initial six-month training course. They were the best-trained men in the squad, and

In communist-controlled East Berlin in 1958, the young troops of a Soviet anti-aircraft unit prepare to return home after a deployment, one of them clutching a photographic souvenir. Note their SKS rifles, fitted with integral bayonets. (Cody/AirSeaLand)

the only ones (apart from the platoon lieutenant and platoon sergeant) who were trained in map reading and basic radio communications. The squad leaders were also usually cross-trained as BTR or BMP drivers and gunners.

The two PKM squad machine guns were allotted 1,000 rounds each, and this was spread out among the squad. Some units used the RPK-74, older RPK or other automatic weapons rather than the PKM. Usually two of the squad riflemen were assigned as assistant machine-gunners for the PKMs. Some units received the AGS-17 automatic grenade launcher in place of at least one PKM. This probably required the attention of two squad members to carry the weapon, the tripod and associated ammunition. The RPG-7 grenadier could be allotted either a pistol or an AK, the latter apparently being more common. Usually one squad rifleman was the RPG assistant, and carried a special rucksack with four additional rocket grenade rounds. Each platoon had a sniper with a Dragunov SVD rifle. Such widespread distribution of sniper rifles was traditional in the Russian Army, and was also rooted in the mass fire tradition explained above, which placed less stress on marksmanship for the average infantryman than, for example, the US Army.

The most sophisticated weapon in the Soviet motor rifle platoon was the Strela-2 (9M32M) air defence missile, better known in NATO as the SA-7 Grail, or the later SA-14 Gremlin. The Strela-2 is a small, man-portable launcher firing an infra-red guided missile; the newer SA-14 Gremlin is a laser-beam-riding guided missile. These missiles provided the platoon with a degree of air defence against low-flying aircraft and helicopters. The missile came in a disposable launch tube; once fired, the tube was discarded, and a new round mounted on the basic gripstock assembly. It would appear that most platoons carried two rounds of missile ammunition.

The two vehicle crewmen attached to the squad, the mechanic/driver and gunner, were both considered specialists and so were usually sergeants. The driver was normally armed with a pistol and the gunner with an AK, but from the advent of the AKSU carbine both may have used this weapon. Special weapons training in the Soviet Ground Forces tended to place heavier reliance on simulators than on live fire. This was particularly true of expensive weapons like the SA-7 Grail. Even small-arms training sometimes featured air rifles for marksmanship practice.

Squad and platoon tactical training tended to be more formalized than in many NATO armies, placing great stress on battle drills and standardized dismounting and attack formations. While this was sometimes cited as evidence of the Soviet tendency to stifle individual initiative, the Soviets felt that battle drills, repeatedly practised and memorized by rote, were more suitable in real combat conditions for the average Soviet infantryman. They contended that under normal combat conditions – with the soldiers exhausted, frightened, or both – the basic drills would be followed automatically, allowing the squad, platoon and company leaders to employ their troops to best effect.

TANK TRAINING

Soviet tankers required more specialized training than infantrymen, so not surprisingly, most crewmen in a tank would be sergeants. The crews of Soviet tanks consisted of four men in the older T-54, T-55 and T-62 tanks, and three men in the newer T-64, T-72 and T-80. The difference in crew size was because the loader could be dispensed with on the newer tanks, which were fitted with an auto-loading system. Generally, on the older tanks, the loader was the only non-specialist in the crew, and the only member who was unlikely to be a sergeant. The three remaining crewmen

The Strela-10 (SA-13 Gopher) is a mobile short-range SAM system introduced into the Soviet armed forces in 1976. The four missiles – which are visually aimed and optical/infrared-guided – are mounted on the back of an MT-LB multi-purpose tracked vehicle. (Cody/AirSeaLand)

In service from 1980, the BMP-2 represented a new generation of Soviet infantry fighting vehicle (IFV). The vehicle featured a 2A42 30mm autocannon (with dual AP and AT ammunition feed) set in its two-man turret and a 9P135M ATGM launcher. (Cody/AirSeaLand)

were the driver/mechanic, gunner and vehicle commander, who received six months of specialized training on induction.

As for the infantry, basic crew weapons training in the Soviet Union placed heavier emphasis on simulators than on actual use of the equipment. Tanks were usually limited to about 250km of travel annually, which was not really sufficient to train and keep the drivers proficient. Soviet tanks tended to use more primitive clutch and brake steering than NATO tanks, and so were more difficult to operate. As a result, driver simulators were used for additional practice. Acquisition of gunnery skills was also somewhat hampered by meagre allotments of training ammunition; Soviet tank crews fired only about a dozen rounds of live main gun ammunition annually, compared to up to ten times that much in the US Army. As a substitute, 23mm sub-calibre devices were fitted into the tubes for firing simulation; this was perfectly adequate for certain gunnery skills, but failed to build up practice in crew interaction such as rapid target acquisition, loading, firing, retargeting, reloading, etc.

As in the infantry, considerable stress was placed on battle drills and standardized formations in tactical training. Most Soviet tank units had small training grounds with a variety of targets for gunnery practice and tactical exercise. One of the main inhibitions to tactical exercises above squad or platoon strength was the limitation placed on the number of hours a tank could be operated annually.

It was not uncommon for a tank regiment to have only a single platoon of tanks operational in each of its three battalions for training purposes, with the rest in temporary storage. These were taken out for periodic battalion- and regimental-scale exercises, which included both tactical and gunnery drills to demonstrate the proficiency of the crews.

Tactical tank training was the subject of a fair amount of criticism in the Soviet military press. Most of these exercises were scored, and it appears to have been an all too common practice to lay out tactical exercises in a very regular and regimented fashion to ensure high scores: low scores would give a poor impression to senior officers, and would do little to improve career chances for the unit commanders. In general, Soviet training doctrine paid a great deal of lip service to creativity and initiative on the part of tank officers, but the actual organizational features of the training cycle served to discourage these principles. Soviet tank training was qualitatively and quantitatively inferior to average NATO training, but it is not clear whether these shortcomings were sufficient to undermine the Soviet Ground Forces' numerical advantages over NATO tank units.

LEADERSHIP – THE SOVIET NCO

As mentioned above, the vast majority of sergeants and other NCOs in the army were regular two-year conscripts who received an initial six-month specialist training at the beginning of their career. The Soviet NCO filled a somewhat different role from his counterpart in Western armies, where there was the tradition of a professional NCO class. NCOs occupied many postings that would be occupied by lower-ranking enlisted men in most NATO armies, and roles requiring any kind of specialized training – including communications and heavy weapons operation – were filled by an NCO. Conversely, because the NCOs were not professional, and lacked broad experience or leadership skills, many leadership roles that would be undertaken by NCOs in NATO armies were undertaken by officers in the Soviet Ground Forces. The Soviets appeared to try to ameliorate this problem in the late 1970s through a warrant officers' programme, but this was seemingly not entirely successful. NCOs made up about a third of the personnel in the Soviet Ground Forces, a somewhat larger fraction than in most NATO armies.

The reason that so few NCOs remained in service was mainly the low pay and low status. A typical junior sergeant's pay of 11.80R monthly was hardly enough for his own needs, and certainly not enough to support a family. In

T-55 TANK, SOVIET ARMY, 1970

1 Idler wheel
2 Road-wheel
3 Gunner's fire controls
4 Gun protective guard
5 Gunner's seat
6 Stowage bin for main gun tools
7 Engine exhaust port
8 Rear stowage bin for tools
9 Lubrication system radiator
10 Rear stowage bin
11 Drive sprocket
12 Unditching beam
13 Stowed snorkel for deep wading
14 External 200-litre fuel drums
15 Cooling fan
16 Transmission
17 External armoured fuel tanks
18 Engine air filter
19 V-55V engine
20 Loader's protective guard

21 Loader's hatch
22 Pintle mount for anti-aircraft machine gun
23 Loader's MK-4 periscope
24 D-10TS 100mm gun
25 Gun recoil cylinders
26 L-2G Luna infra-red searchlight
27 Articulating rod for searchlight/gun alignment
28 Gunner's TShS-32PBM fire control sight
29 Spare track links
30 Main gun tube
31 Fume extractor
32 Turret hand-holds
33 Fuel cap for forward fuel cell
34 Headlights
35 Driver's controls
36 Attachments for mine-rollers
37 Driver's seat

SPECIFICATION
Crew: Four (commander, gunner, loader, driver)
Combat weight: 36 tonnes
Power to weight ratio: 16.1hp/T
Overall length: 9m (hull 6.2m)
Width: 3.27m
Height: 2.7m (with MG, 2.35m without)
Engine: V-55V 580hp (427kW) liquid cooled V-12 diesel
Transmission: Synchronized constant mesh with planetary final drives, five forward, one reverse gear
Fuel capacity: 960 litres integral, plus two 200-litre external drums
Max. speed: (road): 50km/h; (cross-country): 30km/h
Max. range: 500km (integral); 700km with external drums
Fuel consumption: 1.92 litre / km
Ground clearance: 425mm

Armament: 100mm D-10T2S rifled gun
Main gun ammunition: 43 rounds, typically: 6 × UBR-412 HEAT; 9 × 3UBM6 HVAP; 28 × UOF-412 HE-Frag
Muzzle velocity: HE-Frag and HEAT: 900m/s; HVAP:>1,000m/s; AP-T: 1,000m/s
Penetration (vertical armour plate at 1km) HVAP: 200mm; AP-T: 180mm; HEAT: 390mm
Max. effective range: 21km (HE-Frag); effective range 1.5km (probability of a hit >50%)
Gun depression/elevation: 5+18
Armour: turret front: 205mm; turret sides: 120mm; turret rear: 60mm; glacis plate and lower bow: 100mm; hull side: 80mm; hull rear: 50mm

contrast, a junior lieutenant received 220R monthly, plus additional benefits including family housing and a vacation. A young soldier contemplating a professional military career would attempt to join the officers' ranks rather than remaining an NCO. A small fraction, perhaps 5 per cent of NCOs, were extended-service or professional NCOs who received the rank of *starshina* (sergeant-major).

The stereotypical sergeant-major was an East Ukrainian, Belorussian or a rural Russian from some other region who was raised on a collective farm, where the dreariness of life offered little incentive to return to 'Civvy Street'. Soviet peasants did not receive an internal passport that would allow them

DISCIPLINE

The post-war Soviet Army was very conscious of strict discipline. In reply to a question from an officer, a simple 'yes' (*da*) or 'no' (*nyet*) was unacceptable. The proper response was *tak tochno* ('exactly so') or *nikak nyet* ('not at all'). The type and amount of punishment that could be imposed on a recruit depended on rank. A sergeant who commanded a squad could rebuke his troops, and could give them up to seven days of garrison restrictions and up to one day of extra duty, but he could not order confinement. A junior lieutenant, commanding a platoon, could impose up to 21 days of restriction and four days of extra duty.

Only a company commander (usually a *kapitan* – captain) could order confinement in the guardhouse for up to three days. Reduction in rank or revocation of an award, such as a specialist qualification, could come only from a regimental commander or above, meaning usually a colonel or higher.

Attitudes towards punishment varied depending upon the source. Although the Soviet Army was more discipline conscious than many other armies, many line officers did not like to inflict punishments that would be noted officially in the records, such as guardhouse duty. They felt, rightly, that this would be regarded by higher authorities as indicative of poor leadership in the unit. The preferred method of imposing discipline within units was by unrecorded punishment. One of the most frequent forms of punishment was deprivation of leave. Soviet recruits normally got two days' leave a month, which was usually spent in neighbouring towns. In view of the dreariness of life on base, leaves were precious, and the threat of deprivation was often sufficient to convince a recalcitrant recruit to shape up. If this didn't work, officers could get one of the unit's sergeants to beat the recruit – physical bullying could be part of daily life for a young Soviet soldier, and it reached epidemic proportions in the post-Soviet Russian Army.

The other arms of authority took a different view on punishments. The *de facto* military police – the Commandant's Service – was often given quotas to fill when patrolling towns or the like, and so guardhouse time was awarded rather liberally.

A very smartly turned out BMD-I performs for the crowds. The BMD-I was introduced in 1969 as an airborne and amphibious infantry fighting vehicle, for use specifically by the Soviet airborne divisions. (Cody/AirSeaLand)

to travel to the cities seeking work: in this way they were tied to the collective farms, almost as effectively as in the days of serfdom. Collective farmers were very poorly paid, even by Soviet standards, making only about half as much as urban factory workers. In some areas of the country, especially in the Caucasus and Central Asia, this was not quite so important since a fair amount of extra money could be made in black market operations. The singular distinction between serving two years as a conscript sergeant, and accepting another three-year tour of extended duty, was that the extended-tour sergeant-majors received an internal passport, while sergeants serving only their two years of draft duty were obliged to return to their collective farms. This attraction alone enticed a small percentage of the sergeants to remain in the service. These sergeant-majors were derisively referred to as *makaroniki* ('macaroni men') due to their penchant for collecting the annual service duty stripes which were worn to show their seniority.

THE SOVIET OFFICER

There was a much larger gap between Soviet officers and enlisted men than in most NATO armies. A Soviet officer's life was very distinct from that led by the NCOs, and the army tailored the pay and benefits to attract professional officers. Nevertheless, not all officers were professionals. Some university students went through officers' training courses in school rather than enter the army as common conscripts. The lowest officer rank, the junior lieutenant, was intended mainly for such short-term officers. This officer's initial tour of duty was from two to five years, and depended upon the circumstances of the enlistment, for example, the branch of service technical specialization and details of further training. The career pattern of a professional officer was usually different from that of a junior lieutenant interested in little more than serving his time and getting out of the army.

The route into the officer ranks for young men intending to make the army their career varied, but usually started with a posting to one of the more than 140 officers' schools. The sheer number of these schools was due to the fact that the Soviet officer corps made up about 15 per cent of the total personnel of the Soviet Army, which was a larger percentage than in most NATO armies. This was due in some degree to the role of junior officers in the Soviet Army, which as mentioned earlier, was closer in actual tasks to that of the professional NCOs of NATO armies. Also, a portion of the Soviet officer corps was involved in political control as *zampolity*, who had no direct counterparts in NATO armies.

The Soviet officer schools received candidates from three sources: enlisted men with a secondary education, pre-military schools and civilian secondary schools. Although it was not officially admitted, the only enlisted men with a good chance of being accepted for officer school were soldiers of Russian origin (or assimilated non-Russians), with a good military record, and preferably members of the Komsomol youth group. Soldiers who has served with political sections of military units were given special preference. Soldiers could apply for officer schools after their first tour of duty so long as they were not more than 23 years old. The test was the same as that given to students leaving secondary school, but soldiers were accepted for the officers' schools automatically on passing the exams.

There were two kinds of pre-military preparatory schools that provided officer candidates. The nine Suvorov schools, first founded in 1943 for the orphans of servicemen killed in the war, provided five to seven years of education for students who entered the school between the ages of ten and 13 years. Each school provided a basic secondary education as well as preliminary military training. In the 1960s the schools were expanded to permit older students, who had previously completed eight grades of normal civilian schools, to enter the Suvorov schools for the last two years of the courses. The similar Nakhimov schools were also founded during World War II, at locations in Tbilisi (Georgia), Leningrad and Riga (Latvia). Unlike the Suvorov schools, the Nakhimov schools were intended from the outset only to provide two years of education. Students were accepted by competitive examination after completing eight grades of normal civilian education.

Entry to both types of school was on a competitive basis, and about 25–33 per cent of applicants were accepted. The Nakhimov and Suvorov schools provided a high-quality education, and were very prestigious. Their students were predominantly Russian, with a smattering of Ukrainians, Belorussians and other minorities. Students of these schools tended to receive the choicest postings to the officers' schools if their records were good. Graduates wore distinctive insignia throughout their service career, were automatically admitted to officers' school, and were excused from certain entrance exams for later military schooling; they represented the cream of the Soviet officer corps.

Besides these specialized, full-time pre-military schools, the DOSAAF ran about 40 part-time schools. These provided students in the ninth and tenth grades with their NVP pre-induction training, but offered a more concentrated course with better instruction. DOSAAF schools were usually run in association with a particular branch of a service, and students would attend the school on two days a week, receiving 140 hours of instruction over two years (although aviation schools usually required about double

The Soviet May Day (Victory) parade in East Berlin in 1958. The tanks rolling in front of the infantry ranks are T-34/85s, World War II-vintage armour that nonetheless served on well into the Cold War, particularly with Warsaw Pact nations and international Soviet allies. (Cody/AirSeaLand)

that amount). These schools sponsored the special military summer camps that gave their students further specialized training. A typical DOSAAF pre-military school was the Leninist Komsomol Young Paratroopers School in Ryazan, formed in 1972 and located near the Airborne Command School and 106th Guards Air Assault Division, which provided the teachers. The school offered the normal NVP regulation training as well as basic parachute drill, and parachute jumping from towers and aircraft.

Students from normal civilian secondary schools were also eligible for officers' school. Applicants were usually between 17 and 21 years old, and had to pass competitive exams in mathematics, physics and the Russian language. Students who had received a medal or other distinction during secondary education took only one of the tests, which if passed with a grade of 'excellent' admitted them to officers' school. Preference was given to students who had been active in the Komsomol or other Communist Party organizations, and to students who had distinguished themselves in DOSAAF paramilitary clubs, or in pre-military NVP training. To some extent, the Russian language test could be used to weed out many non-Russians, and to identify the most highly assimilated non-Russians.

Soviet officers' schools were more specialized than military academies in most NATO countries due to the sheer number of schools. While the US Army has a single officer academy (West Point), each branch of the Soviet services would have several of these schools. For example, in the Ground Forces, the Armoured Force branch had eight officers' schools, the Artillery had seven, etc. There were three types of officers' schools.

The Military Technical Schools (VTUs) offered three-year courses that trained officers in basic tactical skills for specific types of units; there were about 70 of these schools at one time, but they were gradually upgraded to higher military schools.

The two primary types of officers' schools were the Higher Command Schools (VKUs) and the Higher Engineering Schools (VIUs). The Higher Command Schools, of which there were about 78, were the most common type. These offered four-year courses with about 60 per cent of the time devoted to specialized military subjects, 30 per cent to academic subjects (including mathematics, physics and foreign languages), and 10 per cent to political education. At least six weeks each year were spent training with a line unit from the appropriate branch of service. The Higher Engineering Schools were smaller in number, totalling about 26, and offered a more technical education. The curriculum lasted five years, and placed greater

A Soviet anti-aircraft team of the 1980s, armed with a 9K310 Igla-1 (SA-16 Gimlet). The SA-16 was one of a new generation of Soviet man-portable infra-red homing SAMs. Enhancements over the earlier Strela system included an optional Identification Friend or Foe (IFF) system plus improved target guidance and warhead lethality. (Cody/AirSeaLand)

stress on engineering, mathematics, physics and other technical subjects. Each branch had a mixture of both command and engineering schools. For example, seven out of the Armoured Forces' eight schools were command schools, and one was an engineering school. The command schools provided officers who led tactical units in the field, while the engineering schools tended to provide the staff of research establishments, technical services and the defence procurement bureaucracy.

Soviet officers were assigned on graduation to a staff or command position. They could later attend further military educational institutions if their performance warranted it. Advanced courses were offered, taking up to 11 months' time, and officers were later eligible for entrance into the military academies. In the USSR, the term 'military academies' was reserved for higher officer training institutions that trained officers for command and higher staff positions. There were about 20 such academies, each branch having one or two. There were three types of academies: command, technical and mixed command/technical. The most prestigious was the Military Academy of the General Staff, formerly called the Voroshilov Academy, which trained colonels or major-generals for high staff postings. The academies offered three- to five-year courses, and were an essential step in the training of all senior officers.

The career of a military officer in the USSR was attractive in terms of salary, status and benefits. A junior lieutenant earned about 220R monthly,

The full mechanization of the Cold War Soviet Army is hinted at in this photograph of motor rifle troops on manoeuvres. The vehicles seen here are, at the front, the BTR-50 and further back the BRDM-2. (Cody/AirSeaLand)

and a captain about 250R, compared to a factory foreman (supervising 30 men) who received only 140–160R. Officers' salaries were perhaps a little lower than those of civilians with comparable education; but officers received other benefits, such as the special *voyentorg* stores which gave them access to goods that were hard to find in the civilian economy. Officers' pension benefits were better on average than those in the civil sector, and medical care was often as good or better. The quality of officer housing varied, but no more than in the civil sector.

One drawback of service life, however, was that many Soviet units were stationed on the periphery of the vast Soviet mainland, far from towns or cities of any size, and this could lead to considerable isolation and hardship for the officers and their families. This was not only the case with the Ground Forces; indeed, probably the most unattractive postings were those of the prestigious Strategic Rocket Force, whose silos were located in some of the most god-forsaken reaches of the USSR.

A Soviet officer's career was not significantly different from that in most NATO armies. Efficiency reports (*attestatsiy*) were a regular feature of life, as was the usual process of 'ticket punching' for career advancement. Soviet officers tended to remain in a particular post longer than in the US Army, and there was a more formalized career path alternating between command and staff positions, especially for line officers. Although the Soviets had an 'up-or-out' promotion policy similar to that in the US Army, this was less vigorously pursued. Soviet regulations permitted officers to remain in the service at a particular rank longer than would be the practice in most NATO armies; for example, in the Soviet Army the maximum age for a lieutenant was 40, and the maximum age for majors was 50.

1) Military Police (Commandant Branch), field dress. For traffic duty a chest reflector is worn, with white/pale blue/red belts and arm bands. 2) Lieutenant, Medical and Veterinary Services, summer field dress. Standard women's field dress, with standard field medical kit. 3) Engineer, summer field dress. The jerkin traditional to this branch was misidentified in some Western publications as body armour. (Ronald Volstad © Osprey Publishing)

RESERVE DUTY

Once mustered out of the services, Soviet recruits retained a reserve obligation until the age of 50. Soviet reserve personnel were unlike those in most NATO armies in that they had no further training obligations and were unlikely to be recalled to service except in time of war. On rare occasions some reserves were called up: in the 1968 Czechoslovakia crisis, during the Polish crisis in the early 1980s, in 1979 when Afghanistan was invaded and in 1986 for the Chernobyl powerplant clean-up. However, these call-ups were very restricted in nature, and usually affected only the most recent draft years.

THE SOVIET ELITE FORCES

The Cold War was the era in which what we now term Special Operations Forces (SOF) truly came of age. The spectrum of operations performed by such troops ranged from counter-terrorism and hostage rescue through to major airborne incursions and direct-action raids. The Soviet Armed Forces, despite their overarching emphasis on non-specialized mass, invested heavily in SOF, partly to perform potential small-unit political operations – assassinations, counter-insurgency, etc – within the USSR, Warsaw Pact and beyond, but also to create spearhead units for major land offensive actions.

Of a shadowy nature were the Special Troops of the GRU, the intelligence service of the Soviet Armed Forces and an inter-service organization somewhat akin to the American Defense Intelligence Agency (DIA). This organization was responsible for intelligence troops in the various branches of the armed forces, including reconnaissance and special purpose troops. The Special Troops of the GRU were sometimes publicly called *razvedchiki* (scouts) or *vysotniki* (rangers), although their formal designation was and remains Spetsnaz (an abbreviation of *Spetsialnoye Nazachenie*: Special Purpose). Elements of the Border Troops also warrant characterization as 'elite' formations, as they were in reality far more than border police.

THE VDV AIRBORNE FORCES

The VDV emerged from the war in a state of disarray. On the one hand, the VDV units had displayed exemplary courage and heroism, and some 196 *desantniki* – airborne troops – received the highest Soviet decoration, the Hero of the Soviet Union medal. Yet on the other hand nearly all major airborne operations had been badly managed fiascos. Even though the

An ASU-85 rolls out of the belly of an An-12 Cub aircraft. Note the airborne insignia clearly displayed on the front hull armour plate. (Cody/AirSeaLand)

VDV was part of the Air Force, insufficient aircraft were provided, which foredoomed many of the operations. The issue of airlift would remain a pressing concern of the VDV for the next few decades.

In 1946, the VDV was transferred from the Air Forces to the direct control of the Ministry of Defence to serve as a strategic reserve. Over the next decade the VDV languished, but the future role of the airborne divisions was examined in the light of World War II experience. Assessments of the conduct of airborne operations by other armies were not particularly encouraging. The Soviets concluded that with the exception of the German use of paratroopers in Holland and Belgium in 1940, wartime airborne operations were either failures or had no decisive impact on the conduct of army operations. Moreover, these assessments found that airborne forces gained tactical success only when fighting against severely weakened or disheartened opponents. When facing quality units, as in the encounter between British airborne and German armoured units at Arnhem, the results were usually catastrophic for the airborne units due to their lack of firepower.

Yet the conviction remained that an airborne force had enormous operational potential for wreaking havoc in an enemy's rear area in support of conventional mechanized forces. As a result, the VDV was retained; and efforts were initiated to circumvent the problems with airlift and firepower. In 1956 the VDV was switched to the Ground Forces and came under the control of General Vasily Margelov, a wartime hero of the Soviet Naval Infantry, who would lead the VDV through its modernization programmes over the next decades.

The first substantial enhancement to the VDV came in 1955 with the first flight of the An-8 transport, which was the first modern aircraft of the VTA (Military Transport Aviation) to have any real capability to drop or land airborne forces. The An-8 was followed in 1964 by the more successful An-12, which was the backbone of the VDV's airlift throughout the remaining history of the Soviet Union.

A key shortcoming in VDV firepower was the inability of its units to deal with enemy tanks. The VDV had been the world's first force to be equipped with recoilless anti-tank weapons, in the mid 1930s, but these were never entirely successful. Airborne units began to receive the new B10 82mm recoilless rifle (RCL) in the early 1950s, and this was followed later by the more potent B11 107mm RCL, which benefited from the evaluation of US RCLs captured in Korea. For short-range defence against tanks, the VDV initially received a copy of the World War II German Panzerfaust, the RPG-1, which was followed in the early 1950s by the considerably more potent RPG-2.

Crew-served weapons like RCLs were too bulky to be dropped with the paratroopers, so special containers were developed that could be dropped by even the Il-28 jet bomber. Besides these crew-served weapons, the firepower of airborne divisions was considerably enhanced by the development of special light armoured vehicles. In the early 1950s Soviet design teams worked on a lightly armoured, tracked 76-mm howitzer, the ASU-76, and a similar 57mm gun tank destroyer, the ASU-57. The latter was accepted for quantity production and entered service in 1955, with nine in each airborne regiment. It could be carried in special P-90 parachute containers, one under each wing of a Tu-4 bomber. Later, a heavy load platform was designed for the new An-8 transport which employed a special retro-rocket braking system.

Work followed on a light airborne tank and a light airborne tank destroyer based on the PT-76 scout tank; but only the latter, designated ASU-85, was accepted for production. It entered service in 1960, and 31 served in each airborne division's assault gun battalion. Unlike the ASU-57, it was designed primarily for air-landing from the new, larger An-12 transport.

Over the next decade further improvements were made in the VDV's airlift capability and firepower. In the wake of the Cuban Missile Crisis embarrassment in 1963, the Politburo decided that it must significantly revamp Soviet capabilities to project its power worldwide. As a result, in 1964 the VDV was again shifted back to the direct control of the Defence Ministry as a special force for the Soviet High Command. The reorganization of the VDV as a semi-autonomous branch of the Soviet Army marked a significant watershed in VDV history. It was shortly after this decision that two important changes began to be implemented, which have resulted in a major shift in the complexion of the VDV – changes which continue to this day. In the 1960s the Soviet Ground Forces had undergone tactical and equipment changes to permit their units to fight on a nuclear-contaminated battlefield.

The VDV realized that airborne divisions could be extremely useful in theatre nuclear war by exploiting the devastation created by nuclear strikes. However, their troops could not survive unprotected in the contaminated regions where they would be expected to land and operate. The VDV

A unit of VDV paratroopers conduct a dramatic field exercise. Note their signature blue-and-white striped T-shirts just visible, an item of clothing long associated with the Soviet special forces community. (Cody/AirSeaLand)

selected the same option as the Ground Forces' infantry units: that is, an armoured vehicle that permitted the *desantniki* to fight from within the protection of the vehicle. The VDV initiated development of a smaller, lighter version of the Ground Forces' BMP infantry combat vehicle. This emerged in 1970 as the BMD airborne combat vehicle.

The introduction of the BMD in 1970 marked the shift of the VDV from a force depending primarily on light, air-landed infantry to a mechanized air assault force with considerably more firepower. The BMD was a unique type of vehicle; no other army fielded an armoured vehicle specifically designed for airborne infantry squad action. Initially, the BMDs were used to equip only one of the three regiments in each division. However, as production continued, this gradually expanded to the point where all three regiments in most divisions were fully BMD equipped; there were about 320 BMDs in each division. As the BMD became available, the ASU-57 was gradually withdrawn from service.

The second important change in the VDV came in 1967, when the Soviet Army began experimenting with the tactical use of helicopters. The VDV had always been envisioned as a paratroop or air-landing force. However, air-landing by aircraft implied the ability to seize an airfield in advance of the arrival of the main force. This proved practical in certain peacetime operations against erstwhile allies, like the seizure of Prague airport in the 1968 Czechoslovak invasion and Kabul airport in the 1979 Afghanistan invasion. In wartime, against a mobilized foe, the prospects for such an action were more dubious. In the 1960s, the US Army demonstrated a suitable alternative in the form of the tactical employment of helicopters in this role, notably in Vietnam. While helicopters were hardly new to the military scene, the arrival of new models powered by the more reliable turbine engine made them more practical for this demanding role. In the Soviet Union the Mi-8 began to replace the older, bulkier Mi-4, and this permitted the formation of the first airmobile brigades in the early 1970s. The airmobile brigades were light infantry formations that did not use the BMD; but in the late 1970s air assault brigades were formed – a heavier counterpart, in which two of the four infantry battalions were equipped with BMDs. The BMDs could be carried by the Mi-6 helicopter, but units began to receive the improved Mi-26.

The VDV, from its 1964 subordination to the Ministry of Defence, was used primarily as a strategic strike force for use in sensitive and demanding missions. In the 1968 invasion of Czechoslovakia the 103rd Air Assault

Division was air-landed at Prague airport after it had been seized by a special operations team, a Spetsnaz GRU group. In 1979 the 105th Air Assault Division, supported by elements of the 103rd Air Assault Division, was air-landed at Kabul airport.

By the mid 1980s, the VDV, under the command of Army General Dmitri Sukhorukov, fielded seven air assault divisions, of which one, the

Soviet columns roll through the streets of Czechoslovakia during the Red Army's invasion of that country in 1968. In total, about 250,000 Warsaw Pact forces were deployed, overwhelming the opposition. (Cody/AirSeaLand)

A paratrooper practises a landing during a training jump. He wears the padded jump helmet that was derived from tank crew headgear. (Cody/AirSeaLand)

106th Guards Air Assault Division in the Tula-Ryazan area, was usually earmarked for training purposes. It would also appear that the 44th Guards Airborne Division at Jonava in the Baltic Military District was kept as a skeleton formation for training purposes, but was not war ready, as the other seven divisions were.

These units were under the direction of the Ministry of Defence, and in time of war would serve as the primary strategic reserve of the Stavka (High Command). Besides these units, the VDV was responsible for the airmobile brigades and the air assault brigades. However, in contrast to the airborne divisions, these brigades were subordinate to the Ground Forces in their respective military districts. There were four airmobile brigades, ten air assault brigades and an airmobile battalion with each forward-deployed tank or combined-arms army.

The airborne divisions were based around three airborne regiments with supporting arms. This organizational structure was relatively loose in order to permit the divisions to be deployed in sub-divisional formations. A typical example would be an airborne regiment combat group with attached support units from elsewhere in the division, such as artillery and engineer support. Like the airborne division, the airborne regiment was triadic: its core was formed by three airborne battalions with support provided by an anti-aircraft battery, mortar battery, anti-tank battery and other units.

With a strength of about 6,500 troops, Soviet airborne divisions had considerably less manpower than units such as the US Army's 82nd Airborne Division, but had considerably more firepower with 320 BMDs. The Soviet and American airborne units were also fundamentally different in orientation. Whereas the Soviet units were mechanized air assault units, the US units were light infantry air assault units.

The strategic mobility of the VDV's seven divisions was circumscribed by the airlift assets of the Soviet VTA (Military Transport Aviation). The VTA deployed about 600 medium- and long-range aircraft comprising 370 An-12s, 170 Il-76s and 50 An-22s. The An-12 had a range of 1,400km and could carry one or two BMDs; a single BMD-equipped airborne regiment required 90–115 An-12 aircraft for an operation. The An-12 was slowly replaced by the much-improved Il-76, which had a range of 5,300km and could carry three BMDs or 120 *desantniki*. A BMD-equipped airborne regiment would require 50–65 Il-76s for a mission. The Il-76 and An-12 were supplemented by the enormous An-22 Antei, which could carry 175 troops or four BMDs to a maximum range of 4,200km.

Besides these assets, in wartime the VTA would probably absorb the 200 An-12s and Il-76s in Aeroflot service, although these were not configured for military cargoes. Even with these additional aircraft, the VTA was capable of carrying only about one fully equipped airborne division on any long-range mission, but could airlift two or three more lightly equipped divisions on shorter missions in a single surge. However, it is not at all clear that the entire resources of the VTA could be committed to a single operation due to its other responsibilities.

In spite of the limited airlift capability available to the VDV, its utility in Soviet strategic planning was quite considerable. The Soviets, like the Americans, appreciated that regional conflicts were far more likely to occur than any full-scale confrontation in Central Europe. The VDV was ideally suited for any regional requirement, being very heavily armed, well trained and motivated, and well suited to rapid deployment by aircraft or other means. Significantly, the VDV figured prominently in the two major Soviet military operations – Czechoslovakia and Afghanistan. In the event of all-out war in Central Europe, the VDV could be employed in a variety of fashions. In an operational or strategic role, it could be used to seize key targets in NATO rear areas and to hold on to them until relieved by mechanized units. It was also configured for exploiting tactical nuclear strikes in a conflict involving thermonuclear weapons.

There were probably special KGB teams attached to these divisions for the use of atomic demolition munitions.

On a tactical level, regimental or battalion-sized formations could be dropped or airlifted into the rear of NATO forces to strike at key communication or supply links, to threaten the rear of engaged NATO combat formations, to cut off retreating NATO units, and to wreak havoc in a variety of ways. At lower levels the VDV divisions were configured as combined-arms teams to permit their deployment in small battle groups. The presence of BMDs and Strela-2 SAMs at battalion level provided even these small formations with heavy firepower, anti-tank protection, high mobility and a modest air-defence capability.

The air assault brigades were akin to a miniature airborne division, being somewhat less than half the size with about 2,000–2,600 troops. They consisted of four air assault battalions, two of which were equipped with the BMD. Although paratroop qualified, their primary means of delivery would be by helicopters; as there were no organic helicopters in these formations, they would require the use of helicopters from neighbouring VVS Frontal Aviation units. A brigade with BMDs would require about 40 Mi-8 and 125 Mi-6/Mi-26 sorties, while a brigade without its armour would require 75 Mi-8 and 35 Mi-6/Mi-26 sorties. The airmobile brigade was akin to the air assault brigade, but was much lighter in mechanized equipment and smaller in size, with only 1,700–1,900 troops. It had no BMDs and its only armour was 13 BRDMs, nine of which were the missile-firing anti-tank types. However, some sources claim that the airmobile brigades did have their own helicopters in the form of a composite regiment of 32 Mi-8 and 12 Mi-6/Mi-26. These were not adequate to lift the entire brigade in a single throw, but could lift about half the brigade without additional helicopters. Other sources maintain that the brigades had no organic helicopter support, and would have to rely on local air force units.

The troops of the VDV were far more politically active than in the rest of the army, and about 85 per cent were members either of the Party or of the Komsomol. Although figures are not available, the VDV troops were probably disproportionately Russian, Belorussian and Ukrainian, giving an added factor of political reliability. Beyond basic training, draftees were apparently cycled through an airborne training division before assignment to their division. Training involved a more rigorous course of physical conditioning than in the rest of the Soviet Army, including normal combat jump training as well as more advanced techniques such as high altitude, low

Opposite: A Soviet naval infantryman poses in front of his PT-76 tank, c.1989. The PT-76 was a fully amphibious light tank, first introduced into Soviet service in 1951 for reconnaissance and fire support roles. (Cody/ AirSeaLand)

Russian troops at an artillery observation post make calculations regarding their firing ranges. In artillery, the Soviet Union maintained a superiority in numbers of tubes compared to the forces arraigned against them in Western Europe. (Cody/AirSeaLand)

opening (HALO) for at least a portion of the troops. Officers of the VDV attended a special academy, the Ryazan Higher Airborne Command School. The airborne divisions were, except for the training divisions, Category 1 units, kept near to full strength in men and equipment in peacetime. This is in complete contrast to Ground Forces units, the majority of which were kept at a lower state of readiness.

The VDV remained in the forefront of Soviet efforts to project military power beyond the borders of the USSR. For this reason, modernization of these forces continued up to the fall of the Soviet Union. On the strategic level, the gradual replacement of the An-12 with the far more capable Il-76 began, as did the replacement of the An-22 with the An-400 Condor, with the aim of permitting the VDV to deploy divisions at far greater ranges than was previously possible. On the tactical level, the VDV was at the forefront of adapting the helicopter to traditional VDV roles, leading to a gradual shift of the VDV from being a force relying primarily on paratroop operations, to a more flexible force using air-landing, parachute and heliborne techniques to carry out its operations.

THE SOVIET NAVAL INFANTRY

As we saw in the previous chapter, in World War II Soviet naval infantry were mainly used as ordinary foot soldiers with no particular amphibious training. Indeed, there was no better indication of the true Soviet attitude towards these forces than the decision in 1947 to completely disband

Soviet naval troops make a rather choreographed landing on a beach in Cuba. The Soviets deployed four armoured ground forces combat units to Cuba in 1962, and by the end of the year Red Army troop presence on the island numbered nearly 11,000 soldiers. (Cody/AirSeaLand)

them. What few naval infantry units remained were subordinated to the Coastal Defence Force. Attitudes eventually changed, and in 1961 the Naval Infantry was resurrected; the Soviet Army came to recognize the utility of specialized marine forces for conducting amphibious landings, and each of the fleets was allotted such a unit. Essential to this new policy was the development of amphibious warfare ships, notably the new tank-landing ships (LSTs) of the Alligator class.

The Naval Infantry was divided among the four fleets. From 1961 the Black Sea, Northern and Baltic fleets were allotted a naval infantry regiment, while the Pacific Fleet deployed a brigade. US intelligence assessments from the 1980s indicate that these formations were larger by that time, with brigades deployed by three fleets, and a division with the Pacific fleet.

Each naval infantry regiment comprised three naval motor rifle battalions and a naval tank battalion. The motor rifle battalions each had about 33 BTR-60 amphibious armoured troop carriers, while the tank battalion had a mixed complement of 34 PT-76 amphibious tanks and ten T-55 or T-72 tanks. In battalions with the T-55 tank, three of the ten were often the TO-55 flamethrower type. A naval infantry brigade had two tank battalions and five battalions of naval motor rifle troops, making it nearly double the size of the 2,500-man regiments.

The naval infantry troops, like most Marine forces, were of a higher calibre than normal motor rifle troops of the Soviet Ground Forces. They were better trained than their Ground Forces counterparts, and an increasing percentage were parachute qualified and trained in helicopter-landing operations. There were apparently specialized teams in these regiments trained to employ atomic demolition munitions (ADMs). Soviet ADMs are believed to have been available in several types, weighing 32–36kg each, with an explosive force of 0.1–0.5 kilotons. They would have been used to attack major port or seaside facilities.

The Soviet Naval Infantry force was quite small. It was intended for use on a tactical level as a raiding force, and on an operational level as the spearhead of an amphibious-landing force. Once a beachhead had been seized, further troop landings would be provided by Ground Forces units. For this reason, the Soviet Naval Infantry numbered only about 18,000 troops – compared to the US Marine Corps, which was more than ten times its size. Likewise, the Soviet Fleet's amphibious warfare ships were inferior in number and sophistication to those of the US Navy. The Soviet Naval Infantry also differed considerably from the US Marines in its approach to amphibious warfare. While the US Marines relied on specially designed armoured, amphibious tracked vehicles (amtracs) for landing operations, the Naval Infantry used the normal Ground Forces BTR-60, which had only marginal performance in the open water. This policy was due in no small measure to the difference in the experiences of the two forces. The US Marines had a tradition of preparing for hotly contested beach assaults, such as those of World War II in the Pacific. In contrast, Soviet wartime experience was mainly against targets without formidable beach defences. Current areas where the Naval Infantry might be used, such as the Danish or Norwegian coasts, were not heavily fortified.

Yet the Soviet Naval Infantry was ahead of the US Marines in the adaption of hovercraft for beach-landing operations. The Soviet fleet deployed over 60 hovercraft in classes, most notably 35 of the AIST class, which was capable of carrying four PT-76 tanks, two T-72 tanks or 220 troops; a fourth class of hovercraft, the Uterok, began entering service in the 1980s. Hovercraft have obvious attractions over armoured amphibious vehicles: against lightly defended beaches, they can quickly land an assault force, and return rapidly alongside the ships of the assault fleet to load up for renewed missions to the beachhead.

Soviet troops, possibly naval infantry, conduct self-defence training during the 1970s. One school of Soviet and Russian self-defence training is known as 'Combat Sambo', which in some ways is similar to the techniques of Mixed Martial Arts (MMA), but with an emphasis on lethality and strikes to vulnerable points. (Cody/AirSeaLand)

Judging by the Soviet Navy's shipbuilding programmes of the 1980s, the Naval Infantry remained central to Soviet strategic thinking. The construction of further Ivan Rogov-class landing ships, for example, made the Naval Infantry more suitable for employment outside traditional Soviet waters. The Naval Infantry was no longer confined to LSTs alone: the Ivan Rogov class had habitable berths on board, thus permitting long voyages to more distant destinations.

THE SPETSNAZ

The Spetsnaz were the special operations troops directed by Soviet Military Intelligence, the GRU. In contrast to normal elite formations, Spetsnaz were intended to engage in less conventional, diversionary warfare. They were descendants of specially trained teams who were parachuted behind the lines during World War II to support and inflame partisan activity.

Spetsnaz units of the 1980s were trained primarily for attacking high-value targets such as nuclear weapons stockpiles, theatre nuclear forces, airfields and command and communication centres, as well as other diversionary tasks. The basic Spetsnaz unit was the special operations brigade. There were apparently 16 of these brigades, allotted one per Group of Forces deployed in Warsaw Pact countries or military district in the USSR. Like the airmobile and air assault brigades, the special operations brigades would be commanded by the local army or front commanders in time of war. A proportion of Spetsnaz troops were also trained for more demanding tasks such as assassination, leading communist insurgent groups, or carrying out rear-area sabotage operations. Some Spetsnaz units were also trained to carry out operations disguised as foreign troops.

The special operations brigades had a direct counterpart naval formation, the naval special operations reconnaissance points, which were allotted one to each of the four fleets. These were organized around three battalions of combat swimmers, an airborne battalion, a supporting midget submarine unit, and specialist troops. The naval special operations points were intended to support amphibious operations by beach clearing and scouting; they could also be used for independent offensive operations such as harbour raids. Their closest NATO counterparts were the British Special Boat Service (SBS) or the US Navy SEALS and Underwater Demolition Teams (UDT).

The Spetsnaz were earmarked for especially difficult assignments and were the *crème de la crème* of the elite units of the Soviet Armed Forces. Their existence was, and remains, somewhat shrouded in secrecy, and as a result they were not permitted any distinctive form of uniform or insignia. Their service dress was usually that of corresponding services, such as airborne forces or naval infantry, and their field dress would be much the same. Little is known of Spetsnaz operations, for obvious reasons. There were numerous reports of the use of special commando teams in Afghanistan, which could be Spetsnaz operations, plus sketchy stories of Spetsnaz frogmen operating off the coast of Sweden in the mid 1980s, but there are few hard details.

SECURITY UNITS

The Soviet Union supported two organizations to prevent anti-government actions: the KGB (Committee for State Security) and the MVD (Ministry of Internal Affairs). Both organizations had military units which were part of the Soviet Armed Forces, but which were not under Defence Ministry control. These units were not military elites in the Western sense, and indeed they lacked direct Western counterparts. Rather, they were a form

A frogman conducts a riverine exercise in Czechoslovakia in September 1966. The vehicle appears to be a BRDM-2UM, a turretless command-car variant of the BRDM amphibious vehicle, introduced into Soviet service in 1962. (Cody/ AirSeaLand)

of political/military elite. Recruitment into these units served in lieu of regular military service, and entrance into certain of the units was far more tightly controlled than into most military units.

The security apparatus formed the third leg of the triad of Soviet state power, comparable to the army and the Communist Party. It kept its eye on the other two elements of the Soviet state, as well as on the citizenry in general. In return for loyalty to the security apparatus, members of these organizations were afforded privileges not found elsewhere in Soviet society, such as access to housing and consumer goods that were otherwise difficult to obtain. In some respects, the members of the security apparatus and their families formed a caste separate from the rest of Soviet society. This separation was encouraged by the state, since excessive fraternization with the rest of Soviet society might serve to undermine their commitment to uphold the state against any internal enemies.

The largest KGB military force was the Border Troops, numbering about 175,000 troops. While several European countries had border forces, none matched the military complexion of their Soviet counterpart. The Border Troops had many of the same roles as normal border security forces: they provided the personnel to man immigration check points, airport passport controls, train inspection teams, and border crossings. However, the Border Troops were also responsible for sealing the Soviet borders from both internal and external penetration. Their role was to prevent the unauthorized escape of Soviet citizens from the USSR, to prevent border smuggling, to suppress ethnic dissident movements in the frontier regions, and to repel any incursions by foreign military units until the arrival of other elements of the Soviet Army. For these purposes, the Border Troops were equipped with tanks, APCs, small warships, armed helicopters and light military aircraft.

The Border Troops were organized into nine military border districts, distinct from the military districts of the rest of the armed forces. These districts varied in depth, running 300–600km from the frontier. On average, the districts formed a restricted zone about 42km deep. Within these districts, there were individual border guard detachments, usually responsible for a length of the frontier of 100–600km. These detachments were roughly of battalion strength (about 500 troops) and were organized into an HQ, a motor-manoeuvre group and a *komendatura* (Commandant's Service) unit. The *komendatura* provided the basic outpost service, with five platoon-sized outpost units and a reserve outpost platoon, as well as an HQ and service unit. Each line outpost platoon had three rifle squads, a heavy machine-gun squad and a dog section, plus attached signal and support sections. The *komendatura* absorbed the bulk of the unit's troops. The motor-manoeuvre group was a detachment reserve force to back up any of the outposts in the event of major problems, and usually consisted of two motorized rifle platoons, a light machine-gun platoon and a heavy machine-gun platoon.

Besides the basic border guard detachment, there were a variety of other border guard units, including helicopter patrol and mechanized units. Perhaps the most enigmatic of the border guard units were the Mi-24 Gorbach helicopter units stationed on the Chinese border. As a result of the fighting in the late 1960s, the KGB and Soviet Army co-operated in the development of an armed helicopter suitable for patrolling the long, contested Chinese frontier. The result was the famous Mi-24, which differed from NATO attack helicopters in that it could carry an eight-man squad in addition to its heavy armament. This was developed to make it suitable for carrying small border guard units to inspect or man trouble points along the frontier. In time of war, the Border Troops traditionally served to form special security units,

In a dramatic image, Soviet Border Guards (plus canine support) leap from their truck during a practice alert. (Cody/AirSeaLand)

which were used to suppress anti-Soviet partisan groups in the USSR and neighbouring states, to put down army mutinies, and occasionally to clean up pockets of enemy resistance left behind Soviet lines.

Border Troops were recruited on the basis of a competitive examination, and service in the force counted in lieu of normal Soviet Army service. Although details are lacking, the Border Troops made preferential selection from applicants of Russian, Belorussian and Ukrainian nationality. The Border Troops were the largest, but not the only, military units of the KGB. The KGB also had an elite Kremlin Guard unit, the descendant of the original *Cheka* units of 1917, which guarded the centre of Soviet government. These troops could be distinguished from the Border Troops by their arm-of-service colour, which was royal blue instead of green. The KGB also had special guard units for high state officials, and to protect certain especially sensitive installations, notably nuclear weapons stockpiles. Their shoulder boards were marked with the letters 'GB' instead of the 'PV' of the Border Troops.

The MVD had its own troops which were known as the Interior Army – a larger counterpart to the Border Troops, and as its name implied, responsible for combating anti-state activity inside the USSR. It numbered about 260,000 troops, formed into conventional military units with their own artillery and armour, and equivalent to about 30 motor rifle divisions. The majority of the draftees were trained as static security guards or conventional motorized infantry, but by MVD schools and not the Ground Forces. The MVD seemed to favour induction of politically unsophisticated recruits from developing rural regions, especially Central Asia, who proved more amenable to indoctrination, showing greater appreciation for the modest privileges afforded them, and proved more reliable in carrying out their duties. The Interior Army preferred Central Asian, Russian and East Ukrainian recruits and generally excluded Jews and Balts. When asked why the Interior Army favoured Central Asians, a former Soviet Army officer responded: 'Because they are known for their obedience, stupidity and cruelty. They do everything they are asked without thinking, and are especially mean towards Russians.'

The roles of the Interior Army were quite varied. It provided troops to guard a wide variety of installations, including certain major food storage areas (due to the perennial Soviet problem of pilfering). Probably its most concentrated use was in its guard services for the 1,100 labour camps (gulags) still in operation in the USSR in the 1980s; these required the services of the equivalent of five divisions of interior army troops, although these 'divisions' were essentially administrative structures and not comparable to regular field forces. The Interior Army also served as a counterbalance to the Soviet Army in the event of army mutinies; on major Soviet Army bases, the ammunition stockpiles were under interior army control. Other interior army units were distributed throughout the country, and formed a

1) Senior Sergeant, Armoured Force, summer field dress. He wears standard black coveralls and the black beret used by Armoured Force personnel in place of the *pilotka* or new forage cap (though some units still wore the *pilotka*). Red and white signal flags are still regularly used during periods of radio silence. The AKSU (sometimes called the AKR) is a short carbine version of the AK-74 used by vehicle crews. **2)** Officer Cadet, Armoured Force, winter field dress. The jacket is worn over padded coveralls in extremely cold weather. The PNV-57 night vision binoculars were usually worn by vehicle drivers in lieu of normal metascope or image-intensification periscopes in the vehicles. **3)** Crewman, Armoured Force, summer field dress and IP-46 underwater evacuation gear. The special OPVT kit permits Soviet tanks to be driven underwater for rapid crossing of natural barriers in combat. This is a difficult procedure: even tanks retain some buoyancy, having a very uncertain footing on riverbeds, and in case of stranding crews are issued this rebreathing apparatus. The rubber mask is placed over the head; then the tank is slowly flooded until the hatches can be opened, and the crew swim to the surface. The helmet bears the tank's number: 2nd Battalion, 6th Company (of a nine-company regiment), 3rd tank. (Ronald Volstad © Osprey Publishing)

stiff reinforcement for local militia units if strikes or demonstrations got out of hand. The largest of these units was the Dzerzhinsky Special Operations Motor Rifle Division in Moscow. In most cities, the units were smaller than divisional strength, often consisting of an infantry battalion or less, and backed up by a small number of light tanks and other light armour.

A Soviet tank driver guides his vehicle forward. The distinctive padded fabric helmet, with built-in sections for the radio earpieces, had no ballistic protection at all, unlike many of the armoured vehicle helmets developed for NATO crews at this time. (Cody/AirSeaLand)

Although it might seem superfluous to maintain such a large force as a counterweight to popular unrest in view of the availability of the enormous Soviet Army, several factors argued against using the Soviet Army in this role. To begin with, many units of the Ground Forces did not have the political reliability for such duties, since the troops were apt to be sympathetic to certain popular outbursts. Furthermore, the army has traditionally found such service to be distasteful. The Soviet Army was genuinely popular amongst many elements of Soviet society, and the cultivation of this popularity was not helped by engagement in internal security work. While this sensitivity might seem odd in the army of a totalitarian state, the Soviet Army realized that any popular resentment aroused by its use on internal security duties would probably undermine its efforts to maintain military discipline, and would hamper attempts to persuade draftees to make a career in the armed forces. It is far easier to work in an environment where the army is accepted and even admired, than in a situation where it is deeply resented.

During wartime, the Interior Army continued to be responsible for its regular functions, and had additional war roles. In the past, 'blocking units' had been formed to prevent Soviet Army units or stragglers from fleeing the frontlines. The Interior Army had also traditionally been responsible for forming 'hunter units', used to suppress internal, anti-Soviet partisan groups among disaffected minorities, as well as to root out any enemy forces left behind Soviet lines. In these circumstances, these units tended to fall under KGB control.

* * *

The Soviet Army Forces was a vast military machine. Were it faced by any other opponent than the United States and its Western European allies – with their combined superior military-industrial complex and deep budget pockets – and had there not been international nuclear weapons arsenals balancing out the conventional force equations, the Soviet military would have been an unassailable force. As it was, a conflict between 1979 and 1989 showed that it was anything but undefeatable.

An impressive column of Soviet tanks is overshadowed by
the Afghan mountains in the background. Topography like
this, amongst other factors, has historically defied efforts
to unify Afghanistan into a sovereign state, as it is a loose
collection of tribes and ethnic groups over which, for many
centuries, central governments have seldom exercised more
than a moderate degree of influence, much less actual
control. (GEORGI NADEZHDIN/AFP/Getty Images)

CHAPTER 4

DESCENT INTO DEFEAT: AFGHANISTAN, 1979–89

THE SOVIET–AFGHAN WAR COULD BE considered a perfect metaphor for many of the failings of the Soviet state in the late twentieth century. In less than a decade, it exposed serious defects in the Soviet political structure as well as in communist ideology itself, helped justify and sustain the policy of internal reform led by Mikhail Gorbachev from 1985, and contributed to the decline of the Communist Party at a time when the USSR itself was spiralling into collapse. The conflict rapidly involved other nations with strong political interests at stake in Central Asia, not least the United States, which clandestinely siphoned billions of dollars in aid to the *mujahideen* through Pakistan. Pakistan itself not only supported the resistance in general, but particularly those elements of religious extremists who in the wake of Soviet withdrawal took a prominent part in the internecine struggle between rival *mujahideen* factions that ultimately led to the Taliban's triumph in the autumn of 1996.

In short, the network that became al-Qaeda took root as a direct consequence of the Soviet–Afghan War, in which Osama bin Laden and others like him provided substantial funds to large numbers of *jihadi*.

The rusting remains of a Soviet tank, overlooking Ghazni. The Soviet armour proved particularly vulnerable to IEDs and mines, detonated in combination with ambushes by RPG and recoilless rifle teams. (David Reynolds/DPL)

The international implications soon became apparent. Quite apart from the horrific wave of repression which their regime unleashed, the Taliban offered Afghanistan as a training and recruiting ground for other extremist groups whose political and ideological agenda stretched far beyond the borders of their war-ravaged country. By hosting al-Qaeda on Afghan soil, the Taliban sowed the seeds for the terrorist attacks of 11 September 2001, which in turn triggered a devastating reaction from the United States and the United Kingdom, soon followed by other NATO powers. All of this 'Pandora's box' may be traced to the Soviet invasion of Afghanistan and the ghastly war it inaugurated.

The foundations of a full understanding of the West's involvement in Afghanistan today must rest upon a firm grasp of the causes, course and outcome of the Soviet–Afghan War. The lessons from this confirmed the folly that underpinned Soviet strategy: unrealistic political aims, pursued by armed forces unable to cope with the unconventional methods of an adversary which, though vastly disadvantaged in weapons and technology, managed to overcome the odds through sheer tenacity and an unswerving devotion to freedom and faith.

OVERVIEW

In 1979, political leaders in Moscow directed a sceptical military to intervene in the Afghan civil war in order to maintain in power a nominally communist regime in Kabul, which was struggling against a resistance movement of disparate groups known collectively as the *mujahideen* or 'fighters for the faith'. Deeply unpopular with large swathes of rural, conservative, tribal peoples stretched across a country divided on religious, ethnic and tribal lines, Nur Mohammed Taraki's government of the Democratic Republic of Afghanistan (DRA) controlled urban areas, but very little of the countryside, where tribal elders and clan chiefs held sway. Even within the Communist Party apparatus, rival factions grappled for sole control of the affairs of state, denying them the time or ability to implement the socialist reforms they espoused, including the emancipation of women, land redistribution and the dismantling of traditional societal structures in favour of a more egalitarian alternative.

Leonid Brezhnev, the General Secretary of the Communist Party of the Soviet Union, concerned at the disintegrating situation in Afghanistan and determined to maintain a sphere of influence over the region, ordered an invasion – despite the fact that neither the climate nor the terrain suited Soviet equipment or tactics. When Soviet troops rolled over the border in December 1979, ostensibly in aid of a surrogate government in Kabul, they expected to conduct a brief, largely bloodless campaign with highly sophisticated mechanized and air assault forces, easily capable of crushing Afghan resistance in a matter of months before enabling a newly installed government to tackle the resistance thereafter. Events exploded at least two myths prevalent in the West: the Soviets never intended to remain long in Afghanistan, as supposed in Washington, and their relatively small troop numbers attested to this fact. Nor did the invasion represent the belated realization of the historic Russian drive to establish a warm-water port on the Indian Ocean. Theirs was to be a temporary – albeit an internationally condemned – presence.

Yet the Soviets comprehensively failed to appreciate the quagmire in which they found themselves. Their forces possessed very limited combat experience – none at all in counter-insurgency – and they foolishly assumed their successful interventions in East Germany in 1954, in Hungary in 1956 and in Czechoslovakia in 1968 offered models for any military operation executed against a popular struggle. Western analysts, too, predicted Soviet victory, but the political and military circumstances behind the Iron Curtain offered no parallels with Afghanistan. Unlike the Soviets' client states in Eastern Europe, Afghanistan stood embroiled in the midst of a civil war – not a straightforward, effectively unarmed, insurrection – and thus applying simple but overwhelming military might could only guarantee protection for the central government in Kabul, and perhaps control of larger cities and towns, but not the countryside. Soviet intervention in December 1979 achieved its initial objective with predictable ease: elite troops overthrew the government, seized the presidential palace and key communications centres, killed the head of state, Hafizullah Amin and replaced him with a Soviet-sponsored successor.

The plan thereafter seemed straightforward: stabilize the political situation, strengthen, re-train and enlarge DRA forces to enable them to quell the insurgency on their own, while concurrently performing the more passive roles of garrison duty and, finally, protect the country's key infrastructure such as major roads, dams and its sources of electricity and gas. Thus, within three years, the Soviets, confident in the notion that the Afghan government could stand on its own feet when backed by the continued presence of Soviet advisers including army officers, KGB personnel, civilian specialists in engineering, medicine, education and other spheres, and furnished

with a continuous supply of arms and technology, believed their forces could withdraw across the border, leaving a friendly, stable, compliant and ideologically like-minded regime firmly in power behind them.

None of these objectives stood up to the reality of the situation, however. The civil war continued to spiral beyond the government's ability to suppress it and the DRA forces' morale plummeted further, decreasing their operational effectiveness and causing concern in Moscow that withdrawing its troops would amount to both humiliation and the collapse of all Soviet influence over its client state.

Thus, what began as a fairly simple military operation – overthrowing a government and occupying key positions throughout the country, a task which the Soviet military, trained in large-scale, high-tempo operations could manage with ease – soon developed into a protracted, costly and ultimately unwinnable fiasco. The conflict pitted small, ill-armed but highly motivated guerrilla forces – employing fighting methods bearing no relation to those practised by opponents trained and armed to fight in Central Europe – against troops of utterly different organization and doctrine. Experience soon demonstrated the limited efficacy of heavy infantry, tanks, artillery, and jet fighters in a struggle that decisively depended upon more helicopter gunships, more heliborne troops, and more special forces to meet the demands of the fluid, asymmetric war conducted by the *mujahideen*.

As the years passed and casualties steadily mounted, the war graphically exposed the weaknesses of the Soviets' strategy and the poorly suited structure of their armed forces, which never succeeded in overcoming an ever-growing resistance movement operating over a vast, varied and exceedingly challenging landscape. Indeed, both Soviet tactics and strategy contained fatal flaws. Their doctrine directed the use of armoured and motor rifle units to advance along narrow axes, maintaining secure lines of communication while wreaking destruction upon any resistance they encountered through combined arms (the co-ordination of firepower offered by infantry, artillery, armour and air assault units). With little experience or training in a counter-insurgency role, the Soviet Armed Forces chose a simplistic approach to the problem: especially at first, they merely cleared territory in their path, which translated into the widespread killing of civilians, as well as resistance fighters – who avoided where possible the superior weight of fire which their opponents could bring to bear.

Everywhere circumstances appeared to confirm Alexander the Great's dictum that 'one can occupy Afghanistan, but one cannot vanquish her'. Civilians who survived the onslaught naturally fled, embittered, abandoning their destroyed villages and property to seek refuge in cities or over the border. Such ruthless exploitation of air and artillery power was deliberately meant to clear areas, particularly along the border with Pakistan, so as to deprive the resistance of recruits and local support as well as to aid in the interdiction of supplies crossing over into Afghanistan. This strategy caused horrendous human suffering: only six months after the Soviet invasion, approximately 800,000 Afghans had fled into Pakistan.

At the outset of the war the Soviets' strategy involved persuading the population to support the communist-led Kabul government, thus denying aid to the resistance in the anonymity of the provinces. This soon proved unrealistic, not least owing to the regime's heavy-handed measures. They then turned to denying the insurgents supplies, which led to driving civilians off their land or destroying their livelihoods as a warning to withhold their support from the insurgency. This policy also involved interdicting supply routes that connected the insurgents to the vital materiel moving through Pakistan, the principal source of aid to the *mujahideen*. The Soviet Fortieth Army mounted numerous substantial operations against areas known to be actively supporting the resistance and severed supply lines whenever possible, but the 'drip, drip' effect caused by the guerrillas' constant ambushes, sniping, raids and mine-laying ultimately inflicted politically unsustainable losses on the invader.

The Soviet–Afghan War differed from other conflicts of the Cold War era. Although it was a limited conflict, it was longer than most – slightly over nine years in length – and thus did not share the decisive nature of the Arab–Israeli wars of 1948, 1956, 1967 and 1973, or the Falklands War of 1982. The Soviet imbroglio lacked the scale of either the Korean War (1950–53) or Vietnam (1965–73) and did not conclude with a clear political outcome, in contrast to those proxy conflicts. Nor can it be seen as some sort of Soviet 'Vietnam', especially in terms of scale. The Soviets never deployed anything approaching the numbers the Americans sent to South East Asia, with over half a million personnel by 1968, compared with the average of approximately 118,000 Soviets serving at any given time in Afghanistan. Whereas the Americans conducted numerous operations involving several divisions, the Soviets' entire Fortieth Army in Afghanistan consisted of a mere five divisions, four independent brigades and four independent regiments, plus various small support units.

Numbers as insufficient as these denied the Soviets – by their own faulty strategic calculations – any realistic chance of securing over 20 provincial centres plus various key industrial sites, to say nothing of the manpower required to secure whole swathes of remote and practically inaccessible territory inhabited by a seething population supporting elusive, seldom-visible opponents who moved by stealth, struck at will, and melted back into civilian life with little or no trace. The protection demanded for hundreds of kilometres of roads, communication lines and points of strategic importance – some of which the Soviets had to occupy outright or, at the very least, deny to the *mujahideen* – placed a colossal burden on the invaders, who failed to appreciate both the sheer scale of the enterprise and the immense commitment in manpower it required.

A wrecked T-62 on the former Soviet-Afghan battlefield. The conflict in Afghanistan brought the Soviets some painful lessons in the limitations of conventional weaponry against an insurgent army. (David Reynolds/DPL)

THE SOVIET FORCES AND THEIR DRA ALLIES

The Fortieth Army, which represented the Soviets' military presence in Afghanistan, varied in strength, but averaged around 118,000 men in Afghanistan at any given time. These troops were never intended to play the leading role in subduing the Afghan insurgency – that was to remain the primary responsibility of DRA forces – and never anticipated the scale of the enterprise triggered by their appearance on Afghan soil. As a consequence, and because of the Kremlin's steadfast adherence to the original notion that the Fortieth Army remain a 'limited contingent', these troops failed to establish the substantial presence in the country that subsequent events rendered so necessary. Moreover, with their armed forces structured, equipped and trained to operate on the northern European plain (or Central Front, in NATO parlance), or alternatively on the plains of northern China as the most likely battlegrounds of the future, Soviet strategists expected to conduct fast-paced conventional operations. They certainly did not anticipate undertaking a low-intensity, asymmetric war in Central Asia, and thus their force structure, weaponry and tactics necessarily underwent substantial alteration, a programme which, of course, took time to evolve and implement.

Broadly speaking, Soviet troops engaged in four types of military action in Afghanistan. The first consisted of major operations conducted by both regular and special forces, including artillery and aircraft, and generally in conjunction with DRA units, the purpose being to destroy large groups of *mujahideen* in particular areas of the country. Soviet commanders conducted these operations in phases lasting for several weeks or longer. The second type of operation was carried out on a smaller scale, perhaps by a single regiment with artillery and aircraft in support. This type of operation focused on destroying a specific group of rebels in a location discovered via intelligence-gathering. Such operations tended to be conducted in ten days or less. Third, while such combat missions were under way, units 'combed' villages in search of concealed weapons caches or medical aid stations. Fourth, small units, often company-sized, conducted ambushes along roads, on mountain trails and near villages, with locations selected on the basis of intelligence gathered by Afghan intelligence personnel.

Even so, to a considerable extent the Soviets remained shackled to the methods they knew and understood – large-scale operations in the form of conventional offensives. They continued to launch these regularly, most notably in the Panjshir Valley, despite generally poor results, since none of these major operations achieved more than temporary neutralization of resistance activity in the areas over which the Soviets' ponderous military machine functioned. Experience revealed that heliborne forces operating in conjunction with mechanized forces could function effectively at the battalion and brigade level, but such methods tended to stifle tactical success when carried out on a divisional or larger scale. Counter-insurgency depends on highly mobile, well-led, well-trained and suitably equipped forces capable of fighting guerrillas by employing their own

In this dramatic photograph of Soviet military might, Mi-24 Hind helicopters provide an aerial overwatch for major Red Army tank formations during the campaign in Afghanistan. (Andrei Ivanov/DPL)

methods. Soviet armour, air power and heavily laden infantry dependent on their APCs for transport over difficult terrain could not, despite their impressive firepower, compensate for their inherent shortcomings in a counter-insurgency environment, for the *mujahideen* seldom appeared in concentration, and in any event disappeared before Soviet troops could bring that overwhelming firepower to bear.

The terrain of Afghanistan is heavily mountainous, although the country consists of extensive areas of dry plains, deserts and 'green zones' of river valleys and vegetation as well. This mountainous terrain strongly influenced the strategy adopted by the Soviets, obliging their commanders to convey troops to an operational area via helicopter or convoy. Whenever possible, they sent troops ahead of the main body or inserted advance parties of troops by helicopter on to high ground to cover those following behind. Yet this of course depended on the availability of such aircraft, required proper planning and exposed the limited number of helicopters to ground fire, especially from RPGs, anti-aircraft guns, SA-7s and Stingers (US-supplied hand-held SAM launchers).

Close to the larger cities and along frequently travelled roads, the Soviets established permanent posts consisting of garrisons of between 15 and 40 troops, who controlled the immediate area, guarded the roads and guided artillery fire. Owing to their isolation, they could call on help via radio. Some of the most successful Soviet operations involved combined operations, including air assault forces in support of a mechanized ground attack. Helicopters bearing small contingents of these troops would insert them deep in the rear and on the flanks of resistance strongholds to pin insurgents, prevent their withdrawal, destroy their bases and threaten or cut off their lines of communication. Ground troops would then advance to join up with these heliborne forces and engage trapped *mujahideen*, destroying them with superior firepower. Heliborne forces performed best when inserted behind rebel lines within the range of supporting artillery, unless of course their own guns accompanied them. Operations undertaken without artillery support often ended in high casualties for the Soviets.

As guerrillas received and employed new weaponry and developed fresh tactics, they obliged the Soviets to adapt in turn. For a large conventional force already trying to cope with shifting political circumstances in the country, this pressure proved an unwelcome addition to their existing woes, demanding new approaches to seemingly intractable problems in the field. This meant not simply the modification of tactics, but variations to uniforms, weapons and equipment to suit changing requirements. The Fortieth Army comprised a professional cadre of officers and other ranks, but conscripts formed the bulk of the formation. Like so many American draftees destined for service in Vietnam in the 1960s, they were frequently reluctant or downright unwilling to serve in a war whose purpose they did not understand and in a country about which they knew nothing.

Those with time on their hands, such as the thousands of soldiers based in rear areas involved in maintenance, logistics or communications, could easily fall prey to narcotics addiction with predictable effects on morale, though to be fair homesickness and boredom afflicted rear units more than drug-taking. Naturally the Soviets possessed elite forces, too, but never in adequate numbers. While ground reconnaissance troops tended to be better trained and of a higher quality than the typical conscript belonging to a motor rifle unit, the critical shortage of high-quality infantry often led the Soviets to employ reconnaissance personnel in combat rather

A group of Afghans taken prisoner by Soviet troops in 1987. The soldiers are all armed with the 5.45mm AK-74 assault rifle; Afghanistan was one of the first major combat testings for the smaller-calibre rifle. (E. Kuvakin/CC-BY-SA-3.0)

than in their proper reconnaissance roles. This in turn detracted from the duty of intelligence-gathering on the ground, in compensation for which commanders foolishly relied too heavily on intelligence acquired though aerial reconnaissance, radio intercept and what little access they had to agents in the field. These sources did not always yield much of tactical use, and by assigning reconnaissance units to combat duties the Soviets neglected to make best use of their skills and consequently frequently failed to locate *mujahideen* forces. The most famous elite forces were the Spetsnaz or 'forces of special designation', highly trained and used in long-range reconnaissance, commando and special forces functions such as night-time ambushes. They would be helicoptered in and then proceed on foot to the ambush point, there to lie in wait for their unsuspecting quarry.

Most of the infantry carried the 7.62mm AKM assault rifle, while air assault forces carried the 5.45mm AKS-74, the latter creating more substantial injury. Soviet heavy weapons included two kinds of rocket launchers: the BM-21 Grad (Hail) and the BM-27 Uragan (Hurricane). Smaller weapons included the 12.7mm DShK – a heavy machine gun – as well as RPGs and mortars. The Soviets also deployed various types of aircraft, including MiG-23 and MiG-27 Flogger fighter-bombers and Su-17 and Su-22 Fitter fighter-bombers, plus Tu-16 Badger medium bombers and Su-24 Fencer and Su-25 Frogfoot attack aircraft for bombing missions. Mi-8/Mi-17 Hip helicopters transported troops, ammunition, water and food. Combat helicopters included the Mi-24 Hind attack helicopter, which could provide rapid and accurate firepower for ground attack, convoy escort and patrolling as well as covering troops with close air support. These proved extremely effective against the resistance and were greatly feared. On the other hand, they suffered from vulnerabilities like all weapon systems, and, as helicopters are most exposed when they are on the ground or hovering over a position, the *mujahideen* tended to achieve reasonable success against such aircraft if they caught them in range while landing or disembarking troops.

DRA forces did not enjoy much respect from their Soviet counterparts – and for good reason. Afghan officers could apply for training in a Soviet military college, sometimes within Afghanistan or occasionally in the Soviet Union itself, but they seldom reached a high standard. Apart from volunteers, ordinary soldiers were often acquired by the crude method of virtual kidnapping: troops entered a village and rounded up men of appropriate age. Exceedingly high rates of desertion, sometimes directly into the ranks of the enemy, and numerous instances of DRA soldiers selling their Soviet-supplied weapons to the resistance – including sometimes tanks and armoured vehicles – did nothing to enhance their appalling reputation.

THE *MUJAHIDEEN*

Understanding the Soviet Armed Forces' experience in Afghanistan also requires a sense of their opponents. The *mujahideen* tended to avoid direct contact with Soviet forces of superior numbers and firepower lest they risk annihilation. Unlike the Soviets, they very rarely fought from fixed positions and if threatened with encirclement simply withdrew. Similarly, in the grand tradition of guerrilla operations, the *mujahideen* always sought to achieve advantage through the element of surprise. They benefited enormously from local, intimate knowledge of the ground, possessed years of experience in scouting and reconnaissance-gathering and could transmit intelligence on the movement and strength of Soviet units in rapid fashion and across substantial distances by crude but effective means, including signalling devices that the Soviets could neither interpret nor suppress.

The *mujahideen* were extremely adept at night-fighting, rapid manoeuvre and virtually undetected movement over difficult terrain, and at maintaining a large network of intelligence-gatherers across the country. Boys as young as 11 or 12 fought, carrying Kalashnikovs, together with their fathers and grandfathers. Their motives were various: in rare

In one of the ironies of the Cold War, an Afghan resistance fighter prepares to launch a Soviet-made SA-7 man-portable SAM. Such weapons were channelled to the *mujahideen* via covert suppliers in the Middle East and Pakistan. (DOD/PD US GOV)

exceptions they fought simply for money, but overwhelmingly for the sake of defending their country and affirming tribal loyalty. Whatever other motives existed, without question fighting on behalf of *jihad* or holy war compelled most of them.

A small minority served in the *mujahideen* out of compulsion: fighters simply arrived at a village and threatened to destroy the houses unless men came forward to serve in their ranks, a process that simultaneously prevented DRA forces from adopting the same practice. The number of *mujahideen* actively engaged in fighting varied, but an estimated 85,000 served during the final stages of the Soviet occupation in 1988–89. The *mujahid* prided himself on exhibiting bravery in action and often demonstrated a careless disregard for his own life. He was highly motivated, functioned on very little food, moved considerable distances on foot without complaint, generally performed great acts of endurance over rough and mountainous terrain, and adopted a fatalistic attitude that rendered him the most formidable of fighting men.

In true guerrilla fashion, the *mujahideen* possessed few heavy weapons in the form of aircraft or artillery, and thus depended primarily on small arms. Nevertheless, they did employ heat-seeking, Soviet-made, Egyptian-supplied SAM-7 anti-aircraft missiles, though with very poor results. However, at the end of 1986 the rebels acquired American-made Stingers as well as a few British Blowpipe missiles. They also possessed recoilless mountain guns, mortars and DShK heavy machine guns, which they pronounced 'Dashika'. Some World War II Soviet weapons passed to the Chinese and thence found their way to Afghanistan. The USA purchased and supplied largely Eastern Bloc weapons in order to maintain a policy of deniability, thereby obviating Soviet retaliation in some form. With the Saudis matching US funds dollar for dollar, and various other donor nations including China, Iran and Britain becoming involved in this illicit arms trade, vast quantities of weapons arrived in Pakistan, where that country's Inter-Service Intelligence (ISI) directly controlled their distribution from near Rawalpindi.

The *mujahideen* deployed anti-transport mines such as the 7kg Italian-made TS-6.1, as well as anti-personnel mines, some of which popped up and exploded above waist height, while others were activated by the vibrations of footsteps or by radio, or set off by mine detectors. The *mujahideen* discovered mines to be even more effective by planting bombs underneath them to increase the strength of the explosion. Mines of various types were pervasive and sometimes severely impeded the Soviets' movement.

A WAR WITHOUT FRONTS

By the autumn of 1979, with the Afghan economy in a downward spiral, the regime rent by political infighting, the country racked by fully fledged civil war and the *mujahideen*'s increasingly effective opposition looking certain to end in Amin's downfall, the Soviets felt compelled to act. In the months prior to the invasion, Soviet military and KGB advisers toured the country under various pretences to determine the best method of ensuring a rapid subjugation with a minimum of interference from Afghan forces. But the actual decision to invade did not apparently come until 12 December, during a meeting of the Politburo chaired by Andrei Gromyko and attended by Party General Secretary Brezhnev, Yuri Andropov, the KGB chairman, and the Defence Minister, Dmitry Ustinov.

The first deployments appear to have begun when the 105th Guards Air Assault Division, under Marshal Sergei Sokolov, shifted troops from Termez in Uzbekistan to Bagram air base, north of Kabul, beginning on 29 November. Late on the evening of 24 December, further contingents from the 105th set down at the civilian airport in Kabul, while other units arrived via heavy Ilyushin and Antonov transport planes at Bagram, at the air base at Shindand near Herat, and at Kandahar, the last of the

Soviet troops rush forward to mount their BMP-I infantry fighting vehicles. As with many counter-insurgencies before and since, the Soviets and their Afghan allies could not deploy the requisite numbers and supplies to maintain permanent control over the areas that they cleared of resistance, often obliging them to repeat the same operation. (Cody/AirSeaLand)

major airfields in the country. In addition, units of the 360th Motor Rifle Division crossed the border near Termez en route to the Afghan capital. By launching the invasion around Christmas, the Soviets hoped to lessen the likelihood of any concerted Western objection. Government troops offered no resistance, since they believed the arrival of Soviet forces represented Moscow's desire to uphold Amin in power. As a precaution, Soviet advisers had already removed the batteries from large numbers of Afghan tanks on the spurious ground that the machines required 'winterizing'.

While the Soviet–Afghan War may be divided into distinct phases by historians, it is vital to appreciate that the nature of insurgency defies strict adherence to convenient divisions. Set-piece battles, distinct campaigns and decisive actions indicating the conflict's changing course seldom if ever occur in asymmetric warfare. It is in the very nature of an insurgency, characterized by low- and medium-intensity fighting and the enormous disparity between the protagonists' capabilities, that neither side is capable of inflicting a decisive blow on its opponent via clear-cut encounters. As with all unconventional conflicts, the outcome of the Soviet–Afghan War would depend upon the cumulative effect of years of steadily applied combat power in an attritional contest, in which the winner succeeded in grinding down his opponent through unacceptable losses and a broken will.

Before briefly examining the operational phases of the war, a concise discussion of the basic nature of the fighting may be instructive. From the outset fighting took place throughout Afghanistan, with the highest pitch reached in the east, a fact confirmed by the large proportion of refugees and internally displaced Afghans who fled the area over the course of the nine-year conflict. As this region adjoined the Pakistani border, across which the bulk of foreign aid flowed to the resistance over this period, the country's eastern provinces naturally became the focus of particular Soviet attention, with the establishment of a buffer or cordon sanitaire their principal objective. To that end, the normal course of fighting served well in encouraging or forcing civilians to abandon the region for the safety and refuge provided by nearby Pakistan. Only later did the Soviets institute a deliberate policy of de-populating vast stretches of territory in a bid to deny the *mujahideen* local support in various forms, including food, shelter and basic intelligence. From the beginning of the war and for most of its course, the majority of the operations conducted by the resistance remained consistent with their limited offensive capacity. These consisted of a series of small-scale (albeit seemingly relentless) attacks conducted across most parts of country – the central region of the Hazarajat figuring as a notable exception – in the form of raids, hit-and-run attacks and moderately sized strikes against Soviet and Afghan regime bases, reconnaissance parties and small convoys.

However, the Soviet–Afghan War must not be seen only in the light of elusive guerrilla attacks followed in their wake by the hammer-blows of a superpower wielding numerically superior numbers and advanced technology, for the resistance did not always hold the initiative. Indeed, as early as March 1980 the Soviets launched their first major offensive with a sweep through the Kunar Valley, which left approximately a thousand *mujahideen* and Afghan civilians dead, yet achieved little more than temporarily driving out to other valleys resistance leaders who, in the wake of imminent Soviet withdrawal, resumed their initial positions. Indeed, this scenario strongly characterized the course of the war. The Soviets applied overwhelming force to enable ground troops to establish temporary control of an area after inflicting perhaps sizeable, but seldom crushing and therefore meaningful, casualties on the enemy. These ground troops would then be withdrawn with only a small (and therefore a vulnerable) or no presence left behind, enabling those same opponents to re-establish their former presence

The crew of a Soviet APC talk with who appears to be some form of traffic policeman on a remote road between Kabul and Jalalabad. The rocky surfaces were a gift for *mujahideen* laying well-concealed mines. (Cody/AirSeaLand)

over territory that Soviet and/or regime forces would have to clear again – a frustrating and costly affair that inevitably favoured the insurgency.

Much of the fighting involved insurgent ambushes directed against patrols and convoys. In the case of the former, the *mujahideen* possessed better knowledge of the ground and often struck under cover of darkness, while in the case of the latter, they took full advantage of the limited

1) Motor Rifleman, lightweight winter field dress. From 1985 the Limited Contingent of Soviet Forces/Afghanistan introduced a variety of new uniform items. This new winter jacket, roughly resembling the traditional officers' winter work jacket but with pockets and other features similar to Polish and Czechoslovak equivalents, replaced the clumsy greatcoat. Experience in Afghanistan also led to the introduction of a variety of armoured vests, this example being used by road patrols and truck drivers. Photos taken in Afghanistan in 1986 also show this new chest pouch rig for AK-74 magazines. 2) Motor Rifleman, lightweight summer field dress. Photos from the mid 1980s show this new outfit, including a forage cap. Unusually, some Motor Rifles troops were shown wearing the striped blue and white undershirt previously limited – as a sign of elite status – to Airborne and Naval Infantry forces, possibly as a sign of unit distinction earned in combat. Note the R-105M manpack radio, which could also be accompanied by an amplifier carried by a second soldier. 3) Motor Rifleman, lightweight summer field dress. Some Motor Rifle units were issued the light hooded jacket introduced from 1984, with new gathered trousers, for mountain infantry, and wore it over the normal lightweight summer field dress. Note the LPO-50 flamethrower, in the process of being replaced by the RPO and RPO-A. (Ronald Volstad © Osprey Publishing)

routes available to Soviet and government forces, who found their freedom of movement, even over short distances, hampered by a shortage of roads, particularly paved ones. Regular troops, not trained to confront opponents operating according to radically different doctrine, tactics, and methods of supply and evacuation, could not hope to proceed across hundreds of kilometres of trackless, often mountainous, ground without commensurate support in terms of air power, artillery and supply. Thus, large formations necessarily depended upon the existing network of rudimentary roads – ironically, most of these constructed by fellow Soviets since World War II.

From the Soviet point of view, the war may be divided into four phases: the first involving invasion and consolidation from December 1979 to February 1980; the second, characterized by the Soviets' elusive pursuit of victory between March 1980 and April 1985; the third constituting the period of fighting at its height from May 1985 to December 1986; and the fourth represented by the period of withdrawal from November 1986 to February 1989. These will be examined in turn.

PHASE ONE: DECEMBER 1979–FEBRUARY 1980

The Soviet invasion amounted to a *coup de main* employing a strategy modelled on that used in their last cross-border intervention during a period of unrest (Czechoslovakia in the spring of 1968). Hostilities began in Kabul on 27 December, when air assault and Spetsnaz forces seized the vital Salang Tunnel and key government and communications points in the capital. There Colonel Grigory Boyarinov, leading special forces, specifically sought out Amin, who had recently relocated from the Arg, the presidential palace, to the Tajbeg Palace in the southern part of the capital. There the Soviet assault force surrounded and stormed the building, killing Amin and most of his family, but losing Boyarinov in the process. During the assault, the city's telephone system shut down after a deliberately timed explosion, and on the evening of the 28th the Soviets used a powerful radio transmitter on their own soil to broadcast a recording of exiled communist politician Babrak Karmal announcing Amin's overthrow and naming himself successor. As far as the Soviets were concerned, their seizure of key points across the country, together with the successful installation of Karmal in power, ought to have signalled the practical end of their major military operations in Afghanistan.

A Soviet BMP, manned by airborne troops, rumbles through the streets of Kabul following the Red Army invasion of 1979. The Soviet plan of invasion bore the hallmarks of those employed in Hungary and Czechoslovakia in 1956 and 1968, respectively. (Andrei Ivanov/DPL)

Soviet strategy concentrated on a few key objectives. First, the army was to bring stability to the country by protecting the main thoroughfares, placing large garrisons in the major cities, and guarding air bases and points of logistical significance. Once ensconced in these positions, Soviet troops planned to relieve Afghan government forces of garrison duties and redirect DRA efforts against the resistance in rural areas, where the Soviets would provide support on a number of fronts: logistics, intelligence, air power and artillery. This would enable Soviet forces to take a secondary role in the fighting, thereby both minimizing their contact with the Afghan population and keeping their casualties to an acceptable level. Finally, they planned to strengthen Afghan government forces to the extent that once resistance ceased the Soviets could withdraw their own troops and leave governance and security matters to the 'puppet' regime left in their wake.

The fact that the occupying forces did not anticipate serious resistance may be discerned from their original rules of engagement, which specified that troops were only to return fire if attacked, or to rescue Soviet advisers in insurgent hands. By necessity, these rules rapidly came to be altered owing to the rise in casualties from the very beginning, not least those sustained from urban unrest, the worst of which occurred on 21 February 1980 when approximately 300,000 people crowded the streets of Kabul shouting anti-government and anti-Soviet slogans. The demonstrations continued into the following day when the crowds flowed into the main streets and squares and appeared before the Arg, where Karmal made his residence. Thousands laid siege to government buildings, threw projectiles at the Soviet Embassy and killed several Soviet citizens. After the rioters looted scores of shops, overturned and burned cars and set ablaze a hotel, General Yuri Tukharinov, commander of the Fortieth Army, received orders to block the main approaches to Kabul and stop the demonstrations. This he achieved, but the rising in the capital marked the proper beginning of a resistance movement now extending its remit to foreign forces acting on behalf of Karmal's illegitimate regime.

This left the Fortieth Army with the unenviable task of defeating the insurgency across the country, a task for which, owing to its original remit of the previous December, it was not properly equipped or trained.

In the course of this first phase of the war, that is, the two months from the end of December 1979 to the end of February 1980, the Fortieth Army had already suffered 245 fatal casualties, largely attributable to regular attacks launched against columns of troops and supplies on the main roads from the Soviet Union. The army responded by establishing mutually supporting guard posts (*zastavy*) – typically 12-man sandbagged outposts equipped with heavy machine guns and 120mm mortars – at regular intervals that secured the main roads, principal cities, airports, bridges, power stations and pipelines. These posts observed the insurgents' movements, supported convoy escorts, and could call in air or artillery strikes as necessary.

By the end of February 1980, 862 *zastavy* dotted the landscape, scattered across Afghanistan, containing garrisons amounting in total to more than 20,000 troops, a fifth of the Fortieth Army's manpower. This committed

Kajaki Dam in Helmand province. The Soviets seized the dam in 1979 and built swimming pools and military accommodation. They also planted mines and barbed wire to stop the *mujahideen* from mounting an attack. The *mujahideen*, however, directed hundreds of goats into the minefields to clear a path through, then scaled down into the camp and mounted a brutal attack. Every Soviet in the base was killed. A dozen surviving Soviets took refuge in a guard house at the front of the base, but they were captured, beheaded and skinned. (David Reynolds/DPL)

troops to a necessary yet static function when the Soviets required substantial numbers actually to pursue and engage the insurgents in order to maintain the initiative or at least to deny it to the enemy.

PHASE TWO: MARCH 1980–APRIL 1985

During this period both the Fortieth Army and the *mujahideen* modified their tactics in light of the painful lessons already drawn from the first two months of conflict. No longer would the resistance take on the Soviets in direct confrontations; instead, they turned to guerrilla tactics, with frequent, often small-scale hit-and-run attacks against outposts, convoys and small units, always seeking to employ the advantage of surprise, particularly in the context of an ambush. The insurgents also planted booby-traps and mines along frequently travelled patrol and convoy routes, as well as in abandoned villages. However, the Soviets could sometimes play the game, too, laying ambushes along their opponents' supply routes. Still, more often than not it was the Soviets who were ambushed in this way, and to compound their already formidable problems the *mujahideen* became increasingly ingenious in their methods of laying mines, laying mixed anti-personnel and anti-tank fields along roads and fields, and even suspended mines in trees, there to be caught and triggered by the long radio antennae of the Soviet armoured vehicles.

But the resistance did not rely exclusively on the remote actions of their explosive devices, however numerous and cleverly planted or laid. They supplemented these measures with audacious attacks, as when in the summer of 1980 they bombarded the Fortieth Army's headquarters, less than 7km from Kabul, with rockets. The Soviets did not remain idle, striking at resistance positions that they often located from the air and launching the first of many large-scale operations, notably full-scale sweeps of the Kunar and Panjshir valleys between February and April 1980. The last of these marked the largest single Soviet operation since 1945. This dislodged insurgents from a wide area, but only temporarily, while smaller units left themselves vulnerable to *mujahideen* attacks of their own, such as in August when the 783rd Independent Reconnaissance Battalion of the 201st Motor Rifle Division fell into an ambush at Kisham in Badakhshan province, near the frontier with Tajikistan, and lost 45 men.

The Soviets struck again in the Panjshir Valley in September 1980, followed by other sweeps against guerrillas in November and from January to February 1981. This region, north-east of Kabul, held particular strategic significance owing to its proximity to the road running north–south that connected Kabul and Mazar-e Sharif through the Salang Tunnel and Pul-e Khumri in Baghlan province. This represented the stronghold of Ahmad Shah Massoud, the best-known *mujahideen* leader to emerge during the war. Soviet and DRA forces made nine substantial efforts to clear and hold the Panjshir but never succeeded. Other sizeable operations in 1981 included a largely DRA offensive, which succeeded in securing the Kabul–Jalalabad road near Sarowbi in Kabul province in July. However, regime forces suffered from low morale, performed poorly, and depended heavily on Soviet co-operation, or shamelessly left the execution of major operations entirely to their patrons. This policy applied equally to the Soviets' fourth major offensive into the Panjshir Valley, in August. This, like the others before it, failed, largely owing to paltry troop levels that rendered holding ground all but impossible for any substantial period. As before, the resistance simply re-established itself across the ground from which the Soviets had temporarily driven it by dint of superior firepower. Resistance casualties certainly mounted, but replacements were always to be found amongst those driven from villages destroyed from the air, living in squalid refugee camps over the border, or preparing for *jihad* in one of the hundreds of *madrassas* (religious schools) in Pakistan, whence thousands of displaced Afghans joined the resistance with the promise of martyrdom for those killed in their holy cause.

A MiG-21 at Bagram air base. The MiGs were used heavily for ground-attack missions with cluster munitions, napalm and conventional bombs, alongside other aircraft such as the Su-7. (David Reynolds/DPL)

In the west, around Herat, Soviet and regime forces engaged in heavy fighting with the *mujahideen* in October 1981, with the air base at Shindand, south of Herat, the strong focus of resistance attention. Such actions proved that, despite inhospitable terrain and the great distances across which they

conveyed supplies by mule, donkey, camel and packhorse through the treacherous passes connecting Afghanistan with Pakistan, the *mujahideen* could still undertake operations frequently and on a respectable scale. This circumstance was partly rendered feasible by the large exodus of residents from Herat, who were appalled by the regime's suppression of the rising of March 1979 and consequently drawn to the anti-Soviet cause. Further major encounters in and around Herat between the resistance and Soviet and Afghan forces took place in December 1981 and into January of the following year, with continuous, low-level fighting occurring thereafter.

The Afghan regime's ineptitude came to the fore in April 1982 when *mujahideen* penetrated Bagram air base and destroyed 23 Soviet and Afghan Air Force aircraft. The following month, another major Soviet–Afghan offensive into the Panjshir occurred, followed by another in August and September, perhaps the largest of all the nine conducted in that area. Both failed to make inroads against Massoud's strongholds despite the enormous scale of the operations. As a consequence of the stalemate reached there, the regime negotiated a ceasefire with Massoud that held from December 1982 to April 1984 on what appeared mutually beneficial terms, enabling the Soviets to release thousands of their troops for potentially more successful operations elsewhere. The ceasefire simultaneously provided some relief to Massoud's exhausted forces, and particularly to the gravely stricken local population, whose humanitarian needs the insurgents could not adequately meet in the midst of the Soviet offensive, especially when compounded by the severe winter of 1982/83. Moreover, Massoud's forces had suffered heavily during the offensive, and the ceasefire probably enabled him to recover and regroup before pursuing new operations further north, such as in the Shomali Valley, north of Kabul, where it is thought he struck, in conjunction with other commanders, at Soviet positions near Balkh.

In 1983 the Soviets altered their strategy fundamentally, embarking on a deliberate policy of clearing the Afghan population from rural areas and driving them either to seek refuge in the cities, where Soviet or DRA forces exercised more or less total control, or to other, less strategically vital areas within the country or over the border into Iran (which particularly sympathized with and armed the Shi'a minority in Afghanistan) or Pakistan. At the same time, the Soviets continued to conduct major operations against areas where the resistance appeared in concentrated numbers, a painstaking, exhausting and frequently fruitless undertaking. Owing to poor intelligence, they often directed the focus of their attention in the wrong area of the country, as in the case of the north in the spring of 1983. Here Abdul Qader, known more commonly by his *nom de guerre*, Zabiullah, led as many as 20,000 men and continued to conduct the sort of small-scale operations initiated by him three years before, including attacks, raids and ambushes in Baghlan, Balkh and Kunduz provinces, all north or north-west of Kabul. Amongst numerous *mujahideen* successes during this phase of the war, the victory achieved in May in Mazar-e Sharif, the principal city of northern Afghanistan, figured prominently. Mazar-e Sharif, whose flat and treeless surroundings rendered guerrilla operations particularly difficult, nevertheless witnessed a bold *mujahideen* attack that brought down the civilian airport's control tower.

As was common throughout the country, Zabiullah operated with other local, albeit less powerful, commanders who vied for control of their respective immediate areas, or indeed tried to lay claim to territory well beyond their normal areas of operation. It is vital to appreciate that the *mujahideen* did not operate as a unified fighting force with any common objective beyond that of ousting the Soviets from Afghan soil and overthrowing the communist regime, whether headed by Taraki or Amin before the Soviets arrived, or by Karmal or his successor as President, Najibullah Ahmadzai, thereafter. Rivalry between different *mujahideen*

The air traffic control centre at Bagram airfield. Bagram saw some of the first deployments of the Soviet troops into Afghanistan in 1979, specifically the 105th Guards Air Assault Division. (David Reynolds/DPL)

units, which could consist of merely a dozen to several thousand fighters, sometimes led to open feuds over contested ground; indeed, observers did not rule out the possibility that Zabiullah's death, caused by a mine in December 1984, may have constituted assassination rather than a simple vagary of war. If commanders could agree on a common foreign enemy, they still maintained an eye on Afghanistan's long-term political future and their place in it.

During the course of 1984, in line with their policy of depopulating regions presumed sympathetic to the *mujahideen*, the Soviets conducted a wide-scale bombing campaign in the west, particularly around Herat, driving untold thousands across the border into nearby Iran. In the Panjshir Valley, with the ceasefire over in April, the Soviets opened yet another major offensive that continued into May, with another following in September. The Soviets again employed their new strategy of depopulation through a combination of intensive shell fire, regular bombing raids, and mine-laying. In August, the Soviets sought to relieve the siege of the garrison at Ali Sher in Paktia province. There followed further efforts against the resistance in the east from January 1985, with the purpose of clearing areas in order to create bases along the Pakistani border, both to interdict the movement of supplies into Afghanistan and to weaken the flow of resistance fighters seeking a temporary safe haven in the tribal areas of western Pakistan or in that country's province of Baluchistan further to the south. During this second phase, which ended in April 1985, the Soviets suffered 9,175 fatal casualties – an average of 148 per month.

PHASE THREE: MAY 1985–DECEMBER 1986

During this period Gorbachev, who came to power in March 1985, opened negotiations in an effort to withdraw Soviet forces while simultaneously attempting to reduce the level of casualties during a period when discontent with the war steadily grew. Soviet troops sought increasingly to pass responsibility for making hostile contact with the resistance to their Afghan regime allies, depending themselves more on air and artillery operations, and employing motor rifle units to support DRA forces both operationally and in terms of morale.

As Soviet and Afghan government forces continued to struggle in the east of the country, in June 1985 the resistance struck Shindand air base in the west, destroying about 20 aircraft. Fighting in nearby Herat in July grew so intense that the governor was obliged to leave the city, while at the same time the Soviets launched their ninth and last major offensive in the Panjshir Valley. The DRA regime also continued its efforts: in January 1986 its forces attacked Zendejan in Herat province, inflicting heavy casualties on resistance elements but failing to consolidate their own tenuous control over the region. In the spring, anticipating a Soviet offensive against Zhawar in Paktia province, near the Pakistani border, the *mujahideen* reinforced their base there, strengthening their anti-aircraft positions and placing them about 7km outside their base, complete with defences in depth. They mined the approaches, while small arms, RPGs, mortars and recoilless rifles covered the area. Communications in the form of field telephones and radios kept the various outposts in contact with one another.

The Soviets, in turn, provided one regiment of air assault troops together with 12,000 DRA personnel. Only 800 *mujahideen* defended the base at Zhawar, but they received advance warning of the attack by the presence of two waves of helicopters that approached ahead of the main assault. Air strikes and an artillery bombardment followed, though the attackers could not be certain of the insurgents' positions.

At 0700hrs on 2 April, heliborne troops touched down at scattered landing zones near Zhawar. The defenders shot down two helicopters in the process, but Soviet fixed-wing air support hampered further *mujahideen* success and destroyed several of their positions, killing 18 men. Their commander,

An armoured vehicle labours up through the thin air of the Afghan mountains during the summer months. The arid summers made operations particularly arduous, and dust intake wore heavily on engine components and tracks. (Andrei Ivanovo/DPL)

Jalaluddin Haqqani, and 150 of his men were trapped by debris blocking the cave in which they lay in wait, but by a quirk of fate the carpet bombing that followed cleared the entrance and facilitated their escape. With no answer to the air strikes, the defenders opted to move on to the offensive, thereby remaining close enough to the attackers to avoid fire from the aircraft. Haqqani managed to overrun four landing zones, taking several hundred prisoners in the process – a circumstance that led the Soviets later to alter their tactics to avoid setting down helicopters in the midst of resistance positions that could shower descending aircraft with RPG and machine-gun fire. But the *mujahideen* could do no more: Soviet and Afghan forces managed to outflank Haqqani's position, forcing his men to fall back, and as reinforcements continued to appear around Zhawar, the resistance declined to maintain what amounted to an impossible defence and scattered. DRA troops held Zhawar for a few hours but unaccountably neglected either to carry off the arms and ammunition that remained for the taking, or even to destroy them. Likewise, they made a feeble attempt to destroy the caves with explosives, while their opponents, refusing to withdraw without registering a final act of defiance, fired rockets at regime forces as if to signify the hollow victory that Zhawar represented for Kabul. Indeed, within a few weeks the base returned to operational status, garrisoned once again by resistance fighters, whose losses in the defence of Zhawar amounted to 281 killed and 363 wounded, with government forces suffering similar losses. As hitherto commonly practised, though of course utterly forbidden by international law, the *mujahideen* executed all of the officers they captured and compelled the soldiers to submit to two years' manual labour in rear logistical areas, with the promise of release after serving their time. Zhawar demonstrated that the resistance could not, in fixed positions, hold out against the concentrated firepower of Soviet and DRA forces. Nevertheless, in turn, although outwardly successful, their opponents could not muster the numbers to hold positions seized in the operation.

The capture of the major resistance base at Zhawar in spring 1986 signified a welcome development for regime forces in an otherwise frustrating campaign against opponents who proved exceedingly difficult to pin into position, and who seldom entered an engagement except where the ground, weather, numbers or other factors played to their advantage. But successes such as Zhawar failed to conceal the fact that Soviet and DRA forces could rarely exert more than a temporary impact over a limited area before insufficient numbers and military priorities elsewhere obliged their withdrawal to their bases of operation. Thus, taking ground posed comparatively few problems for conventional forces enjoying vastly superior firepower; holding that ground, on the other hand, required a far greater commitment in manpower than the Soviets were prepared to make. Withdrawal inevitably left in its wake a vacuum that the *mujahideen* quickly filled. In the south, the regime largely controlled Kandahar, but it could never hold down the region permanently against resistance units under such talented commanders as Haji Abdul Latif, or the numerous other smaller rebel factions formed and held together by tribal loyalties or clustered around a particularly charismatic leader.

If fighting in southern Afghanistan, particularly in and around Kandahar, tended to manifest itself in skirmishing, in contrast to the larger-scale operations conducted in the east by Soviet troops, it nonetheless occupied the attention and energy of regime forces for years. The absence of set-piece battles, co-ordinated campaigns and great sweeps may suggest a sense of tranquillity, but nothing could be further from the case. Low-intensity warfare by definition does not yield heavy casualties in the short term (there is no Somme, El Alamein or Stalingrad), but gradual, mounting losses inflicted by the *mujahideen* slowly ground down Soviet morale, encouraging the cycle of atrocity and counter-atrocity so characteristic of irregular warfare. Indeed, both sides committed barbarities against each

Former Soviet tracked vehicles lie stacked by the side of a river near Herat. Historically, the Red Army engaged in high-tempo, large-scale conventional operations to achieve success. In sharp contrast, the war in Afghanistan involved low-level tactics, best conducted by highly mobile units led by platoon, not divisional, commanders with doctrine suited to the fluid nature of asymmetric warfare. (Guy Channing/DPL)

SOVIET/DRA FORCES AND MUJAHIDEEN STRONGHOLDS, 1980s

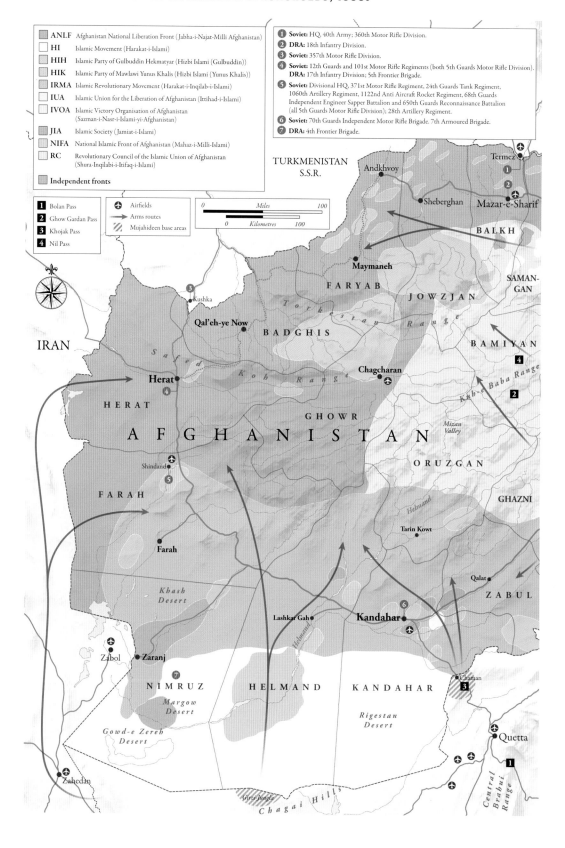

ANLF Afghanistan National Liberation Front (Jabha-i-Najat-Milli Afghanistan)
HI Islamic Movement (Harakat-i-Islami)
HIH Islamic Party of Gulbuddin Hekmatyar (Hizbi Islami (Gulbuddin))
HIK Islamic Party of Mawlawi Yunus Khalis (Hizbi Islami (Yunus Khalis))
IRMA Islamic Revolutionary Movement (Harakat-i-Inqilab-i-Islami)
IUA Islamic Union for the Liberation of Afghanistan (Ittihad-i-Islami)
IVOA Islamic Victory Organisation of Afghanistan (Sazman-i-Nasr-i-Islami-yi-Afghanistan)
JIA Islamic Society (Jamiat-i-Islami)
NIFA National Islamic Front of Afghanistan (Mahaz-i-Milli-Islami)
RC Revolutionary Council of the Islamic Union of Afghanistan (Shura-Inqilabi-i-Itifaq-i-Islami)

Independent fronts

1 Bolan Pass
2 Ghow Gardan Pass
3 Khojak Pass
4 Nil Pass

Airfields
Arms routes
Mujahideen base areas

Miles 0 — 100
Kilometres 0 — 100

1 **Soviet:** HQ, 40th Army; 360th Motor Rifle Division.
2 **DRA:** 18th Infantry Division.
3 **Soviet:** 357th Motor Rifle Division.
4 **Soviet:** 12th Guards and 101st Motor Rifle Regiments (both 5th Guards Motor Rifle Division). **DRA:** 17th Infantry Division; 5th Frontier Brigade.
5 **Soviet:** Divisional HQ, 371st Motor Rifle Regiment, 24th Guards Tank Regiment, 1060th Artillery Regiment, 1122nd Anti Aircraft Rocket Regiment, 68th Guards Independent Engineer Sapper Battalion and 650th Guards Reconnaissance Battalion (all 5th Guards Motor Rifle Division); 28th Artillery Regiment.
6 **Soviet:** 70th Guards Independent Motor Rifle Brigade. 7th Armoured Brigade.
7 **DRA:** 4th Frontier Brigade.

TURKMENISTAN S.S.R.

IRAN

Termez
Andkhvoy
Sheberghan
Mazar-e-Sharif
BALKH
SAMAN-GAN
Maymaneh
FARYAB
JOWZJAN
Kushka
Qal'eh-ye Now
BADGHIS
BAMIYAN
Chagcharan
Torkestan Range
Kuh-e Baba Range
Herat
HERAT
Safed Koh Range
GHOWR
Mizan Valley
AFGHANISTAN
ORUZGAN
Shindand
GHAZNI
FARAH
Helmand
Tarin Kowt
Farah
ZABUL
Khash Desert
Qalat
Lashkar Gah
Kandahar
KANDAHAR
Zabol
Zaranj
NIMRUZ
HELMAND
Chaman
Margow Desert
Rigestan Desert
Quetta
Gowd-e Zereh Desert
Zahedan
Gir-e Jungla
Chagai Hills
Central Brahui Range

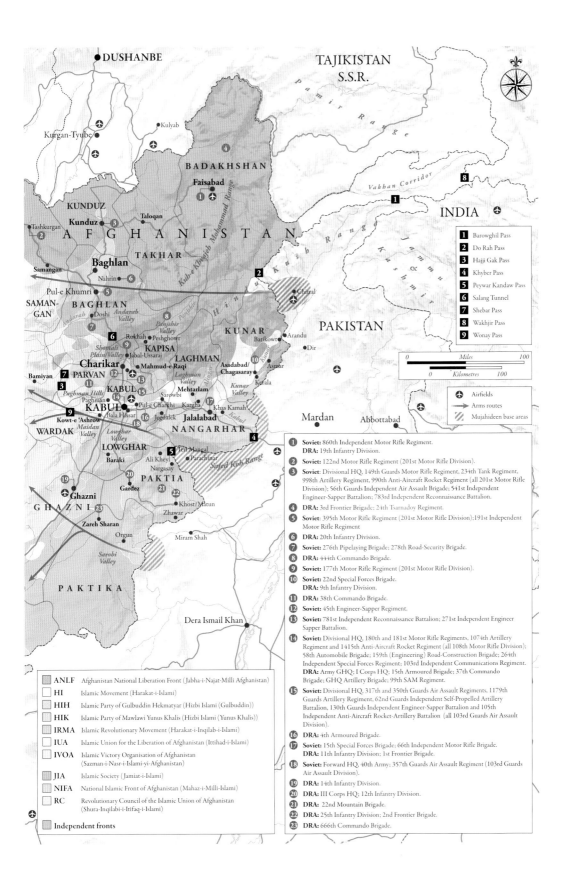

Barowghil Pass
Do Rah Pass
Hajji Gak Pass
Khyber Pass
Peywar Kandaw Pass
Salang Tunnel
Shebar Pass
Wakhjir Pass
Wonay Pass

Airfields
Arms routes
Mujahideen base areas

1. **Soviet:** 860th Independent Motor Rifle Regiment.
   DRA: 19th Infantry Division.
2. **Soviet:** 122nd Motor Rifle Regiment (201st Motor Rifle Division).
3. **Soviet:** Divisional HQ, 149th Guards Motor Rifle Regiment, 234th Tank Regiment, 998th Artillery Regiment, 990th Anti-Aircraft Rocket Regiment (all 201st Motor Rifle Division); 56th Guards Independent Air Assault Brigade; 541st Independent Engineer-Sapper Battalion; 783rd Independent Reconnaissance Battalion.
4. **DRA:** 3rd Frontier Brigade; 24th Tsarnadoy Regiment.
5. **Soviet:** 395th Motor Rifle Regiment (201st Motor Rifle Division);191st Independent Motor Rifle Regiment
6. **DRA:** 20th Infantry Division.
7. **Soviet:** 276th Pipelaying Brigade; 278th Road-Security Brigade.
8. **DRA:** 444th Commando Brigade.
9. **Soviet:** 177th Motor Rifle Regiment (201st Motor Rifle Division).
10. **Soviet:** 22nd Special Forces Brigade.
    DRA: 9th Infantry Division.
11. **DRA:** 38th Commando Brigade.
12. **Soviet:** 45th Engineer-Sapper Regiment.
13. **Soviet:** 781st Independent Reconnaissance Battalion; 271st Independent Engineer Sapper Battalion.
14. **Soviet:** Divisional HQ, 180th and 181st Motor Rifle Regiments, 1074th Artillery Regiment and 1415th Anti-Aircraft Rocket Regiment (all 108th Motor Rifle Division); 58th Automobile Brigade; 159th (Engineering) Road-Construction Brigade; 264th Independent Special Forces Regiment; 103rd Independent Communications Regiment. **DRA:** Army GHQ; I Corps HQ; 15th Armoured Brigade; 37th Commando Brigade; GHQ Artillery Brigade; 99th SAM Regiment.
15. **Soviet:** Divisional HQ, 317th and 350th Guards Air Assault Regiments, 1179th Guards Artillery Regiment, 62nd Guards Independent Self-Propelled Artillery Battalion, 130th Guards Independent Engineer-Sapper Battalion and 105th Independent Anti-Aircraft Rocket-Artillery Battalion (all 103rd Guards Air Assault Division).
16. **DRA:** 4th Armoured Brigade.
17. **Soviet:** 15th Special Forces Brigade; 66th Independent Motor Rifle Brigade. **DRA:** 11th Infantry Division; 1st Frontier Brigade.
18. **Soviet:** Forward HQ, 40th Army; 357th Guards Air Assault Regiment (103rd Guards Air Assault Division).
19. **DRA:** 14th Infantry Division.
20. **DRA:** III Corps HQ; 12th Infantry Division.
21. **DRA:** 22nd Mountain Brigade.
22. **DRA:** 25th Infantry Division; 2nd Frontier Brigade.
23. **DRA:** 666th Commando Brigade.

ANLF Afghanistan National Liberation Front (Jabha-i-Najat-Milli Afghanistan)
HI Islamic Movement (Harakat-i-Islami)
HIH Islamic Party of Gulbuddin Hekmatyar (Hizbi Islami (Gulbuddin))
HIK Islamic Party of Mawlawi Yunus Khalis (Hizbi Islami (Yunus Khalis))
IRMA Islamic Revolutionary Movement (Harakat-i-Inqilab-i-Islami)
IUA Islamic Union for the Liberation of Afghanistan (Ittihad-i-Islami)
IVOA Islamic Victory Organisation of Afghanistan (Sazman-i-Nasr-i-Islami-yi-Afghanistan)
JIA Islamic Society (Jamiat-i-Islami)
NIFA National Islamic Front of Afghanistan (Mahaz-i-Milli-Islami)
RC Revolutionary Council of the Islamic Union of Afghanistan (Shura-Inqilabi-i-Itifaq-i-Islami)

Independent fronts

SOVIET BLOCK AND DESTROY MISSIONS

These operations involved dispatching forces to areas known to contain sizeable concentrations of *mujahideen* and blocking their retreat before engaging and destroying them; several independent *mujahideen* forces would sometimes gather in one place to plan and execute a major operation. In this case, Soviet ground troops operating out of tracked BMP-I infantry fighting vehicles would comb through the villages, killing or driving out into the open any *mujahideen* forces taking refuge among the local population, while various other combat elements, including air assault forces inserted by helicopter, would press the enemy from various directions, denying escape routes wherever possible. It was very unlikely that the Soviet forces would take prisoners; quarter was seldom given.

To this end, three motorized rifle companies - (A), (B) and (C) - together totalling about 300 men, would converge on *mujahideen* positions from three directions by road. A mountain-rifle battalion (D), about 600 men strong, would arrive in BMP-Is, then advance across the heights towards a village below that was known to provide aid to the enemy.

Meanwhile, 12 Mi-24 Hind helicopter gunships (E) would approach to engage the enemy while they remained in open ground; they would arrive in two six-ship groups, both flying in a pattern-eight, one group behind the other. They would approach at low altitude, using flares to distract any infra-red missiles. At 7,500m from their target they would attack with rockets from an altitude of about 80m, but remain beyond 1,500m so as to avoid enemy machine-gun fire. To the south, poised on an eminence, would be a 90-man air assault company (F), inserted by air using Mi-8 Hip helicopters and carrying 82mm mortars, AK-74s and RPK-74 light machine guns. Their mission would be to deploy on heights overlooking a *mujahideen* position and prevent the escape of any enemy forces driven off by other elements of the Soviet offensive. If properly co-ordinated, swift deployment by road and air, including the use of small numbers of tanks, BMPs or BTRs - with or without accompanying dismounted troops - stood to provide the Soviets with decisive results.

other until they became commonplace. The Soviets sometimes cold-bloodedly dispatched prisoners by dropping them from helicopters after interrogation, or simply shooting them in the head. The resistance, for its part, sometimes tortured its captives by means of castration, disfigurement or skinning alive. A lingering death could be created by securing the prisoner to pegs planted in the ground, his death coming slowly under a baking sun, or more swiftly via beheading.

While Soviets were committed to a 'hearts and minds' campaign to win the population over to the government in Kabul, too often this was overtaken by the fear and anger on the ground, and Moscow's forces committed atrocities with shocking regularity against villages suspected of aiding the

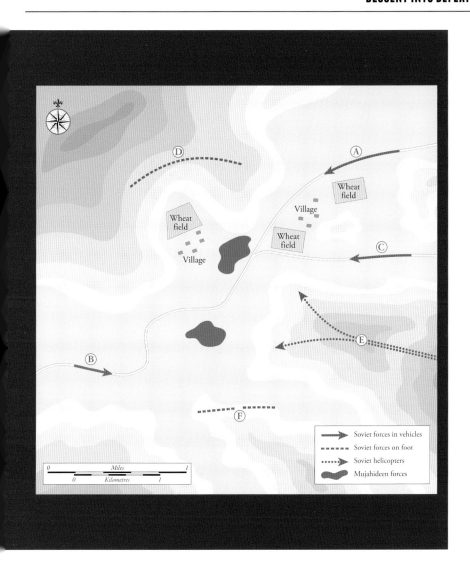

resistance or in retaliation for ambushes. Such ruthless, counterproductive acts certainly forced out vast numbers of the inhabitants – denying the *mujahideen* some of the rural support so vital to their operations – but the short-term advantage thus gleaned by shifting populations and destroying farmland by sowing aerial mines or bombing paled in significance against the numbers of survivors thus driven into the hands of the guerrillas. Thousands joined local *mujahideen* groups, while most fled across the Pakistani border to join the resistance at its base in Peshawar before returning, trained, armed, bitter and vengeful.

Appreciating at last that such counterproductive methods only galvanized the population's defiant stance, and increasingly aware that their military prospects were in decline, in the summer of 1986 the Soviets eased their campaign of driving civilians out of rural areas in favour of seeking to secure their co-operation with, if not allegiance to, the regime in Kabul. This very belated, cynical policy yielded few dividends from a people marginalized by brutality and the forced conscription of their menfolk into the ranks of the DRA forces, as well as by the presence of foreign troops supporting a deeply unpopular regime. Thus, the fighting largely continued as before.

On 6 July, the resistance conducted a co-ordinated and successful attack against an enormous Soviet convoy near Maymaneh, the capital of Faryab province, near the Turkmenistan border, while in August the Soviets, supported by Afghan security forces, conducted substantial sweeps into the Lowghar Valley. On the 26th of the same month, the *mujahideen* set off massive explosions near Kabul when they fired 107mm and 122mm rockets into ammunition dumps at Kargha. Arriving to secure the area and the nearby town of Paghman, Afghan government forces met heavy opposition that left the area in ruins after fierce fighting. At about the same time, intense fighting took place in Herat.

The close questioning of an Afghan prisoner by Soviet troops. If the man was genuinely suspected of being a *mujahideen* fighter, then his prospects for survival following the interrogation would be bleak. (E. Kuvakin/ CC-BY-SA-3.0)

Soviet sappers clear a minefield in northern Afghanistan in 1982. Note how the 30mm cannon of the BMP-2s are trained on the surrounding mountains, to provide immediate covering fire if necessary. (Andrei Ivanov/DPL)

During this third phase of the war the Soviets made more substantial use of special forces in the form of Spetsnaz and reconnaissance units, which sought to interdict the transfer of weapons, ammunition and supplies destined for the *mujahideen* from Pakistan. However, the frequency of contact during this particularly bloody period of the conflict cost the Soviets 2,745 personnel killed, an average of 137 a month. These elite units performed well, and their deployment in greater numbers demonstrated the Soviets' eventual recognition that such forces could fulfil the pressing operational need for highly mobile, highly trained, specialist troops conversant with the tactics of counter-insurgency. But the Spetsnaz and other elite forces never accounted for more than 15 per cent of Soviet combat power and simply could not sustain the extremely punishing levels of continuous deployment imposed on them. Indeed, even as the number of special forces personnel reached its height in Afghanistan, 15,000 other troops withdrew in the summer of 1986, in line with Gorbachev's decision to bring home all field personnel by early 1989.

PHASE FOUR: NOVEMBER 1986–FEBRUARY 1989

In November 1986, Karmal, who had increasingly attracted blame among the Soviet leadership for failures in the war, was removed from power and exiled to Russia. With the war clearly going badly and the Soviets now committed to withdrawing, they were keen to bolster the new president,

Mohammad Najibullah Ahmadzai, the brutish but clever former head of the vicious KhAD. They were particularly enthusiastic about Najibullah's 'Policy of National Reconciliation', a plan to reconcile the government with moderate political and religious leaders of non-communist persuasion while simultaneously strengthening the numbers and capacity of Afghan forces and security personnel, in recognition of the somewhat disconcerting fact that the regime would soon depend largely upon its own wits and resources to defeat the insurgency after final Soviet withdrawal.

Soviet forces naturally continued to support the efforts of the DRA, but by now commanders sought to preserve the lives of men soon to be dispatched home. Part of this process included increasing attacks by air, with heavy bomber strikes originating from the Soviet Union against *mujahideen* positions around Faisabad, Jalalabad and Kandahar, which ground troops had already evacuated. The Soviets also unsuccessfully launched raids against insurgent rocket batteries shelling Kabul on a regular basis, and, as their last forces were withdrawing, aircraft hit the Panjshir Valley in an effort to keep Massoud's forces distracted there. But in this fourth and final phase the Soviets largely occupied themselves with completing their withdrawal, which they carried out in two stages: between May and August 1988 and from November 1988 to February 1989.

Apart from Soviet troop withdrawals, this phase of the war is notable for two other features: the introduction into resistance arsenals of the Stinger ground-to-air missile, whose effectiveness, though often exaggerated, nevertheless manifested itself in the serious blow it inflicted on Soviet air power; and the increasing frequency of raids conducted by the *mujahideen* over the Soviet border. Observers dispute the number of Soviet aircraft downed by the Stinger, but at the very least it induced pilots to fly at higher altitudes, attracting to themselves the derisive appellation of 'cosmonaut'.

Although the *mujahideen* inflicted only small degrees of damage in cross-border raids into the Soviet Union's Central Asian republics, they palpably established the fact that not only had the Soviets failed to bring the insurgency under control, but also that the resistance could penetrate enemy territory almost at will, such as during an operation conducted about 20km north of the Amu Darya River in April 1987, when insurgents bombarded a factory in Tajikistan with rockets.

As before, though, such small-scale operations functioned in tandem with much larger engagements, such as the renewed heavy fighting that took place in Herat on 7 April, when encounters in the streets resulted

Afghan civilians (and possible *mujahideen*) gather around the remains of a Soviet helicopter, shot down over Kabul in 1982. The numbers of Soviet aircraft shot down increased significantly as the 1980s progressed, courtesy of CIA-supplied weaponry. (Andrei Ivanov/DPL)

in over 50 casualties inflicted against Soviet and DRA personnel. The following month the Soviets launched an operation specifically intended to relieve the besieged garrison of Ali Sher in Paktia province. Although a Soviet success, the *mujahideen* struck back to ensure their opponents did not establish a permanent presence in the area, forcing them out in mid June. The following month, on 27 July, particular trouble erupted in the south (never a tranquil place, even before the Soviet invasion), when a *mujahideen* missile brought down a plane containing senior Soviet and Afghan officers while attempting a landing at the airport in Kandahar. At about the same time, the small Soviet garrison at Bamiyan abandoned the city after holding off a *mujahideen* attack. The resistance stepped up its campaign of terror in Kabul when on 9 October it planted a car bomb that killed 27 people, one of many urban terrorist attacks launched by the resistance in towns and cities across Afghanistan.

Further proof of the Soviets' inability to hold much more than the ground on which they stood became evident after the successful relief of the besieged city of Khost, in which 18,000 troops, of whom 10,000 were Soviets, succeeded in re-opening the road between Gardez and Khost to convoys between November and December 1987. The Soviets eventually abandoned these positions at the end of January 1988, in another striking example of their incapacity to secure even positions of significant strategic value while burdened by other pressing demands on troops and supplies. Shortly thereafter, as part of their policy of withdrawal, the Soviets left Kandahar to an uncertain future under tenuous DRA control.

With Soviet forces evacuating the south of the country, activity continued in other regions, where resistance fighters, emboldened by their opponents' withdrawal, struck in Kabul on 27 April 1988. A truck bomb exploded during the tenth anniversary of the communist takeover, killing six and wounding several times more. Bombs planted in vehicles formed only a single aspect of the *mujahideen*'s renewed attacks in Kabul. On 9 May they fired rockets into the city, killing at least 23 civilians, with many more similar attacks to follow over the coming months. Such acts of terror failed to weaken the regime's grip on the city, but they exposed in stark terms the futility of the authorities' efforts to protect the inhabitants from indiscriminate violence and thus to demonstrate a capacity to maintain security even within urban areas, much less within the seat of government itself. In short, by operating in and around Kabul seemingly at will, the *mujahideen* sought to underline the inevitability of the regime's downfall.

In May and June 1988, renewed fighting between local resistance forces and government troops took place in Kandahar, a city no longer garrisoned by Soviet troops, but with no decisive results. Still, the *mujahideen* succeeded on 17 June in seizing Qalat, the capital of Zabol province. As the first such

Photographed after the Soviet–Afghan War, Soviet aircraft wrecks (an Antonov An-12 dominates the photograph) litter Bagram airfield, from where the Red Army mounted its withdrawal airlift in 1989. (David Reynolds/DPL)

city to fall to the resistance, Qalat was a place of symbolic importance. The victory proved short lived, however. Straddling the main road between Kabul and Kandahar, Qalat enjoyed a level of strategic significance which the regime could not ignore lest its retention by the *mujahideen* signal the general defection of other towns and cities across the country. As such, DRA forces took particular pains to retake the city four days later. All told, this last phase of the war cost the Soviets 2,262 fatalities, with an average of 87 deaths per month.

LESSONS LEARNED

An analysis of the operational record of the conflict reveals that the Soviets took too long to to accept that their doctrine and training ill-suited them for the type of war into which they plunged themselves. Fully capable of undertaking operations on a grand scale and in a conventional context, apart from their special forces Soviet troops were not armed, equipped or trained for a platoon leaders' war, which entailed locating and destroying small, elusive, local forces which only stood their ground and fought when terrain and circumstances favoured them, and otherwise struck quickly before rapidly melting away. There were no fixed positions, no established frontlines and rarely any substantial bases of operation for the insurgents. Whereas the Soviets could perform extremely well at the operational level, complete with large-scale all-arms troop movements, this could not be easily adapted to circumstances on the ground – where the war was a tactical one, in which Soviet tactics did not conform to the requirements of guerrilla warfare.

Soviet equipment, weapons and doctrine suited their forces well for a confrontation on a massive scale on the northern European plain, a context in which they were confident in employing massed artillery to obliterate NATO's defensive positions before driving through the gaps created to crush further resistance and to pursue the remnants of shattered units. They were less well suited to a fluid, asymmetric war against opponents taking full advantage of their home terrain, bolstered by faith and dedication to freedom.

Soviet tactics in Afghanistan simply did not accord with their opponents' fighting methods. No benefit accrued by massing artillery to carry out a bombardment of an enemy who seldom concentrated in large numbers and who dispersed at will, re-forming elsewhere for the next ambush or raid. Soviet conscripts and reservists could dismount from a personnel carrier and deploy rapidly for the purpose of laying down suppressive fire on an enemy unit or sub-unit of like composition, but the tactics and standard battle drills of the typical motorized rifle regiment failed to match the attacks of a highly mobile, fluid enemy who refused to fight on terms consistent with Soviet doctrine. Air assault and Spetsnaz forces learned to adapt their tactics to meet the demands of a guerrilla war, and in this regard they achieved some success. But the level of innovation required to defeat such a wide-scale insurgency proved beyond the means of Soviet forces as a whole, and thus must be seen as one amongst many factors that doomed them to ultimate failure.

The Soviets often laboured under the illusion that because the heavy application of military force had succeeded in the past, it was bound also to succeed in current operations. Important precedents existed to support this view, including the numerous campaigns conducted against independence movements as long ago as the Russian Civil War and into the 1920s, when Bolshevik forces put down revolts in the Ukraine, Central Asia, the Transcaucasus and even the Far East. During World War II – quite apart from the Herculean efforts first to oust the Germans from home soil and then to drive on Berlin – Soviet forces quashed serious opposition from Ukrainian and Belorussian nationalists, some of whom carried on the struggle after 1945. After all this, and when their forces easily put down the risings in East Germany, Hungary and Czechoslovakia, Soviet forces could be forgiven for thinking that their might stood invincible against all foes, conventional and unconventional alike.

Afghanistan exploded this fallacy. Even when they adapted to new circumstances, the Soviets failed to deploy sufficient numbers of forces to fulfil their mission. They could not possibly hope to defeat the insurgency when spread across such a vast area. The defence of bases, airfields, cities and lines of communication alone committed the bulk of Soviet forces to static duties when circumstances demanded unremitting strike operations against the insurgents, thereby maintaining the initiative and obliging the resistance to look to their own survival in favour of attacks of their own. Soviet regiments, companies and platoons routinely stood under strength, with

Soviet soldiers welcomed by a local resident upon their return from Afghanistan. The experience in Afghanistan marked a whole generation of young Soviet soldiers. (RIA Novosti archive, image #476785/Yuriy Somov/CC-BY-SA 3.0)

regiments often down to single battalion strength and companies little more than oversized platoons. Much of this occurred despite the large bi-annual troop levies, which certainly furnished the men required, but whose numbers needlessly dwindled enormously due to poor field sanitation practices and inadequate diet, both of which contributed to the widespread dissemination of disease throughout the armed forces. A staggering one-quarter to one-third of a typical unit's strength was diminished by amoebic dysentery, meningitis, typhus, hepatitis and malaria, leaving actual field strength woefully low and so operationally compromised that commanders deemed it necessary to create composite units on an ad hoc basis.

In assessing the tactics and the fighting capacity of the Fortieth Army, one is struck by the generally poor performance of its regular units. As discussed earlier, they were trained to fight NATO forces on the plains of Central Europe, with a strict adherence to orthodox formations and methods of attack. This obliged Soviet infantry to remain close to their armoured vehicles as they advanced down valleys in which the *mujahideen* took full advantage of the ground, much of it familiar to them. Performance improved amongst Soviet units as they examined their mistakes, but the problem of under-strength units regularly dogged their efforts. Little could be done to counter the continuous drain on their morale caused by the anxiety imposed by the never-ending threat of attack by guerrillas who sought out the Soviets' vulnerabilities by day, but especially by night, so wearing down resolve and causing physical and mental exhaustion. The

The Soviet withdrawal begins. The Soviets' failure derived partly from the political hubris of politicians, who grievously underestimated the colossal scale of the enterprise on which they had embarked in 1979 and who failed to establish what has since become known as an 'exit strategy'. (DOD/PD US GOV)

war required immense physical efforts to make contact with an elusive opponent, but many Soviet soldiers lacked the stamina to cross the great distances necessary to come to grips with their enemy, not least across inhospitable terrain. Their training and equipment proved inadequate, and security and intelligence, particularly at the tactical level, proved poor to the extent that even when attempting to surround groups of insurgents, Soviet troops often failed to close the ring, thus allowing the enemy to escape through gaps or otherwise fight their way out. Overly confident in its fighting capacity, an attitude perhaps reinforced by a reputation of military invincibility earned as a consequence of the Red Army's extraordinary performance in World War II, and with no combat experience acquired since that time, the Fortieth Army found itself the victim of breathtaking hubris. Ill-trained for the type of warfare in which it engaged and incapable of achieving the unrealistic aims set for it by Moscow, it launched into the fray regardless.

HOW THE WAR ENDED

Over time neither overwhelming military force nor the internal reforms undertaken by the Soviets and their Afghan protégés could hope to crush the insurgency. While some Afghans, particularly those in the cities and above all the educated classes, collaborated with the Soviets, DRA forces stood distinctively subordinate to their counterparts. In that role, given their consistently poor operational record, morale necessarily suffered and declined. Neither Soviet nor Afghan leaders could offer a political solution to continued resistance, and with an impasse in the field stretching far longer than ever anticipated, stirrings in Moscow began to encourage withdrawal, not least because the *mujahideen* demonstrated no inclination to negotiate under circumstances where compromise offered them nothing.

Accordingly, Moscow began to appreciate in 1985 that the war had become unwinnable. Konstantin Chernenko and Yuri Andropov, both of whom succeeded Brezhnev as Party Secretary for brief periods (November 1982–February 1984 and February 1984–March 1985 respectively), suffered from ill health during their entire periods in office, during which they failed to exercise the energy and leadership required to keep the insurgency under control, much less destroy it. Coming to power on 10 March 1985, Mikhail Gorbachev inherited an intractable war, but he represented a fresh start in Soviet foreign policy as well as in domestic politics. He was a leader

A *mujahideen* village wiped out by the Soviet forces is inspected by local fighters. Such material and human attrition left little room for mercy on either side. (DOD/PD US GOV)

whose policy of *glasnost* (openness) had from the beginning of his time in office already tolerated internal – and even public – criticism of the war, and who recognized the strategic errors committed by his country.

Gorbachev's desire to extricate troops from Afghanistan centred on three key motives. First and foremost, the failing prospects of the war rendered further operations pointless. Second, withdrawal would provide a mechanism by which to improve the Soviet Union's relations with the West, particularly with the United States at a time when the issue of nuclear disarmament remained high on both countries' agendas. Indeed, even if the Carter administration's (1977–81) boycott of the 1980 Moscow Olympics and the embargo of American grain shipments to the Soviet Union had constituted nothing more than irritation, Carter's and the subsequent Reagan administration's (1981–89) refusal to continue talks to try to ratify the proposed SALT II restrictions on nuclear weapons meant that the treaty stood indefinitely postponed as a result of the invasion, and Gorbachev could countenance this no longer. Third, with domestic discontent partly assuaged by the troops' return and military expenditure reduced, he could concentrate on the social, economic and political reforms urgently needed within the USSR.

A T-54A and T-55 at Bagram air base. Soviet materiel left behind from the Soviet–Afghan War would fuel further conflicts in Afghanistan, including those fought against Coalition forces from 2001. (PHI (SW) Arlo K. Abrahamson, USN)

The origins of the decision to withdraw require brief examination. Anatoly Dobrynin, the Soviet ambassador to the United States between 1962 and 1986, claimed that at a Politburo meeting of 17 October 1985 Gorbachev declared, 'It's time to leave', to which the other members raised no objection. They fixed no date for final withdrawal, but the die had been cast. Debate continues about the degree to which this meeting represented the first concrete decision to bring an end to the war, but any doubts may be cast aside by the decisive results of the Politburo meeting held on 13 November 1986, in which Sergei Akhromeyev, the Chief of the General Staff, made a devastatingly prescient and unchallengeable assertion: 'We have lost the battle for the Afghan people.' Accordingly, Gorbachev proposed that the Soviet Union should withdraw its forces over a two-year period, with half to be removed in 1987 and the rest to leave the following year, a recommendation to which the other members gave their assent. Here stood the idea in principle; now Gorbachev needed the mechanism by which to implement it.

To lay the groundwork for troop withdrawal, Soviet authorities sought to expand DRA forces to enable them to take a more active combat role. However, this did not achieve the desired effect, since government military personnel continued to perform unreliably against their compatriots in the resistance, leaving Soviet troops to continue to bear the greatest burden in combat. This compounded anxiety over the likelihood of a smooth transition of security affairs to the Kabul regime, already looking grim in light of Najibullah's continuing failure successfully to implement his programme of reforms. In short, it became clear that Moscow would eventually have to withdraw from Afghanistan in as honourable a fashion as possible and thus leave Najibullah to his own devices, albeit heavily subsidized with food, weapons and materiel.

The United Nations (UN) stood as the obvious intermediary between the belligerents. Gorbachev depended on it to achieve this role, with the Afghan government effectively representing Soviet interests and Pakistan acting on behalf of the *mujahideen*, since Islamabad unofficially supported the resistance, while the United States by extension supported the same through Pakistan. As such, negotiations conducted by the UN, if successful, stood to benefit the interests of all the principal parties to the conflict, belligerents and non-belligerents alike. Having said this, accords brokered by the UN necessarily set some limitations on its freedom of action in light of the Soviet Union's position as a permanent member of the UN Security Council.

That fact had protected the aggressor in 1979, since the Soviet Union could veto the UN's original condemnation of its invasion. Now, nearly a decade later, for the sake of extricating themselves from an unwinnable

An abandoned T-55 tank near Jalalabad, guarded by a young child fighter, armed with an AKM assault rifle. Many millions of AKs came into *mujahideen* hands from across the border with Pakistan. (Mike Peters/DPL)

war, the Soviets were happily prepared to regard the UN as a third party in the process of 'conflict resolution' by accepting its 'good offices' and the shuttle diplomacy it could offer. Specifically, the Secretary General, by the authority of the UN, could engage in negotiations unilaterally, supported by the UN Secretariat.

The Geneva Accords were signed on 14 April 1988; by these the Soviets agreed to remove their forces from Afghanistan. The passing of Soviet troops back over the border went largely unchallenged by the resistance, though the Soviets themselves, anxious to prevent attacks on their forces as they withdrew, staged a campaign of terror, largely with concentrated artillery fire, against villages along their route towards the frontier so as to intimidate the *mujahideen* into restraint. Thousands streamed away from their villages as vast Soviet columns trundled through the smoke of the devastation left in their wake. Finally, on 15 February 1989, General Boris Gromov, commander of the Fortieth Army and the last Soviet soldier to leave the country, crossed the bridge at Termez, so putting an end to a tragic adventure fraught with human folly and misguided ambition.

CONCLUSION AND CONSEQUENCES

Statistics connected with the Soviets' role in the war make for depressing reading. Total forces deployed over the whole course of the conflict amounted to approximately 642,000 personnel. Of these, approximately 545,000 served in the regular forces, while another 90,000 came from armed KGB units. Perhaps 5,000 belonged to the MVD. Statistics for the dead and missing vary according to the source consulted, but range between 13,000 and 15,000 personnel. Some 10,751 soldiers became invalids, many as amputees. Yet these already substantial figures must be seen in light of the 469,685 sick and wounded – or over 70 per cent of the total force – who were discharged and repatriated.

Statistics for those stricken with disease tell an even more revealing story: a staggering 415,932, of whom 115,308 men suffered from infectious hepatitis and 31,080 from typhoid fever. The sheer scale of this suffering reveals the dreadful state of hygiene prevalent within the Soviet forces and their appalling conditions in the field. The pressure on Soviet hospitals – particularly with respect to the long-term sick and the disabled – can only be reckoned to have been enormous, with correspondingly serious implications for society as a whole.

In sharp contrast to their fathers who had defended the country against the German menace during World War II, soldiers returning from Afghanistan not only received no hero's welcome but often felt shunned by a public detached from, if not actually hostile to, the war. The loss in materiel and hardware also helps place in perspective the scale of the conflict, and offers a sharp lesson to those who would slavishly depend on technology alone as some sort of magical recipe for success: 118 jets, 333 helicopters, 147 tanks, 1,314 APCs, 433 artillery pieces and mortars, 1,138 radio sets and CP vehicles, 510 engineering vehicles and 11,369 trucks.

There is no question that the Soviet war effort suffered from poor or virtually non-existent political direction. Either the series of ineffective political masters in Moscow or the regularity with which they sickened and died off during the 1980s contributed in no small way towards Soviet failure. Brezhnev, not healthy at the time of the invasion, became incapacitated the following year and did not succumb to his illness until November 1982, leaving all decisions to committees exercising collective leadership. His successor, Yuri Andropov, lasted less than two years, and upon his death in February 1984 Konstantin Chernenko carried on for little more than a year until his own demise. During this whole period the conflict was allowed to carry on with little in the way of decision-making over substantial issues concerning the conduct of operations or the overall objective of the war. When at last Gorbachev took the helm and found that the war could not

This view of a Soviet mechanized patrol illustrates the stark reality of Afghanistan's winter terrain. The Soviet rifleman depended on his personnel carrier both for his own transport and for his equipment that the vehicle conveyed, with the specifications of his uniform and gear naturally reflecting this. (Cody/AirSeaLand)

Airborne troops man a Zu-23 23mm anti-aircraft gun, covering armoured units as they cross a dusty summer Afghan track. Such cannon were useful for long-range direct fire against elevated *mujahideen* mountain positions. (Cody/AirSeaLand)

be brought to a conclusion within a year – in fact Soviet casualties rose to record levels during that period – he sought a means to withdraw in a dignified fashion, which, as we have seen, the United Nations provided.

Even before the troops returned the impact of the war at home had become palpable. The Soviet military experience in Afghanistan amounted to a slow, attritional effort, which not only demonstrated the declining combat effectiveness of the USSR's armed forces, but revealed stark, irreparable cracks developing within the Soviet political infrastructure. Society itself underwent change owing to the rotation in and out of Afghanistan of conscripted troops, whose disappointments, stories of hardship and frustration permeated Soviet society, undermining morale and sowing seeds of doubt respecting both the war effort and also the people's confidence in the political and economic system as a whole.

Thus, problems experienced in Afghanistan manifested themselves back home, or one could contend that internal disintegration reflected on Soviet troops' morale in theatre. The two, in any event, proved mutually destructive, albeit within a process that must be seen as gradual, like that of the growing body count of the war. While only a small percentage of the population served in the war or was touched by it as a consequence of the loss of a son, brother or husband, the Soviet experience in Afghanistan created a large body of disaffected veterans of the conflict. Known as the *afgantsy*, these veterans' disillusionment at home manifested itself over a range of emotions, from unexpressed derision of Moscow to outright criticism of the Soviet system in general. Such veterans largely did not organize themselves into any form of political movement or lobby, but in light of Gorbachev's growing liberalization of Soviet society as a consequence of his policies of *glasnost* and *perestroika* (literally 're-structuring', involving wholesale changes to the Soviet state), the attitudes of Afghan veterans nevertheless played some part in influencing public opinion and contributing to the general atmosphere of disgruntled citizens now prepared to question decisions made at all levels of government, including the Kremlin. In short, the war became a metaphor for systemic problems within Soviet society, and thus accelerated the rate of social and political change under way since Gorbachev came to power in the spring of 1985. Criticism of communist rule, or at least its existing form, also developed from within, for the war led to a loss of faith in the party leadership amongst the middle and upper echelons of the Communist Party itself.

Whereas before and during the Brezhnev era the party elite tended to operate on the basis of intra-party consultation, this practice had rapidly

In the highlands near Kabul in 1986 an officer of the Fortieth Army conducts live-fire training with troops just arrived from the Soviet Union, teaching them how to use the 30mm AGS-I7 automatic grenade launcher. (E. Kuvakin/CC-BY-SA-3.0)

declined during the years of intervention in Afghanistan, prompting those of a reformist disposition to use the failing military effort as a means to push through their agendas and thus speed the process of change. Many analysts point to the declining Soviet economy, the inability of the state to continue to bear the burden of subsidizing communist allies around the world, Afghanistan included, and the impossibility of trying to match the United States in the nuclear arms race as the prime movers in the collapse of the Soviet Union. In the end the Soviets had intervened on the basis of supporting a notionally communist state; in reality, from 1978 the succession of Afghan regimes only attracted widespread domestic condemnation followed by open hostility and civil war. The fact of Soviet withdrawal in 1989 – with little to show for it but a deeply unpopular satellite government condemned to hold down an insurgency that even the Soviets had failed to contain, much less defeat – went far in eroding the long-held Soviet doctrine that socialism represented a positive and irreversible movement for the political, social and economic good of peoples across the globe.

The Soviet–Afghan War demonstrated that the Soviets had embarked on an adventure based on unattainable goals. The British Army field manual *Countering Insurgency* concisely sums up Soviet errors:

> Soviet activity failed due to several key strategic factors:
>
> - They failed to remove the extensive external support provided to the *Mujahideen*;
> - Inability of the Soviets to exploit internal weaknesses among the insurgents;
> - Absence of a stable government in Kabul commanding popular respect;
> - The Soviets failed to adopt an effective counter-insurgency strategy;
> - There was no integration of military and political objectives and tactics;
> - [No] immediate exploitation of intelligence;
> - They focused almost exclusively on search and destroy operations;
> - They had no understanding of the local community;
> - They failed to restrict the enemy supply lines and communications networks.

Numerical superiority was lacking – an estimated Soviet and Afghan Government force of 400,000–500,000 was required. Endurance, will and moral commitment were lacking.

(MoD 2010: Section 3-15)

The war also revealed, as had Vietnam for the Americans 20 years earlier, that victory remains elusive even for a superpower when it confronts an opponent driven by deep ideological or religious convictions and bolstered morally, but above all materially, by generous external allies. Like the Vietminh and Viet Cong in the 1950s and '60s, the *mujahideen* proved themselves an exceedingly formidable force to reckon with, notwithstanding their initial acute deficiencies in weapons, ammunition and supplies. Once adequately armed, equipped and fed, and with limited access to safe havens providing training and rest, the motivation and drive of an exceptionally robust, utterly determined, ideologically driven foe employing tactics suited to the circumstances produced the most intractable of opponents: one with time on his side and a willingness to accept horrific losses many times in excess of his adversary. Here lay the ingredients of the Soviet Union's military demise and the concomitant ruins of its political ambitions in the region.

Russian Spetsnaz troops, followed by a T-72 tank fitted with a mine roller, enter the Chechen stronghold of Bamut, a village in western Chechnya, in May 1996. Federal forces eventually took the fortress-like village, which once housed a Soviet rocket base, although the village had little strategic value. (Alexander Nemenov/AFP/Getty Images)

CHAPTER 5

THE POST-SOVIET ARMY: DEFEAT IN CHECHNYA

THE COLLAPSE AND PARTITION OF the USSR from 1989 onwards was a traumatic experience for the Soviet military, which was already embroiled in local ethnic conflicts and coping with problematic withdrawals from Central Europe. Even while the Soviet Union still stood it had already begun its painful retreat from empire. The Warsaw Pact – ostensibly a military alliance, but in reality the fiction that allowed Moscow to base troops in and control its Eastern European satellites – had become increasingly untenable. Many of these countries were restive, and Moscow could no longer afford the economic, political and military cost of keeping them under its thumb. On 7 December 1988, in a momentous speech to the United Nations, Soviet President Mikhail Gorbachev announced that he would start drawing down troop deployments in Eastern Europe.

What was intended to be a phased and partial withdrawal soon became overtaken by events, as communist governments across the region started to fall in 1989–90. In Poland, Czechoslovakia, Hungary and Bulgaria new governments were elected; the DDR (East Germany) effectively collapsed; and a violent uprising saw Romanian dictator Nicolae Ceausescu toppled and executed. On 25 February 1991, the Warsaw Pact was formally disbanded. This left half a million Soviet troops (and 150,000 dependants)

Airborne troops move through Grozny in 1996, riding on the hull of their armoured vehicle just as Red Army infantry did in World War II half a century earlier. (ITAR-TASS/Anatoly Morkovkin/Getty Images)

stranded in countries technically no longer under their control, nor even especially friendly. The situation forced an accelerated withdrawal, often before there were barracks or bases ready to accommodate them. While what was then still West Germany helped pay for the removal of Soviet troops from the DDR – a process that would take until 1994 – elsewhere the situation was less orderly. The USSR simply had nowhere to put its returning legions: as of July 1990, 280,000 military families were reportedly without housing.

These soldiers and families were returning to a country itself in the midst of collapse and re-creation. The late Soviet era saw nationalist risings which were sometimes quashed violently by the use of troops, as in Tbilisi, Georgia (1988) and Baku, Azerbaijan (1990). Meanwhile, in the heartland Soviet republic of Russia, anti-communist politician Boris Yeltsin was rising in influence. Eventually Gorbachev opted for a policy of democratization and power-sharing with Yeltsin and other local leaders, which would have dramatically changed the very basis of the Soviet Union – not least at the expense of the military and the KGB political police. As a result, on 19 August 1991 a group of eight Communist Party hardliners, including Marshal Dmitry Yazov, put Gorbachev under house arrest and declared a state of emergency.

Although the plotters had counted on the support of the military, it soon became clear that there was little enthusiasm for their efforts to hold the old Soviet Union together, let alone a willingness to fire on the protesters who came out onto the streets against the coup. Some paratroopers and elements of the 2nd Tamanskaya and 4th Kantemirovskaya Divisions of the Moscow garrison deployed into the centre of the city, but several promptly defected to Yeltsin. Eventually, it was soldiers such as the paratroop generals Alexander Lebed and Boris Gromov who persuaded Marshal Yazov that any attempt to storm the Russian parliament building (known as the White

Some aspects of military life are enduringly timeless. Here a young Russian soldier digs a trench the old way. The Russian Ministry of Defence emphasizes in its publicity that a military career is a good way of picking up new skills for future employability. (Andrei Ivanov/DPL)

House) and arrest Yeltsin would result in massive civilian casualties. Yazov, who had thought the coup would be virtually bloodless, decided to stand down the military, in effect bringing the 'August Coup' to a close on the 21st, just three days after it had started.

Gorbachev was freed, but his power base had been broken, and Yeltsin used the opportunity to block any further attempts to reform the Soviet Union. Recognizing the futility of his position, Gorbachev's last act as Soviet president, on 25 December 1991, was to resign his position and sign the USSR out of existence.

THE NEW RUSSIAN ARMY

In practice, control of Soviet military forces and assets devolved to whichever newly created republic they found themselves in, but at first there was a distinct lack of clarity as to their future. Yeltsin had taken over control of the Soviet nuclear launch codes and systems, but according to the 1991 Belavezha Accords agreed by the leaders of Russia, Ukraine and Belarus, a loose new union called the Commonwealth of Independent States (CIS) was formed. This entity had its own supreme military commander – Marshal of Aviation Yevgeny Shaposhnikov – and provisional control over joint forces. This was never an especially comfortable or practical solution, and after initially announcing that Russia would form its own 100,000-strong

In an example of lingering traditionalism, a Soviet flamethrower unit in the late 1980s unleashes jets or flame at training targets. The flamethrower model appears to be the LPO-50. Today flamethrowers are largely a thing of the past, although might occasionally make an appearance for duties such as foliage burning. (David Reynolds/DPL)

National Guard, in March 1992 Yeltsin established the Armed Forces of the Russian Federation (VSRF), subsequently appointing paratroop commander General Pavel Grachyov as his defence minister. By the end of 1993 it was clear that there was no real future for the CIS as a military structure, and it was relegated to being simply a channel for co-operation within the post-Soviet region. More than two million soldiers – the majority of the old Soviet military – ended up under Moscow's control.

As remaining forces withdrew from East Germany, Russia had to consider what kind of an army it had and needed. In November 1993 it adopted a new Military Doctrine – the foundational document describing when and how Russia might go to war – which spoke of the nation's role as a regional power, and of the need to modernize and professionalize the army. These were fine words; but Moscow, in the midst of economic crisis, lacked the resources for any wholesale modernization of the Soviet military machine it had inherited. Grachyov was also out of his depth; an able field officer, he lacked the strategic vision or political skills to handle his new position. (He also infamously acquired the nickname 'Pasha Mercedes', for his alleged acquisition of luxury cars with embezzled funds meant to cover the withdrawal of forces from East Germany.) Besides, it soon became clear that while the charismatic (but alcoholic) Yeltsin had stood initially on a reformist platform, the pressures of office would bring out his authoritarian streak, and this would see the army embroiled in controversial and debilitating domestic conflicts.

THE EARLY 1990S: STUCK IN SOVIET PATTERNS

Through 1993, Yeltsin and the Supreme Soviet – the communist-dominated parliament he had inherited from the USSR – were increasingly at odds. This came to a head in September, when Yeltsin, in violation of the constitution, declared the Supreme Soviet dissolved. Legal niceties quickly gave way to the arithmetic of force; the Supreme Soviet gathered armed defenders, who tried to storm the Ostankino TV centre. However, Yeltsin was able to persuade the security troops of the Ministry of Internal Affairs and elements of the 2nd Tamanskaya Division to take his side. Tanks emplaced on the Novoarbatsky Bridge in front of the White House shelled the building and, when it was subsequently stormed, the parliamentarians and their supporters surrendered. Yeltsin went on to rewrite the constitution to retrospectively legalize his actions, and replaced the Supreme Soviet with a new, less powerful body, the State Duma.

Russian airborne troops conduct unarmed combat training, one man going flying after receiving a heavy kick. Russian combat training is still known for its realism and occasionally its brutality, especially in the SOF units. (Iain Ballantyne/DPL)

Politics might have changed, but meaningful reform of the army was largely stalled. This was to a considerable extent due to a lack of both ideas and money, but also reflected the conservative bias of the officer corps. Yeltsin's army was to a large extent the Soviet Army in organization, culture and role – just smaller, and poorer. As of 1996 it numbered 670,000 officers and enlisted personnel, divided among eight military districts and the separate Air Assault Forces (VDV). There were 85 divisions, but given the shortfall in personnel and the very officer-heavy distribution of these forces – more than one soldier in three, 290,000, were commissioned officers, and far too many of them colonels – the majority of these divisions were more notional than actual. At best, they were structures ready to accept reservists in case of national mobilization, but at worst they were simply 'paper' formations kept in being in order to find something for the professional soldiers to do.

There was talk of creating a Rapid Deployment Force, and of a smaller, all-professional army, but these dreams came to nothing. For most of the 1990s the army was consumed by a desperate struggle simply to survive, in a decade of social turmoil, economic crisis, rampant crime, and political unrest. In 1995 a Defence Ministry spokesman warned that 'if no radical decision is made shortly, the Russian Army may well find itself on the verge of starvation'; reports were coming in that in parts of Siberia recruits were being given animal feed, and even soldiers in the Moscow Military District were having to beg in order to survive. Although the situation would ease in the latter half of the decade, this was hardly an army capable of modernization and reform.

A particularly toxic legacy of Soviet times was *dedovshchina* – 'grandfatherism' – a distinctive and brutal Russian seniority-based hazing culture that led to hundreds of deaths among conscripts every year. No army is immune to bullying and abuse, but in the Soviet military the cycle of spring and fall call-ups for soldiers to fulfil their two-year national service obligation meant that at any given time the conscripts were divided into four six-monthly cohorts. This generated an unofficial progression through stages of military life: a newly arrived *molodoy* ('youngster') could expect to be lorded over by the *dedy* ('grandfathers') who were more than halfway through their service, and by the *dembely* (from 'demobilizing') who were serving their last hundred days. Newer recruits were forced to serve the older ones – to perform their duties, hand over food (especially that sent from home), and even go through the ritual of the 'hundred days', putting a cigarette under the pillow of a *dembel* every night until the end of his service. This culture was enforced by often brutal means, including everything

Heavily armed Spetsnaz soldiers listen to an officer's briefing as they prepare for a mission on 18 May 1995 in Khankala on the eastern outskirts of Grozny. Note the suppressors on their assault rifles. (Alexander Nemenov/ AFP/Getty Images)

from humiliations to beatings. In Soviet and even early post-Soviet times, *dedovshchina* was officially decried but unofficially tolerated, because it was believed to offer an alternative form of discipline. For a relatively small and often under-trained junior officer corps, without adequate numbers of seasoned NCOs on whom to rely, the senior conscripts offered a means to keep the rest in line, in return for the officers turning a blind eye to their bullying. Yet *dedovshchina* was dangerously corrosive of morale and counterproductive in combat, when squads must stick together, and it also made military service extremely unappealing, contributing to widespread draft-dodging and making it hard to attract volunteers.

Nor was 'grandfatherism' the only problematic legacy with which the Russian military had to struggle. It was receiving only 30–40 per cent of the budget it needed simply to maintain its fighting condition, let alone modernize and reform. Every unit was actually under-strength. The cohesion of units was often appallingly bad: there was no professional NCO corps to speak of – sergeants were conscripts with a few months' extra training and junior officers performed many of the roles carried out by NCOs in Western armies – and morale was generally rock bottom. After all, pay was low and often late (as of mid 1996, pay arrears had reached $889 million) and even basics such as food and heating in winter were never guaranteed. With pay often in arrears, food scarce and even power supplies sporadic, officers and men alike turned to crime to survive. Much of this was petty and opportunistic, such as the pilfering of stores. (In Chechnya it reached the extreme of soldiers selling weapons to the very rebels they were fighting, in return for food and money.) Some officers created criminal business empires, along a spectrum from illegally hiring out soldiers as labourers, to using military convoys (which were exempt from police and customs checks) to smuggle drugs from Asia and stolen cars from Europe. Investigation of such scandals was discouraged: for instance, when journalist Dmitry Kholodov began to look into embezzlement of army funds in 1994, an anonymous tip-off directed him to a briefcase in a left-luggage locker. When he opened it, he was killed by a bomb that the police later described as being made the way Spetsnaz commandos were trained to build booby-traps.

It was clear that the post-Soviet army of the early 1990s had enough work contending with its own internal issues and was in no fit state to commit to a major conflict. Yet such is exactly what it did in Chechnya from 1994. In the remainder of this chapter and the beginning of the next, we will explore

This haunting portrait of a Russian soldier shows youth being steadily erased by the terrible experiences of war. There were many instances of desperately miserable Russian conscripts trading their weapons to Chechen dealers for alcohol and drugs to escape the horror. (Malcolm Linton/Liaison)

the utter Russian disaster of the First Chechen War (1994–96) through to its eventual victory in the early 2000s. For as much as these wars illustrate the near catastrophic faultlines running through the new Russian Army, they also demonstrate the infamous Russian resilience, and the army's canny ability to adapt to reality.

THE FIRST CHECHEN WAR (1994–96)

Post-Soviet Russia fought its first war – the First Chechen War – in 1994–96. In effect, it lost: a nation with a population of 147 million was forced to recognize the de facto autonomy of Chechnya, a country one-hundredth its size and with less than one-hundredth of its people. A mix of brilliant guerrilla warfare and ruthless terrorism was able to humble Russia's decaying remnants of the Soviet war machine.

But this was a struggle that had already run for centuries. Russia licked its wounds and built up its forces for a rematch, invading again in 1999 and by 2009 declaring the Second Chechen War won (see next chapter). However, this did not mean peace in Chechnya, much less in the wider North Caucasus region, which seems to have been infected by insurrection.

If only Boris Yeltsin, first president of post-Soviet Russia, had been more aware of his history. After all, it is hardly surprising that the first and most serious direct challenge to Moscow's rule after the collapse of the USSR came from the Chechens. An ethnic group from the North Caucasus mountain region on Russia's southern flank, the Chechens – who call themselves *Nokhchy* or *Vainakh* – have lived in the region for thousands of years, their land defined by the Sunja and Terek rivers to the north and the west, the Andi mountains to the east and the mighty Caucasus range to the south. Their reputation has been as a proud, fractious, raiding people. This is, after all, a land of mountains and valleys. Diagonal ranges cut the country from north-west to south-east, with the lowland valleys and hillsides in between often thickly forested. This is perfect bandit and guerrilla country, but also a geography that worked against the rise of any strong central power.

Instead, what emerged was a people politically divided between clan (*teip*) and family, but with a shared culture characterized by a close-knit sense of community, based on tradition, kinship and a fierce sense of honour, which valued independence to an immense degree. The Russians came to realize this when their own imperial expansion brought them to the North Caucasus in the eighteenth century, their eyes fixed on other prizes: Georgia to the south, and beyond that, Safavid Iran and the Ottoman Empire. Of all the North Caucasian mountain peoples, the Chechens put up the fiercest resistance to the Tsarist Russian invaders of the eighteenth and nineteenth century and Soviet occupiers of the twentieth.

FLASHPOINT: 1994

On 25 December 1991, General Secretary Mikhail Gorbachev resigned his post, and on the last day of December the USSR formally ceased to exist, creating 15 new states, including the Russian Federation. However, this was a new nation created by default and from the first would encounter challenges between the centralizing impulses of Moscow and the national aspirations of some of the members of this federation. Originally, Yeltsin had suggested that constituent members of the Russian Federation would be free to chart their own destinies, but as ever this proved a promise easier to make while seeking office than to keep once in power. The head of the Chechen-Ingush Autonomous Soviet Socialist Republic, Doku Zavgayev, had failed to repudiate the August Coup and had been hounded out of office. In October 1991, a referendum was held to confirm Dzhokhar Dudayev, then the head of the informal opposition All-National Congress of the Chechen People, as president. He immediately declared the republic independent – something the minority Ingushetians questioned and Yeltsin flatly refused to accept. Moscow declared a state of emergency and

dispatched an MVD VV regiment to Grozny. However, when the lightly armed security troops touched down at Khankala air base outside the city, they were surrounded by a far greater number of Dudayev's forces. Gorbachev refused to let the Soviet Armed Forces get involved and Yeltsin shied away at the time from escalating, so after some tense negotiations the MVD VV troops were allowed to leave by bus. Moscow had challenged Grozny and Grozny had won, the first round at least, leaving Dudayev a national hero and Chechnya believing itself finally free.

In March 1992, a new Federation Treaty was signed as the foundational document of the Russian state and Chechnya refused to take part. As a result, in June Ingushetia formally split from Chechnya, petitioning successfully to be incorporated into the Russian Federation as the Republic of Ingushetia. Meanwhile, the self-proclaimed Chechen Republic of Ichkeria (ChRI) affirmed its own statehood, with a flag and national anthem – even if no international recognition.

This was not a tenable state of affairs. On the one hand, Yeltsin was increasingly worried about the long-term implications of allowing Chechnya's withdrawal from the federation as a precedent. Indeed, Dudayev was eager

A column of Russian troops, with armour and anti-aircraft cannon, heads across Chechnya on 11 December 1994. The convoy was photographed about 50km from Grozny and contained at least 200 armoured vehicles. (Alexander Grek/ AFP/Getty Images)

A Russian unit's lead T-72 tanks, one mounted with a mine-clearing system (right), halt near Samashky, some 40km from Grozny, on 13 December 1994. (Ivan Shlamov/AFP/Getty Images)

to create a federation of the Caucasian *gorsky* ('mountain') peoples, although his Confederation of Caucasian Mountain Peoples never amounted to much. The much larger and economically important Republic of Tatarstan had already negotiated for itself special membership terms and there were even fears that territories east of the Urals might seek to break free some day.

Not that the ChRI was stable in any sense. While three of Chechnya's 18 constituent regions were threatening secession, Dudayev began to talk of the forced re-incorporation of Ingushetia. Conversely, the Terek Cossack Host laid claim to parts of Chechnya. There appeared ample scope for unrest, local insurrection, even civil war, given that under Dudayev, Chechnya was becoming a virtual bandit kingdom. Organized crime flourished, not least within the new ChRI state apparatus. The Chechen State Bank, for example, was used to defraud its Russian counterpart of up to $700 million using fake proof of fund documents. Russian oil pipelines which ran through Chechnya were not only at risk of destruction but also being tapped illegally and even though Grozny was still a hub for oil refining, in the first two years of independence not a single new school or hospital was built and industrial production fell – largely as a result of under-investment – by 60 per cent.

Chechnya was becoming a genuine threat. At least as important, Yeltsin needed to prove that no one could challenge Moscow with impunity. There was also a political dimension: increasingly unpopular at home as the economy collapsed, he wanted an enemy and a success to distract the public. A conflict became increasingly inevitable. In August Yeltsin was still describing a military intervention by federal forces as 'impermissible' and 'absolutely impossible'; it was not that he was ruling out action, just that he hoped to rely instead on Chechens opposed to Dudayev, who had formed the Provisional Chechen Council.

In October and November 1994, forces of the Provisional Chechen Council, essentially a puppet rival government formed, armed and encouraged by Moscow to oppose Dudayev (and supported by Russian airpower), launched abortive incursions into Chechnya. This proved a disaster; they were easily defeated by Dudayev loyalists, who captured Russian soldiers among them and paraded them on television. To an extent, this reflected the unexpected level of support Dudayev's regime still had, but it was also a product of poor planning on the Russian side. The Provisional Chechen Council was essentially a tool of Russia's domestic security agency, then still called the Federal Counter-Intelligence Service (FSK), but later the Federal Security Service (FSB). It was the FSK that was pushing for intervention and the troops involved, while drawn from armed forces units, had actually been hired by the FSK without the explicit

A Chechen fighter intimidates several Russian soldiers who were captured during a Russian offensive on 13 January 1995. The future prospects for prisoners on either side were horribly bleak. (Pascal Guyot/AFP/Getty Images)

clearance of the armed forces High Command. According to the testimony of captured soldiers, FSK recruiters had offered them the equivalent of a year's pay to prepare tanks for the operation, and the same again to crew them in support of the irregular forces of the Provisional Chechen Council. They were also told that Dudayev had already fled, his forces were demoralized and the people of Grozny were ready to welcome them with flowers and cheers. Instead, of the 78 Russian soldiers accompanying the irregulars into Chechnya in November, only 26 made it home, with the rest killed or captured.

When Major-General Boris Polyakov, commander of the elite 4th Guards Kantemir Tank Division, heard that some of his soldiers had been hired by the FSK without his knowledge, he angrily resigned his position. Russia's Chechen 'Bay of Pigs' put Yeltsin in a position where he could either escalate or back down. Characteristically, he escalated, encouraged by his compliant defence minister, General Pavel Grachev, who airily reassured him that he 'would solve the whole problem with an airborne regiment in two hours'. On 28 November, a secret session of select members of the Security Council met to consider next steps and decided to invade. This was then put to the full Security Council the next day, but with Yeltsin and his closest allies set on intervention, there was no real scope for debate, even though Yevgeny Primakov, head of the Foreign Intelligence Service and a veteran Middle East specialist, counselled caution. As a result, on 30 November, Yeltsin signed Presidential Decree No. 2137, 'On steps to re-establish constitutional law and order in the territory of the Chechen Republic.'

Even ahead of that vote, on 28 November the Russian Air Force bombed Chechnya's small air force on the ground and closed its two airfields by cratering the runways. Meanwhile, an invasion force was mustered in three contingents. The first, based in Mozdok, North Ossetia and commanded by Lieutenant-General Vladimir Chilindin, numbered 6,500 men. It was based on elements of the 131st Independent Motor Rifle Brigade, nine MVD VV battalions and the 22nd Independent Spetsnaz Brigade.

The second, mustering at Vladikavkaz, North Ossetia, was under Lieutenant-General Alexander Chindarov – the deputy head of the Airborne Forces – and comprised 4,000 troops from the 19th Motor Rifle Division and the 76th Airborne Division, as well as five MVD VV battalions. The third, under Lieutenant-General Lev Rokhlin, assembled at Kizlyar, Dagestan, with 4,000 troops drawn from the 20th Motor Rifle Division and six MVD VV battalions. Together with other forces, including the air assets committed to the operation, the total force was around 23,700 men, including 80 tanks, under the overall command of Colonel-General Alexei Mityukhin, commander of the North Caucasus Military District.

1) Conscript, 1992. This disgruntled-looking private sitting on top of a BTR-70 personnel carrier is contemplating his IRP-P rations box. The old rations (since replaced with a plastic-wrapped version) contained a day's-worth of food – mostly canned, but also including so-called 'army loaf' crackers and, of course, tea – and a hexamine-based folding stove. The daily ration provided 3,100 calories, but in the 1990s it was often distributed well beyond its formal use-by date. The soldier wears the standard summer-weight *afganka* field uniform and high, uncomfortable boots. **2)** Major, paratroops; IFOR, 1996. This unit commander, part of the Russian brigade contributed to the multi-national Implementation Force in Bosnia-Herzegovina in 1995–96, is briefing his junior officers before the day's patrols. He is wearing a VSR winter camouflage jacket with a major's star on the epaulets, and a Russian national patch on his left sleeve; as was then often the case, he still sports a Soviet cap badge on his winter hat of synthetic 'fish fur'. He carries a slung AK-74 assault rifle. **3)** Machine-gunner, First Chechen War, 1996. This infantryman manning a 12.7mm NSV heavy machine gun is desperately defending his position during the Chechen rebels' successful operation to retake Grozny in August 1996. He is wearing a two-piece KLMK camouflage uniform and an old-pattern SSh-68 steel helmet. **4)** Russian KFOR sleeve patch, 1999. Such formation patches are normally worn on the upper right sleeve. The wording around the edge reads 'Russian Military Contingent', with 'Kosovo' at the bottom. The letters 'MS' in the centre stand for Mirotvorcheskiye Sily, 'Peacekeeping Forces'. The motif above, of two stylized aircraft with a parachute canopy and a red star, echoes the insignia of the Air Assault Force (VDV), reflecting the paratroopers' primary role in the KFOR mission. (Johnny Shumate © Osprey Publishing)

On 11 December, as Yeltsin disappeared from public view reportedly for a minor operation – but really to avoid embarrassing questions – federal forces moved into Chechnya along three axes that then split into six. Already that represented a deviation from the original plan, which had envisaged starting on 7 December, but the forces had not been ready. Within three days they were meant to be ready to storm Grozny, but in fact local resistance, bad weather and a rash of mechanical difficulties meant they were not emplaced around the city until 26 December. Nevertheless, they had reached the Chechen capital and the real war was about to begin. When the Russians moved in on 31 December, they were met not by cheering crowds throwing flowers and kisses at their liberators, but by a population mobilized for war and charged by a 200-year history of struggle.

THE FIRST BATTLE FOR GROZNY

The Russians' assumption was that seizing Grozny would mean the end of the war. This planning decision not only showed that they had forgotten the experiences of past wars with the Chechens, or even the Soviet invasion of Afghanistan in 1979; it also drove them to try to push towards and into the city more quickly than they should have. Federal forces were gathered in a special Joint Group of Forces (OGV) that was predominantly made up of units from the Soviet Armed Forces and the MVD, but also included FSB units (including some Border Troops, subordinated to the FSB), elements of the separate Railway Troops and detachments from the Ministry of Emergency Situations (MChS). Co-ordination between these various forces was inevitably going to be problematic, especially as the preparations had been hurried, and this was another factor behind the relatively simple 'drive to Grozny'.

The plan was that these task forces would push directly to Grozny and surround it. While MVD troops locked down the countryside, armed forces units would assault the city from north and south, seizing key locations such as the presidential palace, main railway station and police headquarters before the Chechens had had the chance to prepare proper defences, and then mop up any remnants of Chechen resistance as remained. However, the plan ran into problems from the first. The three task forces – which had had to advance along multiple routes because of the geography and the width and quality of roads – all failed to keep to schedule, so Grozny was never effectively blockaded, especially to the south, allowing its defenders to be reinforced with volunteers and raising their numbers to perhaps 9,000 by the height of the battle. With the Russian first wave only numbering some 6,000 men, given the advantages for the defence in urban warfare, this was a serious development for the federal forces. They were to have to throw substantially more into the fray before they eventually took the city and levelled much of it in the process.

The Chechens had also had longer than anticipated to prepare. Under military Chief of Staff Aslan Maskhadov, the Chechens had established

The pile of spent artillery shells here indicates the intensity of the Russian bombardments during the First Chechen War. The Russians deployed nearly 400 artillery pieces, as opposed to the 100 guns possessed by the Chechens. (Georges DeKeerle/Sygma via Getty Images)

three concentric defensive rings and had turned much of the centre of the city into a nest of ad hoc fortifications. Buildings were sandbagged and reinforced to provide firing positions, while – knowing the Russian propensity for the direct attack – the few tanks and artillery pieces the Chechens had were emplaced to command those roads wide enough for an armoured assault, notably Ordzhonikidze Avenue, Victory Avenue and Pervomayskoye Avenue. Further out, there were defensive positions at chokepoints such as the bridges across the Sunzha River, as well as around Minutka Square south of the centre.

The Russian plan called for assault elements of the 81st and 255th Motor Rifle regiments to attack from the north under Lieutenant-General Konstantin Pulikovsky, supported by the 131st Independent Motor Rifle Brigade and 8th Motor Rifle Regiment. Meanwhile, elements from the 19th Motor Rifle Division under Major-General Ivan Babichev would move in from the west, along the railway tracks to seize the central station and then advance on the presidential palace from the south. From the east, Major-General Nikolai Staskov would lead assault units from the 129th Motor Rifle Regiment and a battalion of the 98th Airborne Division again along the railway line to Lenin Square and thence capture the bridges across the Sunzha River. From the north-east, elements of the 255th and 33rd Motor Rifle Regiments and 74th Independent Motor Rifle Brigade under Lieutenant-General Lev Rokhlin would take the central hospital complex,

A young Russian soldier sits in shock during the fighting for Bamut in 1994, with one of the many Russian dead behind him in an APC. (Georges DeKeerle/Sygma via Getty Images)

from where they could support other advances. Finally, units from the 76th and 106th Airborne Divisions would be deployed to prevent the rebels from firing the Lenin and Sheripov oil-processing factories or chemical works, as well as blocking efforts by the rebels to attack the assault units from behind.

The attack began on 31 December after a preparatory air and artillery bombardment and soon ran into trouble as Chechen resistance proved fiercer than anticipated. The western advance soon bogged down in fierce street-to-street fighting. The eastern group was forced to detour and found itself in a kill-zone of minefields and strongpoints. The northern group managed to push as far as the presidential palace, but there likewise found itself unable to break dogged resistance, and dangerously exposed by the failure of the other groups. Furthermore, a lack of training, the use of forces cobbled together from elements from different units, and poor morale quickly proved problematic. Advances became snarled in traffic jams of armoured vehicles, friendly-fire incidents proliferated and units coming under fire showed a propensity to halt and take cover, rather than press on as intended.

The First Battle for Grozny

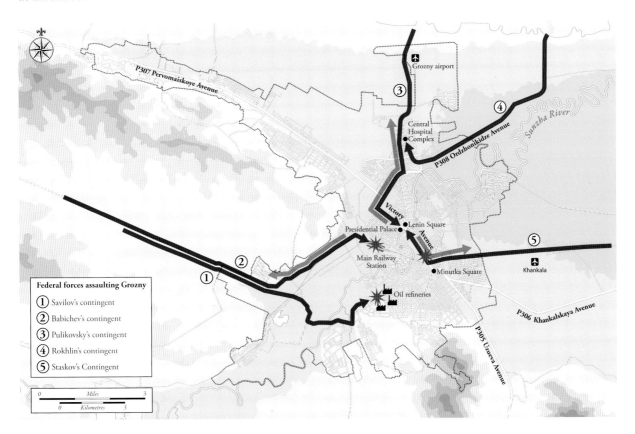

Federal forces assaulting Grozny

① Savilov's contingent
② Babichev's contingent
③ Pulikovsky's contingent
④ Rokhlin's contingent
⑤ Staskov's Contingent

Perhaps the most striking reversal was the fate of the 1st Battalion of the 131st Independent Motor Rifle Brigade, which by the afternoon of the first day had reached the main railway station and had assembled at the square outside it. There it was ambushed by well-positioned Chechen forces in buildings all around the square, which soon became an inferno of small-arms and RPG fire. When survivors fled into the station building, it was set on fire. When other elements of the 131st tried to support their comrades, they were ambushed and blocked. The battalion lost more than half its men and almost all its vehicles; in effect, it had ceased to exist.

By 3 January, the Russian attack had effectively been beaten back. Their only forces still in the city in good order were Rokhlin's group, which had not been expected to drive to the presidential palace and had thus avoided the worst of the fighting and had been able to dig in.

Even so, this could only be a temporary respite. The Russians redoubled their air and artillery campaign against the city, and adopted a much more cautious campaign, slowly grinding their way through the city. On 19 January, they seized the presidential palace – or what was left of it after it was hit by bunker-busting bombs – and although fighting would continue in the south of the city for weeks to come, Grozny had essentially fallen. But it was a ruin, strewn with the bodies of thousands of its citizens – estimates range up to 35,000 – in a bloodbath that the Organization for Security and Cooperation in Europe (OSCE) would describe as an 'unimaginable catastrophe'. This would not, however, be the last battle for this ill-fated city.

YELTSIN'S MESSY WAR

On 6 January 1995, the Security Council had announced that military actions in Chechnya would soon be coming to an end; it took almost another two weeks before they even controlled the ruins of the presidential palace. Contrary to Russian expectations, though, the fall of Grozny did not end the war. Instead, what would follow would devolve into a messy series of local brawls, sieges, raids and feints. The towns of Shali, Gudermes and Argun held out for months and federal forces seemed to show little enthusiasm to engage in further urban warfare.

In what became a traditional way of expressing disapproval of the progress being made, Yeltsin decided to change commanders and on 26 January, Deputy Interior Minister General Anatoly Kulikov, head of the MVD VV, was given overall charge of the operation. At the same time, efforts were being made to negotiate a settlement and on 20 February, Maskhadov met his Russian counterpart, Chief of the General Staff General Anatoly Kvashnin. But there was no real scope for agreement: the Russians would accept nothing short of complete capitulation. From the Russians' point of view, at least the pause gave them a chance to regroup and reinforce. More and better troops were rushed to Chechnya, from wherever they could be found: part of the MVD VV's 1st Independent Special Designation Division – the elite 'Dzerzhinsky Division' from Moscow – as well as the Vityaz anti-terrorist commando unit, Naval Infantry from the Northern, Pacific and Baltic fleets (though the commander of one Pacific Fleet battalion refused his orders) and the Armed Forces' elite 506th Motor Rifle Regiment. In total, the OGV was brought to 55,000 personnel from the MVD and military. The FSK set up a Chechnya directorate. In short, having realized that this was hardly going to be the quick or neat operation it had anticipated, Moscow hurriedly looked to raise its game.

A young Russian machine gunner on the streets of Grozny, his torso heavily clad in body armour. At the small-unit level, the Chechens had just as much firepower as the Russian forces. (Antoine Gyori/Sygma via Getty Images)

Ceasefire talks broke down on 4 March; the next day, federal forces began their assault on Gudermes, although this would prove a lengthy, on-and-off process before the town was taken. Argun fell more easily, on 23 March, and by the end of April, most main centres were loosely in federal hands, even

if attacks continued regularly. Having originally suggested that Grozny was returning to normal, in May the Russians were forced to introduce a curfew and admitted that hundreds of rebel fighters remained within the city. Colonel-General Mikhail Yegorov, the temporary acting field commander of the OGV, spoke of 20 per cent of the country still being in rebel hands, in the southern highlands around Shatoy and Vedeno – they themselves claimed almost twice that.

Nevertheless, the Russian offensive ground on, with Kulikov asserting that no more than 3,000 fighters still supported Dudayev, a figure that remained suspiciously constant throughout the war. On 13 June, the Russians claimed – and the Chechens admitted – that they had taken Shatoy and the nearby town of Nozhay-Yurt. Moscow began to believe that the end of the war was close. However, the Russians' notion that this was a conflict whose progress could be charted by map was flawed. Although the rebels only controlled a small portion of southern Chechnya, the Russians had neither the numerical nor the moral strength to be said to control the rest. By day, the armed forces and MVD patrolled the cities while Mi-24 helicopter gunships tracked along roads and pipelines. There were sporadic bomb and sniper attacks in the cities and ambushes outside, but in the main the Russians did not try to penetrate too deeply into the highlands and villages and the Chechens knew that a direct confrontation with the federal forces would bring a devastating response. By night, though, the Russians largely withdrew to their bases, mounting only occasional and heavy patrols in main cities, abandoning the country to the rebels, who used these times to regroup and relocate. This allowed the rebels to be able to mount attacks throughout the country still. Besides, what was looming was the start of a whole new type of war, one for which the Russians were distinctly unprepared.

Even as the Russians were making their grandiose assertions, a convoy of trucks was travelling up the P263 highway, into Stavropol Region. Some 195 Chechen fighters under rebel commander Shamil Basayev bluffed and bribed their way past successive police checkpoints, pretending to be carrying the coffins of dead soldiers home. Basayev had hoped to get further into Russia, but on 14 June, they reached a roadblock just north of the southern Russian city of Budyonnovsk 110km north of the Chechen border. Basayev had spent $9,000 in bribes and had run out of money, so instead his party turned round and drove back into Budyonnovsk. They seized the mayor's office and police station and when security forces

converged on the town, withdrew to the local hospital. There, they took some 1,800 hostages, mostly civilians and including some 150 children.

Basayev demanded that Moscow end its operations in Chechnya and open direct negotiations with the ChRI government. He threatened to kill the hostages if the Russians moved against him, tried to prevent his access to the media, or refused to accept his terms. Several times, government forces tried to storm the building but were driven back. Eventually Russian Prime Minister Viktor Chernomyrdin personally negotiated a resolution that in effect granted the Chechens their demands. On 19 June, Basayev and his remaining fighters, accompanied by over 100 volunteer hostages, including journalists and parliamentarians, were allowed back into Chechnya. Much of Budyonnovsk was in ruins, 147 people were dead (many from Russian fire), but perhaps most comprehensively shattered was Moscow's confidence and its claims that the war in Chechnya was going easily to be won. Chernomyrdin was no dove, but seizing the moment while Yeltsin was away at a conference in Canada, he was shrewd enough to know when to cut a deal.

Basayev's men had suffered just 12 casualties, yet their act of terrorism had not only humbled their enemies – FSK director Sergei Stepashin and

Russian Interior Ministry soldiers sit atop an APC near Grozny, January 1995. The man in the foreground is armed with an AKS-74 with under-barrel grenade launcher. (Malcolm Linton/ Liaison/Getty Images)

Interior Minister Viktor Yerin, both hawks, were forced to resign because of the mismanagement of the crisis – it had changed the course of the conflict. It did not end the war, but it demonstrated convincingly that the Russians were asymmetrically vulnerable to unexpected threats. Nevertheless, although negotiations and ceasefires came and went over following months, something of a bloody stalemate seemed to be emerging.

The Chechens could not dislodge the federal forces, nor, as in history, meet them in open battle. However, the Russians were unable to bring their forces properly to bear on the rebels and end the war. A case in point was the battle of Gudermes in December 1995. On 14 December, the very day on which Chechens were meant to be voting for their new – Moscow-approved – republican president, some 600 rebels under Salman Raduyev attacked the country's second-largest city.

They managed to take large tracts of central Gudermes, by then considered one of the most secure federal strongholds in Chechnya, although they were not able to storm its military headquarters. For two weeks, federal forces launched repeated assaults, interspersed with artillery barrages, but while Raduyev's men could not expand their grip on the city, nor were the Russians able to break them. Eventually, a local ceasefire was agreed and Raduyev and his forces were allowed safe passage out of the city. Gudermes returned to federal hands, but at the price of allowing the rebels out to fight another day.

That they did. On 9 January 1996, Raduyev led some 200 fighters into neighbouring Dagestan to attack the air base at Kizlyar. They only destroyed two helicopters there – most were elsewhere or on operations – but when federal forces responded, seemingly more quickly than he had anticipated, Raduyev took a leaf out of Basayev's playbook. His men retreated to the nearby town, took over 1,000 hostages and holed up in the city hospital and an adjacent building. A deal was struck allowing them to return to Chechnya in return for the hostages. Most were let go, with some 150 kept as human shields. However, the Russians were not willing to let Raduyev strike a third time. Just short of the border, the Chechen convoy came under fire from a helicopter and the guerrillas seized the nearby village of Pervomayskoye, taking more hostages and digging in.

There followed three days of sporadic assaults by Russian special forces, which led to heavy casualties on their side but no progress. They resorted to bombarding the village, claiming that the hostages had already been killed, while commanders competed to put the blame on others and some units seemed on the verge of mutiny. On the eighth night, though, most of the surviving Chechens managed to break through the Russian lines and flee, assisted by a diversionary attack launched by other rebel forces which had come to support them. Raduyev was among them, and would continue to elude the Russians until his capture in 2000; he died in the Russian Bely Lebed (White Swan) maximum-security prison camp in 2002.

The Kizlyar/Pervomayskoye operation encapsulated the dynamics on both sides. The Chechens retained the initiative, and could win when they struck unexpectedly. They also still had forces with the morale, weapons and will to fight. On the other hand, their 'army' was shattering into various autonomous forces under charismatic warlords who often had their own agendas. Dudayev, after all, would contradict himself as to whether he had or had not ordered the Kizlyar attack. Raduyev, though, was one of a new generation who had little time for negotiation or moderation; whereas many of his colleagues would drift into Islamic extremism, he simply seems to have lived for the fight, whatever the costs. He had no qualms about extending the war beyond Chechnya's borders, nor over merging war and terrorism. Meanwhile, the Russians were still slow to respond. They were also deeply divided over tactics and aims and also between institutions and officers. Many within the military, especially veterans of Afghanistan, believed that they should withdraw. Others felt that policies of brutal suppression and ethnic cleansing were needed.

Meanwhile, with no clear sense of direction and no strong political pressure encouraging them to consider Chechen hearts and minds, the Russians too often relied on indiscriminate firepower to solve any problem. In the process, while rebels were dying, others were joining up. In part this was because actions such as Budyonnovsk, Gudermes and Kizlyar were considered victories by some, but it was also in part because often-brutal Russian tactics helped galvanize resistance. In a country where avenging fallen family members and slights to one's kin is still a strong part of national culture, the Russians were virtually Dudayev's recruiting sergeants.

Dudayev himself, though, was hardly much of an asset to the rebel cause. He issued stirring pronouncements from time to time, but was neither a battlefield tactician, nor a negotiator able to use the sporadic and often half-hearted negotiations with the Russians to reach any kind of a deal. The 'peace plan' he proposed to Yeltsin, for example, demanded that he arrest the current and former commanders of the OGV, sack his prime minister and key security ministers and purge his parliament! Arguably

Dudayev's greatest and last gift to the Chechen cause took place on 21 April 1996, when he put a satellite phone call through to a liberal parliamentarian in Moscow and was killed by Russian homing missiles for his pains. His death meant that formal power devolved to his vice-president, Zelimkhan Yandarbiyev. However, this poet and children's author wielded relatively little real authority among members of the rebel movement, who instead looked to Aslan Maskhadov for leadership. He, in turn, knew that the Chechens were unlikely to win a war of attrition with the vastly more numerous Russians, especially as the latter were beginning to adapt to the circumstances of this war. Already, the new forces Moscow had deployed were beginning to make their weight known on the battlefield.

Instead, like all great guerrilla commanders, Maskhadov knew that his struggle was essentially political. Budyonnovsk had brought the Russians to negotiations, even if ultimately that chance had been squandered. He needed an equivalent, or even greater, 'spectacular' to convince Moscow to come to terms, and not an act of terror but something to demonstrate that the Chechens could also win on the battlefield. His gaze turned to Grozny.

THE SECOND BATTLE FOR GROZNY

On 1 January 1996, Lieutenant-General Vyacheslav Tikhomirov had been appointed head of the OGV. Tikhomirov was a career armed forces officer, unlike his two predecessors, Kulikov (who became Interior Minister after Yerin) and Lieutenant-General Anatoly Shkirko (another MVD VV veteran). With his arrival, the Russian forces stepped up their efforts to win on the battlefield, but in the main all that happened was that offensives would take ground, only to lose it once the tempo slackened. With Dudayev's death in April, Maskhadov was eager to seize the military and thus political initiative. Yandarbiyev's representatives and Moscow's continued arm's-length, on-again off-again talks about talks, which led to sporadic ceasefires but no real prospect of true agreement. Indeed, Yandarbiyev could not even claim to be speaking for the whole rebel movement, as Basayev said he should be deposed for talking to the Russians.

At the same time Maskhadov, who was taking an active role in peace talks being held in Nazran in Ingushetia, was also working on a fall-back option, assembling a coalition of warlords willing to take part in a daring strike. Meanwhile, the tempo of guerrilla attacks slackened somewhat, allowing the Russians to begin to think they were winning. This also allowed Moscow to make a point of doing something it had been promising to do: bring forces home. A conscript army is inevitably subject to regular rotations of units and men, and as units were withdrawn from Chechnya, they were not matched by new elements being deployed. At the end of May, Yeltsin visited Grozny – under very tight security – and told assembled soldiers from the 205th Motor Rifle Brigade, 'The war is over, you have won.' Reflecting this upbeat mood, by then federal forces had been allowed to shrink from their peak of 55,000 personnel to just over 41,000: 19,000 armed forces and 22,000 MVD VV, OMON and other security elements. Further reductions, especially to the armed forces contingent, were to follow: the aim was that eventually no more than one MVD VV brigade and the 205th Motor Rifle Brigade were to be left by the end of the year.

By July, the Russians had decided to escalate their operations in the south, hoping to force the rebels into accepting their terms. As they focused their forces to seize such remaining rebel strongholds as the village of Alkhan-Yurt, they pulled forces out of Grozny, including not just MVD VV garrisons but also police officers of the pro-Moscow regime. Anticipating this, though, Maskhadov had assembled forces in a daring counter-strike on Grozny itself,

Russian artillery bombardments in Chechnya were some of the heaviest the world had seen since World War II. Here a Soviet artilleryman places an artillery shell on the auto-loader of what appears to be a 152.4mm 2S19 Msta-S. (TASS via Getty Images)

timed to overshadow the inauguration of Boris Yeltsin, who had just been re-elected to the Russian presidency in a poll widely regarded as rigged.

On the morning of 6 August – the very day federal forces were launching their assault on Alkhan-Yurt – some 1,500 rebels from a number of units were quietly infiltrating Grozny in 25-man units. Although the defenders had established a network of checkpoints and guard stations, their reluctance to venture out at night, as well as their reduced numbers, meant that it was relatively easy for the rebels to move into their city. At 0550hrs, they struck, attacking a wide range of strategic targets including the municipal building, Khankala air base, Grozny airport and the headquarters of the police and the FSB, as well as closing key transport arteries. They placed mines in some garrisons and set up firing stations to command the routes along which federal forces could sally.

Within three hours, most of the city was in Chechen hands, or at least out of meaningful federal control. Although Russian forces and their Chechen allies (who had a particular fear of being captured) were holding out in the centre, around the republican MVD and FSB buildings and also at Khankala, the speed and daring of the attack led to disarray and downright panic among the numerically superior defenders. There had been some 7,000 armed forces and MVD VV personnel in Grozny, but most fled or simply hunkered down in their garrisons. The rebels did execute some collaborators and also in several cases refused to take prisoners.

The rebels' numbers only grew as news of this daring attack spread. Some pro-Moscow Chechens switched sides, some city residents took up arms and further reinforcements arrived from across Chechnya. Desperate to regain the city, the Russians did not wait to gather their forces but instead threw them into the city piecemeal as soon as they became available, allowing Maskhadov to defeat them in detail. On 7 August, a reinforced battalion from the 205th Motor Rifle Brigade was beaten back and another armoured column was ambushed and shattered the next day. On 11 August, a battalion from the 276th Motor Rifle Regiment managed to make it through to the defenders at the centre of the city, delivering some supplies and evacuating a few of the wounded, but they failed to make a real breakthrough.

After another week of desultory clashes, the city remained largely in rebel hands. Their numbers had grown to some 6,000 fighters, while around 3,000–4,000 federals were still trapped behind their lines. Lieutenant-General Konstantin Pulikovsky, acting commander of the OGV while Tikhomirov was on a singularly ill-timed holiday, lost his patience and on 19 August issued an ultimatum demanding that the rebels surrender Grozny within 48 hours or an all-out assault would be launched. Even before that ultimatum had expired, on the next day air and artillery bombardments began and the flow of refugees out of the city increased dramatically. By 21 August, an estimated 220,000 people had fled Grozny, leaving no more than 70,000 civilians in a city which before the war had been home to 400,000. However, the ability of the Chechen rebels, long described as a defeated and dwindling force, to retake Grozny had a dramatic impact on Russian politics.

Even while Pulikovsky was gathering forces for a massive bombardment of Grozny that would have led to casualties among federal forces, civilians and rebels alike, opinion against the war in Moscow was hardening. Although a number of politicians had long expressed their doubts, the crucial constituency was that of disgruntled armed forces officers, especially veterans of Afghanistan, who saw Chechnya as an equally unwinnable and pointless war.

Such figures as General Boris Gromov (former last commander of the Fortieth Army in Afghanistan) had long been calling for a withdrawal. However, the prospect of massive friendly fire and civilian casualties in Grozny galvanized the highest-profile member of this camp, Security Council

A Russian Army T-72 passes by a destroyed house during fighting in the Chechen stronghold of Bamut, May 1996. The tank is covered liberally with explosive reactive armour (ERA) plates, which partly counteract the detonation of an incoming RPG or AT missile. (Alexander Nemenov/AFP/Getty Images)

Secretary (and Soviet–Afghan War veteran) Alexander Lebed. A blunt, even tactless man nevertheless idolized by the VDV troops who served with him, Lebed was decorated for his service in Afghanistan and had refused to back communist hard-liners during the 1991 August Coup when they ordered him to deploy his 106th Airborne Division against Yeltsin's supporters. In the June presidential elections, he had come third with 14.5 per cent of the vote, but then threw his weight behind Yeltsin in the run-off poll, in return being appointed to the politically pivotal role of Secretary of the Security Council and Yeltsin's national security adviser. If Yeltsin had thought this would tame the outspoken Lebed, he was wrong, but by the same token Yeltsin was clearly in poor physical health and was worried that the Communist Party might be able to make a renewed bid for power. He was eager, too, to extricate himself from a war that seemed now to have no end.

On 20 August, Lebed returned to Chechnya and ordered federal forces around Chechnya and in the south alike to stand down and observe a ceasefire. Thanks to the assistance of the OSCE, he opened direct talks with Maskhadov and on 30 August they concluded the Khasav-Yurt Accord. This shelved the question of Chechnya's constitutional status but instead recognized Chechen autonomy and promised a full withdrawal of all federal forces by 31 December. Further treaties would follow, which would formalize Maskhadov's willingness to cede claims of outright independence for an end to the fighting and an unprecedented level of autonomy within the Russian Federation. In effect, so long as Chechnya pretended to be part of Russia, Moscow would not try to assert any actual control over it. The First Chechen War was over.

RUSSIAN FORCES

It is difficult to argue that the First Chechen War was anything other than a defeat for Russia: a nation with a population of 147 million was forced to recognize the effective autonomy of Chechnya, a country one-hundredth its size and with less than one-hundredth of its people. A mix of brilliant guerrilla warfare and ruthless terrorism was able to humble Russia's decaying remnants of the Soviet war machine. Just as in wars past, this would be an asymmetric conflict from the first – although the Russians would eventually learn a hard-fought lesson, that the best way to fight a Chechen is with another Chechen. In the main, though, the two Russo-Chechen wars saw a conventional military machine and a nimble local insurgent movement each seeking to force the other to fight on their terms.

Moscow certainly had all the advantages on paper. At the time of their first invasion, at the end of 1994, the Russian Armed Forces officially numbered more than two million. However, this was a war machine whose gears were rusty, whose levers were broken and whose fuel was sorely lacking. It was really just an exhausted fragment of the old Soviet Armed Forces, unreformed and largely unfunded.

The bulk of federal forces in the Joint Group of Forces (OGV), especially in the First Chechen War, were standard motor rifle infantry, mechanized infantry in Western parlance. They moved in trucks sometimes, but otherwise BTR-70 and BTR-80 APCs or BMP-2 infantry combat vehicles, and their units were leavened with T-72 or T-80 tanks. Already rather dated, these tanks were poorly suited for operations in cities and highlands, especially as the reactive armour that might have helped defeat the simple, shoulder-fired anti-tank weapons wielded by the Chechens was available but generally not fitted.

Units would cycle in and out of the OGV over the course of the conflicts, but for most of the time they comprised conscripts from the units of the North Caucasus Military District , serving two-year terms, whose training – like their equipment – was still essentially based on Soviet patterns. As such, they were geared towards fighting mechanized mass wars on the plains of Europe or China. The painfully won lessons of Afghanistan had often

A Spetsnaz soldier searches for mines in Grozny on 18 May 1995, while another soldier covers him with his PKM machine gun. (Alexander Nemenov/AFP/Getty Images)

been deliberately forgotten or ignored by a high command that thought it would never again be fighting a similar war. Likewise, the last specialized urban-warfare unit in the Russian military had actually been disbanded in February 1994. Furthermore, units were often cobbled together from elements drawn from other parent structures, without having had time to train together and cohere. As a result, the Russian infantry was largely unprepared for the kind of scrappy yet often high-intensity fighting it would face in Chechnya, lacked effective low-level command and initiative and was often forced to improvise or fall back on raw firepower to make up for other lacks, a factor that contributed to civilian casualties and the federal military's poor reputation with the civilian population.

All that being said, the federal forces should not be considered entirely or uniformly degraded. Some of the units deployed were of distinctly higher calibre, especially the Spetsnaz commandos and the VDV airborne troops, as well as particular elements of the Russian Armed Forces and the MVD VV (Ministry of Internal Affairs Interior Troops). Indeed, once the qualitative weaknesses of the federal armed forces became clear, there was something of a scrabble to find better-trained and better-motivated forces to deploy there, including Naval Infantry marines and OMON (Special Purpose Mobile Unit) police riot troops (who were at least professionals, and who were well prepared for urban operations).

Much of the equipment with which the Russians fought had serious limitations or was ill suited to this conflict. Nevertheless, there were also elements of the Russian arsenal which certainly carried their weight. The Mi-24 Hind helicopter gunship, while a design dating back to the late 1960s, nonetheless would demonstrate its value in scouring the Chechen lowlands and hillsides alike, just as it had in Afghanistan. By the same token, the Su-25 Frogfoot ground-attack aircraft proved a powerful weapon in blasting city blocks with rockets and bombs, even though ten were lost through the two wars to enemy fire and mechanical problems. However, much of the key fighting was against snipers and ambushers, and weapons able to bring overwhelming firepower rapidly to bear in these conditions were often crucial. For example, the man-portable RPO-A Shmel incendiary-rocket launcher was often called 'pocket artillery' for its ability to blast a target with a thermobaric explosion equivalent to a 152mm artillery round.

Beyond this, the Russians learned and improvised. When it became clear that their APCs were all too vulnerable to Chechen rocket-propelled grenades, they began welding cages of wire mesh around them to help defeat the enemy's shaped charges. Likewise, the ZSU-23-4 and 5K22 Tunguska self-propelled air-defence vehicles, armed with quad 23mm and double 30mm rapid-fire cannon respectively, were pressed into service as gun trucks; they could elevate their weapons high enough to sweep a hilltop or building roof and lay down withering fire. The acute lack of decent maps of Chechnya, a serious problem in the early days of the invasion, was partly remedied by scouring the closed-down bookshops of Grozny.

CHECHEN FORCES

Although the Chechen Republic of Ichkeria (ChRI) formally had its own security structures, they did not last long once the war began and the fight was soon in the hands of more irregular units, even if at times they were able to display unusually high levels of discipline and co-ordination. When the Russians invaded in 1994, they faced a Chechen Army, a National Guard and the Ministry of Internal Affairs (Russian bombers had essentially destroyed the Chechen Air Force on the ground on the eve of invasion). These forces were at the same time more and less formidable than they seemed.

The sense in which they were less formidable was that many of the units were far smaller than their titles suggested. The army, for example, fielded a 'motor rifle brigade' that was actually little more than a company, with some 200 soldiers; the Shali Tank Regiment (some 200 men, with 15 combat-capable tanks, largely T-72s); the 'Commando Brigade' (a light motorized force of 300 men); and an artillery regiment (200 men, with around 30 light and medium artillery pieces). To these 900 or so troops could be added the 'Ministry of Internal Affairs Regiment', another light motorized force of 200 men. However, about two-thirds of the ChRI's field strength of 3,000 had been drawn from the so-called National Guard. This was a random collection of units, ranging from the gunmen of certain clans through to the personal retinues of particularly charismatic leaders as well as Dzhokhar Dudayev's own guard. These had such picturesque names as the 'Abkhaz Battalion' and the 'Muslim Hunter Regiment', few of which truly reflected their real size or role.

However, this ramshackle assemblage of forces did have several significant advantages. They knew the country well and while they were no longer quite the hardy outdoorsmen of the nineteenth century, having adapted to the age of the car, central heating and college, their traditions did grant them a certain *esprit de corps*. They also knew their enemy, most having served their time in the Soviet or Russian military. Indeed, given the martial reputation and enthusiasm of the Chechens, a disproportionate number had served in the VDV or Spetsnaz, experience which would serve them well in the coming wars. In age, they spanned the full range from adolescents to pensioners, although the typical fighter was in his mid to late twenties.

While some units still retained a more formal structure modelled on the Russian forces, in the main they fought in units of around 25 men broken into three or four squads. They were largely armed only with light personal and support weapons, especially AK-74 rifles, RPG-7 anti-tank grenade launchers, disposable RPG-18 rocket launchers, SVD sniper rifles, grenades and machine guns. However, thanks to their martial tradition, as well as the preceding years of rampant criminality which had seen guns smuggled into the country and state arsenals opened, they had plenty of those, not least the ammunition and spares the lack of which is often the guerrilla's bane.

Besides which, their numbers would quickly be swollen by volunteers from across the country, from the Chechen diaspora elsewhere in Russia and, eventually and ultimately counterproductively, from Islamist militants from the Middle East. This would be an 'army' of warlords and their followings, even if during the First Chechen War and the early years of the Second there was still some sense of a command structure, largely anchored around the person of Aslan Maskhadov, the Chief of Staff of the Chechen military and later their elected president. Even so, this was a force whose size fluctuated by the season and the day, not least as individuals might take up arms for a particular operation and then return to their civilian activities until the next.

Above all, they were characterized by a fierce determination and excellent tactics. These were often unconventional, but rooted in an understanding of how their enemies operated. Knowing the Russian propensity for the artillery barrage, for example, in urban warfare they 'hugged' Russian units, keeping within a city block or so of them so that the Chechen forces were safe from bombardments. Likewise, the Chechens were well aware that the guns of Russian tanks could not depress enough to engage basement positions, in which they built makeshift bunkers from which to attack Russian advances. Finally, they drew on their strengths, from sticking to using the Chechen language Nokhchy for their communications, knowing the Russians could intercept their radio traffic but not generally understand it, to drawing the federal forces into traps and ambushes in the cities and mountains that they knew so much better.

THE 'HOT PEACE' (1996–99)

For the Grozny operation, Maskhadov had had to assemble a coalition of warlords, commanding some, haggling and negotiating with the rest, including Akhmad Zakayev, Doku Umarov and Ruslan Gelayev. This was a warning sign, that Chechen politics had already become fractured among rival leaders, clans, factions and platforms. Maskhadov would discover that navigating Chechen politics would prove every bit as difficult, as well as dangerous, as fighting the war. In October, President Zelimkhan Yandarbiyev formally appointed him prime minister of the ChRI and in January 1997 Maskhadov was elected president in a landslide victory, winning over 59 per cent of the vote. Radical warlord Shamil Basayev came second with 23.5 per cent, Yandarbiyev received only 10 per cent and none of the other 17 candidates could top even 1 per cent. Translating this vote of confidence into real power, though, was the challenge.

In May 1997, Maskhadov travelled to Moscow, signing the final peace accord with Yeltsin. But peace did not mean amity, and not only would there be those in both Russia and Chechnya who wanted to resume hostilities, the

Two disabled T-72 tanks in Chechnya, 1995. Although the Russian Army could easily outclass the Chechens in terms of armoured resources, heavy armour actually had limited applications in the main urban and highlands battle zones. (TASS / Vladimir Shneerson/via Getty Images)

challenge of rebuilding this shattered country was formidable. Moscow was not willing to pay reparations and the cost of reconstruction was estimated at $300 million. Unemployment reached 80 per cent and pensions and similar benefits simply were not being paid.

Maskhadov did what he could, but that often was not very much. He could not disarm the warlords, so instead he brought them into the ChRI's military structure, granting them ranks and official status in the hope that it would tame them. In the main, it did not. Some became virtual local dictators and bandit chieftains. The economy was still disastrous and people were disillusioned with peace. In July 1998, after the fourth assassination attempt on Maskhadov, he declared a state of emergency, but his capacity to crack down on the estimated 300 separate armed groups numbering a total of around 8,500 men in the country was limited, not least because any that he targeted could turn to the jihadists for support. He then tried to reconcile the increasingly powerful jihadists by going against his own secular tendencies and introducing sharia law, but they were not willing to compromise. Instead, this simply led to splits within the Chechen government and an increasing sense of disillusionment among Maskhadov's core supporters.

All that was needed was a spark, and Saudi-born al-Qaeda field commander Emir Khattab and rebel commander Shamil Basayev were determined to provide one. Neighbouring Dagestan had been experiencing its own rise in anti-Russian and jihadist violence. In April, Bagauddin Magomedov, self-proclaimed 'Emir of the Islamic Jamaat [Movement] of Dagestan', and an ally of Khattab, had appealed for a 'free Dagestan'. On 7 August 1999, Khattab and Basayev led a mixed force of some 1,500 Chechen, Dagestani and Arab fighters across the border, proclaimed the 'Islamic State of Dagestan' and began advancing on Botlikh, the nearest town.

Federal forces were characteristically slow in responding, but – just like those federal forces when they invaded Chechnya – Khattab and Basayev's 'International Islamic Peacekeeping Brigade' would face a rude awakening. Magomedov had assured them they would be welcomed as liberators, but instead they were met not only by tenacious Dagestani police, but also by spontaneous resistance from ordinary locals. This helped slow the invaders down long enough for the inevitable deluge of Russian firepower. The attack stalled and in the face of combined ground and air attacks, was forced back into Chechnya. A mix of armed forces units, the MVD VV's 102nd Brigade, Dagestani OMON and Russian Spetsnaz demonstrated a

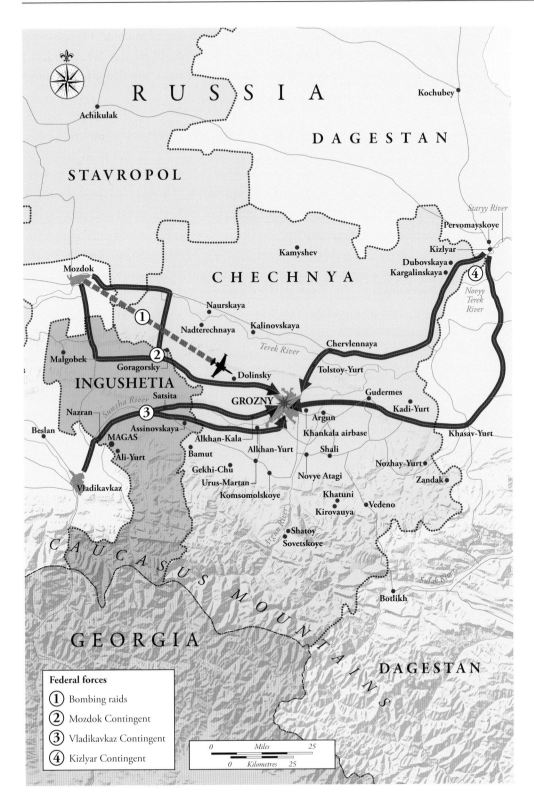

Federal forces
1 Bombing raids
2 Mozdok Contingent
3 Vladikavkaz Contingent
4 Kizlyar Contingent

The First Invasion

level of competence that had rarely been seen in the First Chechen War. On 5 September, a second incursion was launched further north, striking towards Khasav-Yurt, but this too was blocked after an initial surprise advance, then driven back by local and federal forces. The Russians launched cross-border bombing raids first to try to strike the rebels as they withdrew and then to punish the Maskhadov government for letting this happen, as the attacks shifted to Grozny.

Maskhadov had realized the danger of the attacks and condemned them from the first. He announced a crackdown on Khattab and Basayev and pledged to restore discipline over the warlords. It was too little, too late. After all, there were also rising forces in Moscow looking to reassert control over Chechnya.

THE 1990S: POWER PROJECTION

Despite the Chechen disaster, in less widely publicized external operations during the 1990s it should be noted that the army succeeded – largely by relying on elite units and commanders – in simultaneously asserting the Kremlin's agenda and also demonstrating that it still had certain capabilities. Often these operations amounted to tipping the balance in political and inter-ethnic conflicts as violence flared across post-Soviet Eurasia. In Moldova, in a sliver of land on the east bank of the Dniestr River populated largely by ethnic Russian colonists, rebellion broke out against an anti-Moscow regime in 1992. The Russian Fourteenth Army was still based there; while officially neutral, it supported the rebels with artillery barrages and weapon transfers. The outcome was the creation of the unrecognized but *de facto* mini-state of Transnistria – the Pridnestrovian Moldavan Republic (PMR) – which survives to this day, and remains a handy launch pad for Moscow's political influence in the region.

Also in 1992, a civil war erupted in Tajikistan, pitting an authoritarian Soviet-era government against minority ethnic groups and Islamic extremists. Russia's 201st Motor Rifle Division, which had not yet been withdrawn, openly sided with the regime. Over the next five years the 201st, largely recruited locally but led by Russian officers, was often at the forefront of military operations against the rebels. Renamed the 201st Military Base in 2004, it continued to prop up the government in Dushanbe and, by extension, to maintain Moscow's authority in Central Asia.

After Yugoslavia fragmented in 1991–92, Russia played a role within UNPROFOR, the UN Protection Force that sought in 1992–95 to underwrite a tenuous peace in Bosnia-Herzegovina and Croatia. The Russian contingent grew from 900 soldiers when UNPROFOR was formed, to an airborne brigade of 1,500 paratroopers in the Implementation Force (IFOR) and Stabilization Force (SFOR) that replaced the 'blue helmets' in 1996. The largest non-NATO force in these organizations, the Russian contingent played a useful role not just on the ground, but also in making the case that, for all its troubles, Russia should still be considered a serious global player.

When IFOR and SFOR were formed a Russian general was invited to become a Special Deputy to the NATO Supreme Allied Commander, Europe (SACEUR) in order to resolve command and control issues. However, tensions and suspicions remained, and would come to the fore during the 1998–99 Kosovo War. This ethnically Albanian region was then still controlled by the Federal Republic of Yugoslavia, which by that time consisted only of the dominant Serbia and smaller Montenegro. Terrorist attacks by the Kosovo Liberation Army prompted a heavy-handed Serbian response, which in turn provoked a NATO air campaign

Russian troops move through the countryside in Kosovo in their BTR-80. The BTR-80 entered service at the end of the Soviet era, and through numerous upgrades and variants has remained relevant to modern combat conditions. (Tim Ripley/DPL)

against Serbia. Moscow, which had historic ties to Serbia, was unhappy with this from the first, and when, following a peace deal, a multinational Kosovo Force (KFOR) was established under NATO auspices, it insisted on taking part. From the very first day – 11 June 1999 – Russia's determination that NATO should not get everything its own way was demonstrated when 250 Russian paratroopers rushed from their SFOR base in Bosnia to seize Pristina International Airport in Kosovo's capital

Major-General Anatoly Volchkov was the commander of the Russian troops during the confrontation with NATO forces at Pristina Airport in the former Yugoslavia. (Tim Ripley/DPL)

before NATO forces could get there. After a tense stand-off in which KFOR's commander, Britain's Lieutenant-General Mike Jackson, ignored confrontational orders from SACEUR general Wesley Clark (Jackson reportedly declined 'to start World War III for you'), a deal was struck that allowed both sides to stand down. The 'Pristina Dash' heartened a Russian public and military starved of good news. It might also be said to have set the tone for future Russian interventions, relying on élan, surprise, and a willingness to bluff and gamble on the other side's restraint. These were exactly the kinds of characteristics that appealed to the man who, in 1999, had just been appointed prime minister, and was about to become president: Vladimir Putin.

A Russian tank passes a checkpoint on the Gori–Tbilisi road near the village of Khurvaleti on August 22, 2008, towards the South Ossetian capital Tskhinvali. (DIMITAR DILKOFF/ AFP/Getty Images)

CHAPTER 6

VICTORY AND RESURGENCE

I N THE LATE NINETEENTH CENTURY, Tsar Alexander III is famously supposed to have remarked that 'Russia has only two allies: its Army and its Navy.' If that is true, then since its emergence from the dissolution of the Soviet Union at the end of 1991, modern Russia has been singularly exposed. After all, it inherited from the USSR a portion of an army that was not only in serious decline, beset by problems of indiscipline, demoralization, backwardness and decay, but also designed for the kind of war – a full-scale confrontation with NATO – that the new regime could not envisage ever fighting. Meanwhile, Moscow lacked the money, the political will, and even the vision to be able to reform this disintegrating relic.

The result was disastrous, not least, as we have seen, during the First Chechen War, when the army used brutal and heavy-handed tactics that led to massive civilian casualties, yet was still, in effect, defeated by a smaller but more disciplined and imaginative rebel force. The 1990s were a time of chaos and redefinition across Russia, and nowhere more so than within the military. In 1993, in defiance of the constitution, President Boris Yeltsin used the army to shell his unruly parliament in Moscow's 'White House' into submission. Officers who dared to criticize the Kremlin were dismissed; soldiers moonlighted as mafia hitmen; deserters terrorized remote communities; and officers embezzled as much as they could, while forced to live in unheated tank sheds and condemned apartment buildings.

Yet for all that, there were faithful torchbearers within the once-proud military who did not forget the professionalism and discipline of past times, while both the geopolitical challenges facing Russia and its rich martial mythology energized those within the leadership who were eager to see a revival of their country's military strength.

The rise to power of Vladimir Putin at the end of 1999, coinciding with a recovery of the Russian economy, at last permitted the start of

A Russian soldier in the uniform of the late 1980s, as worn in Afghanistan. Since the early 2000s, the Russian soldier has seen a progressive upgrade in many aspects of his equipment and weaponry. (Andrei Ivanov/DPL)

The modern face of the Russian Army – a Spetsnaz soldier pictured during Arctic warfare training. His helmet fittings, equipment and weapon accessories would scarcely look out of place on a US Navy SEAL or British SAS soldier. (Andrei Ivanov/DPL)

a process of long-term re-armament and reform. Since the early 1990s Russia's new army has undergone a turbulent transformation, from the scattered leftovers of a decaying and partitioned Soviet military into the disciplined forces that seized Crimea virtually overnight in 2014. In the space of 25 years they fought two wars in Chechnya, one in Georgia and another in Ukraine. They battled insurgents in Tajikistan and Syria, sheltered rebellious clients in Moldova, and contributed to multi-national peacekeeping operations in the Balkans. Their modernization programmes are still a work in progress, but by 2017 Russia was spending 4.3 per cent of its GDP on the military, making it the fourth-ranking nation in global defence spending behind only the USA, China and Saudi Arabia. This is a process that may yet become stalled by the country's current economic problems linked to the massive fall in world oil prices; nevertheless, for the moment and the foreseeable future, it ensures that Russia is still the pre-eminent Eurasian military power, with the capacity not only to defend the Motherland but also to project the Kremlin's interests well beyond its borders.

THE SECOND CHECHEN WAR (1999–2009)

When Boris Yeltsin stood down as president at the end of 1999, he handed power to his prime minister, Vladimir Putin. An ambitious and fast-rising young KGB veteran, Putin had made a name for himself as a pragmatic fixer, able to protect his friends (and his corrupt predecessor), but also to get things

Russian SOF troops of Alfa Group meet with President Vladimir Putin. The man shaking hands appears to be armed with an AK-103, but with an M4-style collapsible stock plus attachments that include a close-combat optic and an infrared/laser illuminator. (Andrei Ivanov/DPL)

done. Initially as acting president, and then from 2000 as elected president, Putin quickly outlined a programme of measures intended to re-establish both Moscow's control across the Russian Federation and Russia's standing in the world. The armed forces had a crucial role in his vision for the country, as simultaneously the final guarantors of state power, a symbol of Russian revival, and an instrument to ensure regional hegemony.

To this end, Putin's priority was ending the stand-off with Chechnya and wiping the slate clean of the embarrassing defeat in 1996. On 1 October 1999 Putin formally declared that the Chechen government was no longer recognized by Moscow and that federal forces would be deployed to re-establish control over the region. A nationalist and a statist, Putin made no secret of his desire to reverse the weakening of central control under Yeltsin and his determination to make the world recognize Russia as a great power once again. He had enjoyed a meteoric rise thanks to powerful patrons within the system but was relatively unknown to the Russian public; he needed some high-profile triumph, some dramatic opportunity to prove that the Kremlin was now occupied by a determined and powerful leader. Chechnya seemed perfect for this. While Khattab and Basayev were giving him the grounds to tear up the treaty with Grozny with their incursion into Dagestan, he began instructing his generals to prepare for a second war. Contingency plans for an invasion had, after all, started to be developed in

March and for over a year the Russian military has been actively wargaming invasion plans. In July 1998, for example, an exercise across the North Caucasus had seen 15,000 armed forces and MVD troops practise fighting against 'terrorists'.

Putin was determined that this time the Russians would muster adequate forces, prepare properly and plan for a guerrilla war. Furthermore, the Russian public would be readied for the inevitable casualties. In September 1999, a mysterious series of bombs exploded in apartment buildings in Moscow (twice), Buynaksk and Volgodonsk, killing 293 people. Still to this day there is controversy over these bombs. There is certainly a serious body of belief that these were provocations arranged by the Russian security agencies, not least given that a similar bomb was found by chance in Ryazan and connected to the FSB, which then claimed this had been a training drill. Nevertheless, the Kremlin presented this as an escalation of the Chechens' terror campaign and at the time many ordinary Russians were frightened and angry, looking to the government for security and revenge.

The bombing campaign which had followed the Dagestani incursion was expanded steadily, hammering Chechen cities until the flood of refugees into Ingushetia was exceeding 5,000 people a day. Overall, perhaps a quarter of the total remaining Chechen population would flee and while this put great pressure on neighbouring regions to deal with the influx of refugees, drawing on Mao's famous analogy that guerrillas move among

By the early 2000s, Grozny was a wrecked city, littered with ordnance of every type and description. Here is an unexploded 300mm rocket from a multiple launch rocket system (MLRS). (Antoine Gyori/Sygma via Getty Images)

the population like fish in the sea, it also drained much of the 'sea' to allow the Russians to spot the 'fish' that much more easily. 'Filtration camps' were established behind the army lines, to hold and process refugees, identifying suspected rebels for interrogation and detention.

On 1 October, Putin formally declared Maskhadov and the Chechen government illegitimate and reasserted the authority of the Russian Federation over its wayward subject. Meanwhile, federal forces started moving. Instead of the foolhardy direct assault of the first war, the Russian plan was a staged and methodical one. The first stage was as far as possible to seal Chechnya's borders, while forces were assembled. All told, these numbered some 50,000 armed forces troops and a further 40,000 MVD VV and OMON personnel, some three times as many men as had taken part in the 1994 invasion. Overall command went to Colonel-General Viktor Kazantsev, commander of the North Caucasus Military District.

Then, Moscow announced that in the interests of securing the border and establishing a 'cordon sanitaire', units would have to take up positions which 'in a few cases' would be 'up to five kilometres' inside northern Chechnya. Next, saying that the terrain meant that it was impossible to secure this line, it warned that units would advance as far as the Terek River, occupying the northern third of the country. By 5 October, they had taken these new positions. Fighting was at this stage sporadic and localized, in part because Maskhadov was still trying to make peace. Again, the Russians were in no rush. They spent the next week consolidating their forces – and ignoring Maskhadov's overtures – until 12 October, when they crossed the Terek, pushing towards Grozny in three fronts. The Western Group drove through the Nadterechnaya district until it reached the western suburbs of Grozny; the Northern Group pushed down across the Terek at Chervlennaya; while the Eastern Group swung past Gudermes and likewise moved to flank Grozny from the east.

It is important to note that there was a distinct difference between the federal forces that fought in the First Chechen War and those of the Second. (Much of this transformation will be explained in the next chapter, but here we can provide an overview of some of the most significant changes.) By 1999 the military and political leadership had learned many of the lessons of their initial humiliation. They had spent time and money preparing for the rematch and assembled forces that were far more suited to this conflict. Much more, and better, use was made both of special forces and MVD VV units. The latter are essentially light infantry, although some units are

mechanized, with a particular internal-security and public-order role. As a result, they were more prepared for operations in Chechnya, especially those involving mass sweeps of villages hunting for rebels, arms caches and sympathizers. The MVD also disposes of a range of elite forces, from the OMON police units through to its own Spetsnaz units, many of which were rotated through Chechnya. Alongside them were deployed a larger number of other elite security forces, including the Alfa anti-terrorist commando unit of the Federal Security Service (FSB).

More generally, the Second Chechen War also saw a greater use of new weapons and equipment, from body armour and night-vision systems for the soldiers to reconnaissance drones in the skies. However, the main changes were in the preparations made beforehand, a willingness to adapt to Chechen tactics – such as by creating special 'storm detachments' for urban warfare – and a more sophisticated overall strategy. If in the First Chechen War the implicit assumption was that Chechens were all threats to be neutralized, in the Second the Russians adopted a two-pronged approach. On the one hand, they were ruthless in their control of the

The Mi-24 Hind, heavily used in Afghanistan and Chechnya, is still at the forefront of Russia's attack helicopter force. Most recently it has been used in operations over Syria, and on 9 July 2016 the Russian Ministry of Defence reported that a Russian Mil Mi-35M helicopter (an export version) was shot down by ISIS, killing two pilots east of Palmyra. (Andrei Ivanov/DPL)

Chechen population, but on the other, they eagerly recruited Chechens, including rebel defectors, to a range of security units, realizing that such fighters were often best suited to taking the war to the rebels. The Russians, after all, had the firepower, but their Chechen allies could often best guide them as to how and where to apply it.

As they advanced, the federal forces met relatively little resistance, with local settlements' community leaders often protesting their loyalty and claiming that there were no rebels in their areas. These settlements would be searched for weapons and fugitives and then MVD forces would establish guard posts. Where the Russians did come under fire, they would typically fall back and liberally use artillery and air power to clear potential threats and obstacles in their path before continuing. On 15 October, they seized the Tersky Heights, which commanded Grozny from the north-west.

Accepting that no truce was possible, Maskhadov declared martial law and called for a *gazavat* (holy war) against the Russians. Within the next few days, the Russians slowly encircled the city, taking outlying towns and villages such as Goragorsky (one of Shamil Basayev's bases) and Dolinsky.

Batteries of D30 122mm howitzers ready themselves for firing on Chechen targets in 1999. The reliance upon massive artillery fire was intensified in the Second Chechen War, as the Russians hoped to avoid some of the close-quarters casualties of the previous conflict. (ITAR-TASS/Valery Matytsin/via Getty Images)

Meanwhile, Grozny itself came under sporadic but heavy bombardment, including strikes by OTR-21 Tochka short-range ballistic missiles with conventional warheads, one of which hit a marketplace on 21 October, killing more than 140 civilians.

Again in contrast to the first war, the Russians were willing to leave Grozny until they had consolidated their rear. In this, they were also the beneficiaries of the years of in-fighting within Chechnya, which had broken the discipline that had held the rebels together before. Gudermes, for example, fell to the Russians to a large extent because of the defection of the Yamadayevs, the dominant local family of the Benoi *teip* (clan), who had their own private army (known officially as the 2nd ChRI National Guard Battalion). Pragmatists, the Yamadayevs had been very much on the secular, nationalist wing of the rebels. In 1998, they had clashed with the notorious warlord Arbi Barayev and units of the jihadist Sharia Regiment and might have destroyed them, had pressure not been brought to bear to arrange a ceasefire. Squeezed between an increasingly jihadist rebel movement and the approaching federal forces, the Yamadayevs opted to make a deal with the Russians. Their forces would become the basis of the Vostok (East) Battalion, set up by the GRU (Military Intelligence) and commanded first by Dzhabrail Yamadayev and then his brother Sulim. They would not be the only defectors.

Through November and December, the Russians concentrated on taking and holding urban centres, forcing the rebels either to cede them and be forced into the countryside during the bitter North Caucasus winter, or else to stand and fight where they could be battered by federal firepower. The village of Bamut, which had held out for 18 months in the first war, fell on 17 November, bombed and shelled to rubble. Argun fell on 2 December, Urus-Martan on 8 December. In December, the federal forces turned to Shali, the last rebel-held town outside Grozny, which had fallen by the end of the year, although efforts were made by the rebels to retake it and Argun in January.

THE THIRD BATTLE FOR GROZNY

The defenders had had time to fortify Grozny. They dug trenches, laid mines, built fortified positions inside some buildings and booby-trapped others. However, the Russians were also far more prepared for the latest battle for Grozny. Chief of the General Staff General Anatoly Kvashnin, who had been responsible for the initial and disastrous New Year's

Eve attack on Grozny in 1994, was determined to atone for his earlier failure. Beyond a few skirmishes and probing raids, through October, November and much of December, the Russians confined themselves to bombardments using aircraft, Scud and OTR-21 ballistic missiles, artillery and TOS-1 fuel-air explosive rockets. Only some 40,000 civilians were left in the ruins of the city, along with perhaps 2,500 rebels under Aslambek Ismailov. On 5 December, the Russians starting dropping leaflets, urging those remaining to leave by 11 December, while opening up a safe corridor for them. Although many Chechens mistrusted this offer, not least as the Russians checked the documents of those leaving, there was no mistaking that the Russians were preparing for an assault.

They mustered some 5,000 troops for the assault itself: the 506th Motor Rifle Regiment, two MVD VV brigades and in total some 400–500 Spetsnaz, who were particularly used for reconnaissance, sniper and counter-sniper duties. They were backed by extensive artillery elements and OMON (who would be used for rear-area security). In what was a portent of the future, they were also supported by some 2,000 pro-Moscow (or at least anti-rebel) Chechen fighters in a militia commanded by Beslan Gantemirov, a convicted embezzler whom Yeltsin had pardoned in return for his becoming the mayor of Grozny in the new regime. He recruited a force of volunteers, patriots, mercenaries, opportunists and criminals whom the federals trusted little – the MVD only issued them outdated AKM-47s from reserve stocks, which had been phased out of military use in the 1980s – but who nevertheless knew the city and were fierce and flexible, like their ChRI counterparts.

The siege forces started moving in on 12 December, infiltrating reconnaissance elements to draw rebel fire and then hammering the rebels with airstrikes and artillery. By the end of the next day, Khankala air base was back in federal hands. One exploratory push into Minutka Square by the 506th was ambushed, although the new T-90 tank proved much more resistant to RPGs than the old T-80 had, one surviving seven hits. The fighting was fierce: about a quarter of the soldiers of the 506th were killed or wounded, so it was withdrawn and replaced with fresh troops of the 423rd Guards Yampolsky Motor Rifle Regiment. In the main, though, the Russians were content to draw their ring slowly closer. That put the pressure on the Chechens to seek to break out or distract the federal forces with other attacks. This they did, in one case managing to take back the outlying village of Alkhan-Kala south-west of Grozny, but each time they

did so, they took casualties they could not afford and, thanks to the siege of the city, could not replace.

On 15 January, Kazantsev decided the ground had been prepared well enough. Federal forces moved into the city along three axes, facing both tough rebel resistance from the 2,500 or so remaining defenders and also the problems of trying to move through a city not only liberally strewn with mines, traps and unexploded ordnance but also pounded into rubble. This, along with the Russians' new-found caution, kept advances slow. Even so, the rebels were able frequently to infiltrate the Russian lines, lay more mines and stage lightning attacks, in one case managing to kill Major-General Mikhail Malofeyev, commander of the Northern Group, in the assault. Nevertheless, the best they could do was slow the Russian advance. By the end of the month, running low on men and ammunition, the rebel commanders opted to abandon the city, regroup at the village of Alkhan-Kala and make for the highlands in the hope of regrouping and following the same trajectory as in the First Chechen War. Already, though, the new divisiveness of the rebel movement was becoming visible, as Ruslan

A Russian soldier scans for targets from a half-ruined building in Grozny in January 2000. The battles for Grozny gave the Russian Armed Forces a costly laboratory for the art of urban warfare. (Sovfoto/UIG via Getty Images)

A heavy machine-gun emplacement is manned by troops of a Russian Border Guards detachment in the south of Argun Ravine in Chechnya, where some extremely intense fighting occurred during the Second Chechen War. (Sovfoto/UIG via Getty Images)

Gelayev – following a disagreement with the jihadist elements of the rebel command – withdrew his forces from the city, allowing them to slip out in small groups all around the perimeter.

At the end of January, as federal forces continued to grind into the centre of Grozny, the rebels attempted to break out of the city under the cover of a heavy storm. Some tried to bribe their way through Russian lines, others to slip out hidden among groups of refugees, while others tried to use stealth when possible, firepower when not. This would be a disastrous and humiliating flight, as rebels blundered into minefields outside Alkhan-Kala, were scoured by artillery-fired cluster rounds (in some cases bringing Russian fire down onto civilians, too) and were harried by helicopters and Spetsnaz. Of the perhaps 1,500 rebel fighters left in Grozny, some 600 were killed, captured or wounded in the retreat, including Ismailov. The survivors largely scattered, some simply drifting home, most heading south.

Meanwhile, on 6 February the Russians formally declared Grozny 'liberated'. Even so, the city was in ruins and it would take a month for OMON and Gantemirov's militia to mop up a few remaining hold-outs in the city and a year for the bodies from the battle to be found and buried.

Although on 21 February the traditional Defender of the Fatherland Day parade was held in central Grozny, supposedly as a mark of the return of normality, this would be a brutal, vengeful time, as apartments were looted, men accused of being rebels were dragged off to a filtration camp (or simply shot in the street) and stray rebels continued to mount bomb and sniper attacks. The 21,000 civilians remaining of the city's Soviet-era population of 400,000 were often forced to camp out in the ruins, eating whatever they could scavenge.

PUTIN'S WAR: THE PACIFICATION

Grozny was the last major urban centre to fall and the federal forces quickly moved towards consolidating their positions across the country. Even while Grozny was under siege, the Russians had been pushing forwards on two separate fronts. The first was in the south, where armed forces units were trying to break into the southern highland strongholds. The second front was in the rear, where the MVD was establishing not just its own network of strongpoints and garrisons of VV and OMON personnel, but also launching aggressive patrols and search operations to locate rebels, arms caches and safe houses. With the shattering of resistance in Grozny, these other federal forces were well placed to block, intercept, capture or eliminate larger concentrations of rebels.

A Russian military helicopter flies over the Chechen war zone on 21 November 2000 at dusk, the cockpit instruments on night illumination mode. As in Afghanistan, in Chechnya attack helicopters were one of the more successful tools of Russian military muscle. (Scott Peterson/Getty Images)

In April 2000, Colonel-General Gennady Troshev was appointed head of the OGV. Although the Russians were still estimating that there were some 2,000–2,500 rebels, they were satisfied that they were largely scattered around the country and posed relatively little serious challenge to federal control. They were both wrong and right. Wrong in that rebels still could cohere in units numbering several hundred and engage in operations which could cause serious Russian casualties. Right, though, in that these attacks never posed a serious threat to the federal forces' overall grip on the country. For example, one of the last major pitched engagements of the war took place in March, at Komsomolskoye, a village south of Grozny and the home village of warlord Ruslan Gelayev. An OMON unit from Russia's Yaroslavl Region first encountered Gelayev and his men there, as they prepared to break through to the cover of the Argun Gorge. Once their numbers became clear – estimates ranged from 500 to 1,000, but the real figure was closer to the lower end of that scale – the OMON settled for trapping them in the city and calling for support. The OMON were promptly reinforced by an MVD VV regiment and OMON and special police units from Irkutsk, Kursk and Voronezh. After four days of almost constant bombardment, including sorties by Su-25 ground-attack jets and salvoes from TOS-1 220mm multiple rocket launchers firing thermobaric rounds, the federal forces stormed the village. The fighting was fierce and unpredictable, even though a wounded Gelayev managed to slip out of the village, and it took another week and a further bombardment before Komsomolskoye was pacified.

This was one of the bloodiest battles of the war, with the official butcher's bill being 552 Chechens and more than 50 Russians. The village itself was all but levelled; journalist Anna Politkovskaya called it 'a monstrous conglomerate of burnt houses, ruins, and new graves at the cemetery', though she put the blame not just on federal forces but also on Gelayev, wondering 'how could he ever think of taking the war home, to Komsomolskoye, knowing in advance that his own home village would be destroyed?' This was a serious clash, but hardly something to make Putin think twice.

Ambushes continued, sometimes substantial ones in which the Chechens could muster as many as 100 fighters and could inflict distinct losses, but with some 80,000 federal soldiers still present in-country and the Kremlin keeping a much tighter control of the media reporting on the war, nothing generated the kind of public and elite dismay that had been present during the First Chechen War. Furthermore, Putin moved quickly to re-establish the forms of constitutional order so as to give the appearance of normalization. In May, in a half-step forwards, Moscow announced that it was taking over direct rule of Chechnya. This at least ended its previous ambiguous state of being a conflict zone essentially outside the regular laws of the state and was a prelude to establishing a local puppet government. In June 2000, Putin appointed Akhmad Kadyrov as the interim head of the Chechen government. Kadyrov was the most prominent of the former rebels who had defected to Moscow. The Chief Mufti of the ChRI, he was a prominent rebel during the First Chechen War but he was an outspoken critic of the Wahhabist jihadi school and this new generation regarded his moderate Islamic views with equal suspicion. In 1999, he and his son Ramzan broke with the ChRI and joined the federal side, bringing with him Kadyrov's personal militia. This force of Kadyrovtsy ('Kadyrovites') was to expand dramatically, not least as other deserters from the rebel cause flocked to join. After all, Kadyrov still retained considerable moral authority, paid well – and was known to ask no questions as to previous

On the Russian–Chechen border in 1999, a Russian paratrooper scans the landscape through a telescopic sight mounted atop a 12.7×108mm NSV heavy machine gun, which has a 700–800rpm rate of fire. (Konstantin Zavrazhin/Getty Images)

activities. In another attempt to portray the conflict as all but over, or at least no more than a police action now, from 2002 successive OGV commanders came from the MVD VV, not the armed forces.

Assailed not just by federal forces but by Chechen militias such as the Kadyrovtsy, the Yamadayevs' Vostok Battalion, as well as a separate Zapad (West) Battalion recruited by the GRU as a counterweight, the rebels were increasingly pushed onto the defensive and limited to small-scale raids and ambushes. They turned ever more to terrorist tactics and even suicide attacks (never previously a feature of Chechen guerrilla struggles). Controversially, this extended to terrorist attacks against Russian civilians, albeit probably without Maskhadov's approval. In October 2002, for example, some 40 terrorists seized the Dubrovka Theatre in Moscow, taking some 850 hostages. After two days of failed negotiations, a narcotic gas was pumped into the building, which was then stormed by the Alfa counter-terrorist team. The terrorists were killed, but so too were 179 hostages, almost entirely because of adverse reactions to the gas.

Later, in September 2004, another effort was made, when 32 jihadist terrorists seized School Number One in the North Ossetian town of Beslan on the first day of the new school year. Of the 1,100 hostages taken, most were children. On the third day of the ensuing siege, when one of the terrorists' bombs exploded, the building was stormed: 334 hostages died, including 186 children. However, whereas during the First Chechen War the authorities had been willing to compromise, under Putin the Kremlin took a tough line and continued its campaign to pacify Chechnya. If anything, he used it as the reason to intensify his efforts; after Beslan, he said: 'We showed weakness, and weak people are beaten.'

In March 2003, a new Chechen constitution was ratified by referendum, explicitly declaring the republic part of the Russian Federation, with Akhmad Kadyrov being formally sworn in as Chechen president later that year. While the rebels were down, they were not yet out, though. Attacks continued, most strikingly on 9 May 2004. Akhmad Kadyrov was receiving the salute at Grozny's Dinamo stadium during the annual Victory Day parade when a bomb exploded, killing him along with a dozen others.

Although his son Ramzan, who commanded the Kadyrovtsy, was too young formally to succeed him as president – Interior Minister Alu Alkhanov was sworn in as a stopgap replacement – in effect he took over his father's role. In keeping with the rich Chechen tradition of the feud, he also redoubled his efforts to wipe out the remnants of the rebel movement. As it was, though, the rebel movement was already a shadow of its former self. Their leaders killed one by one, the rebel movement shrank and radicalized, with more and more nationalist guerrillas simply drifting quietly home when their hopes of a free Chechnya receded and their leaders increasingly seemed more interested in a greater holy war. Federal forces in-country were reduced to the newly formed 42nd Motor Rifle Division and MVD VV assets, but along with the Kadyrovtsy these were more than enough for the task. Meanwhile, the real focus of insurgency shifted to new conflicts elsewhere in the North Caucasus. Ingushetians, Dagestanis, Kabardins and other local peoples began challenging Moscow's rule and corrupt and ineffectual local governments.

THE END OF THE WAR

The Second Chechen War ended with a whimper rather than a bang. By March 2007, when Ramzan Kadyrov finally succeeded his father as Chechen president, large-scale combat operations had long since ended. Khattab, who had survived being blown up by a landmine and shot in the stomach with a heavy machine gun, had died in March 2002 when an FSB undercover agent passed him a letter that was steeped in poison. In February 2004 Yandarbiyev died in exile in Qatar, when a bomb blew up his car. The men convicted of his killing were eventually extradited to Russia – where they received a hero's welcome, apparently being GRU agents.

In March 2005 Maskhadov, long since by then a general with no army, was killed by federal forces in Tolstoy-Yurt. Shamil Basayev was killed by a Russian booby-trap in July 2006. Doku Umarov, who took up the poisoned chalice of titular head of the resistance movement in 2006, proved a lacklustre figure whose talents beyond staying alive were limited. In 2007, he declared the formation of the Imarat Kavkaz (Caucasus Emirate), aiming to unite the nationalist and jihadist movements of the North Caucasus into a single common movement, but this never amounted to much on the ground. In 2014, even his capacity to survive was exhausted and he died in circumstances still unclear, but probably from an earlier wound.

The rebel movement was increasingly dispersed, demoralized and divided. The Chechen population was exhausted by years of brutal war and draconian security measures. Ramzan Kadyrov's government, buttressed by his personal force of Kadyrovtsy, seemed to have the situation in hand. Thus, on 16 April 2009, the National Anti-Terrorism Committee of the Russian government issued a statement that the decree 'declaring a counterterrorist operation in the territory of the [Chechen] republic' was being repealed, so as to create 'the conditions for the future normalization of the situation in the republic, its reconstruction and development of its socio-economic sphere'. Through this banal press release, the Russian government in effect declared victory.

Russian forces in Chechnya had been reduced to around 10,000 soldiers, in the MVD VV's 46th Independent Special Designation Brigade and the armed forces' 42nd Motor Rifle Brigade. They were supported by the MVD VV's 34th Special Designation Detachment, a small counterterrorist commando unit, as well as the MVD VV's 352nd Independent Reconnaissance Battalion and the MVD VV's 140th Artillery Regiment. The bulk of forces within Chechnya were Chechen MVD forces, built on the basis of the Kadyrovtsy: the 141st Akhmad Kadyrov Special Purpose Police Regiment in Grozny, the 249th Independent Special Motorized VV Battalion Yug (South) in Vedeno (formerly known as Neftepolk, the 'Oil Regiment'), the 424th Independent Special Designation Brigade and 359th Independent Special Police Motorized Battalion in Grozny and the 360th (Shelkovskaya), 743rd (Vedeno) and 744th (Nozhay-Yurt) Independent VV Battalions. While these technically were from the first subordinated to the North Caucasus VV District headquarters in Rostov-on-Don in southern Russia (now the North Caucasus District of the National Guard), in practice it is widely acknowledged that their primary loyalty was and has always been to Grozny and Kadyrov. By contrast, the rebels were down to no more than a few hundred fighters, largely stranded in the highlands, with perhaps 500 trying to integrate back into civilian life, whether back with their families or hidden amid the population of displaced persons. In theory, they could be considered sleepers, ready to return to the fray when the time was right, but in practice most appear to be hoping or determined to turn their backs on the fight.

The wars, however, had a serious impact on the rest of Russia. The official casualty figures for the first war were 5,500 federal police and soldiers dead, with a further 5,200 for the second, although these tallies have been questioned, not least as they may omit those dying of their wounds later in hospital. Beyond these figures, though, are the many less seriously wounded or those traumatized by what was an especially vicious and disturbing conflict, which saw atrocities committed by both sides. Beyond that, even though the public was more supportive of the Second Chechen War, a fear

of ending up being sent to Chechnya during either conflict was one of the factors behind massive levels of draft-dodging. In 2000 alone, following the invasion, it rose by 50 per cent. The wars also contributed to the rise of movements such as the Committee of Soldiers' Mothers, which campaigned to force the Kremlin to address issues of indiscipline, *dedovshchina* and the poor treatment of draftees, often with only limited success.

Indeed, the wars had a significant impact on the military as a whole. The First Chechen War in particular was a disaster in almost every respect. Looting, rape, murder and rampant crime were a constant factor (rebels would often re-arm themselves simply by buying guns from soldiers desperate for some food or drink). Morale hit its absolute nadir: some 540 NCOs and officers – including at least a dozen generals – resigned rather than serve in the war, or on receiving especially objectionable orders. Lieutenant-General Rokhlin, one of the few commanders to come out of the first battle of Grozny with any credit, refused the Hero of Russia medal – Russia's highest military honour – saying that he saw nothing glorious in fighting a war on his native soil. Although the Second Chechen War was less catastrophic, and allowed some units, especially the MVD VV and the

A Russian Army Mi-26 helicopter takes off over a destroyed jet on 29 March 1995, from Khankala airfield on the eastern outskirts of Grozny. The Mi-26 can carry up to 90 troops or 20 tonnes of cargo. In August 2002, Chechen separatists shot down an overloaded Mi-26 with a SAM missile; the unfortunate helicopter crash-landed in a minefield and all 127 people on board were killed. (Alexander Nemenov/AFP/Getty Images)

VDV, the chance to build up some combat experience among their cadres of professional soldiers, it could not be said to have been a great boon, either. There is little public enthusiasm or sympathy for the veterans and the lacklustre performance of the Russian Armed Forces in the three-day war with Georgia in 2008 overshadowed the Russians' ability to beat the Chechens the second time round.

The conflicts also became something of a testing ground for the new Russian media. There were courageous journalists who risked their lives – and lost them – reporting on the realities on the ground. Anna Politkovskaya, an unflinching observer of the horrors meted out by both sides, was murdered in Moscow in 2006, in a killing widely believed to be because of her stand on Chechnya. On the other hand, an awareness of the extent to which critical media coverage undermined public support for the First Chechen War meant that Putin made great efforts to control the story during the Second, putting further limitations on media already under considerable state pressure. After all, there was one clear beneficiary.

In 1904, Russian Interior Minister Vyacheslav von Plehve had advocated hostilities with Japan because 'a nice, victorious little war' was, he felt, just what Russia needed to regain its cohesion and self-esteem. Disaster in the Russo-Japanese War brought Tsarist Russia the 1905 Revolution, international contempt and bankruptcy. However, victory in the Second Chechen War was the making of Vladimir Putin, a perfect opportunity for a still-unknown figure to construct his image as the tough-talking and decisive defender of Russian national interests. From his early visits to the North Caucasus to be seen with the troops, to his street-slang references to the Chechens (in 1999 he memorably warned that 'if we catch them on the toilet, we'll whack them in the outhouse'), he used it masterfully to his political advantage. It may have led to widespread international condemnation, but domestically it allowed him to show a strong hand.

One price of this, though, was a string of terrorist attacks in Russia. Mass attacks such as Dubrovka (2002) and Beslan (2004) have increasingly given way to bombings, suicide or otherwise. The most serious of these were bombings in Stavropol (2003), on the Moscow metro (2004) and two passenger airliners (2004), in the Moscow metro again (2010), at Domodedovo airport (2011) and on the St Petersburg metro (2017). Although these have not yet shaken Russia's resolve – if anything they have simply heightened traditional xenophobia towards people from the North Caucasus – they do reflect a continuing threat.

THE 2000s: FURTHER REFORMS

The Second Chechen War was a political victory for Putin, and it did help restore some of the credibility of the Russian military, but it hardly demonstrated any great progress. Success had been due to Moscow's avoidance of the more serious blunders of the first war; to its Soviet-style willingness to throw massive force into the operation, unleashing devastating firepower regardless of civilian casualties; and also to its 'Chechenization' of the conflict, relying on ex-guerrillas to take the battle into the hills. However, Putin was still determined to reform the Russian Army, and to this end in 2001 he appointed his close ally Sergei Ivanov as Defence Minister. Touted as 'Russia's first civilian defence minister', Ivanov was actually a fellow veteran of the KGB (as many of Russia's senior central and regional government figures would also be, by 2004). Ivanov was committed to trying to modernize the army, but in practice he found himself increasingly stymied by the scale of the challenge after years of neglect and mismanagement, as well as by the conservatism of a high command that feared change. Nonetheless, he did manage to make some progress, especially in terms of increasing the proportion of volunteers within the ranks and of shortening the draft. In 2007 the national service term was reduced from 24 to 18 months, and then to 12 months in 2008. This was unpopular with many generals, who complained – not without reason – that it meant that conscripts were properly trained and able to be deployed for only about three months of their service. However, it was politically popular, and reflected a desire to rely in due course on so-called *kontraktniki*, volunteers serving on longer-term contracts, rather than on draftees.

One problem was that the former political policeman Ivanov not only had limited military knowledge and authority of his own, he was also overburdened – as a deputy prime minister from 2005 – with additional responsibility for the defence industries. Most important, it became clear that meaningful reform would take two things: vast amounts of money, and some means of forcing the recalcitrant High Command to commit to the programme. Ivanov was granted some increased budgets, but most were wasted in the absence of any clear blueprint for change. In 2007, he was promoted to the position of First Deputy Prime Minister and relinquished the defence portfolio. His successor, the former head of the tax service (and former furniture salesman) Anatoly Serdyukov, proved to be the unexpectedly successful figure who would finally bring reform to the Russian Army.

2008: GEORGIAN TURNING-POINT

The Russian forces' invasion of Georgia to teach the defiant President Saakashvili's regime a lesson proved to be a crucial turning point in military reform. The Russians won, as they inevitably would – but they did so much less smoothly and efficiently than they had anticipated, and not without a range of problems coming to light. For example, abandoned airfields were bombed because of faulty intelligence; friendly fire claimed many lives; and communications breakdowns forced officers to pass on their orders by civilian cellphone. This all provided the new Defence Minister Serdyukov and Chief of the General Staff General Nikolai Makarov with ammunition to force the conservative High Command to accept serious reforms.

The small independent country of Georgia had long been an irritant to Moscow, which considered it as a natural part of its sphere of influence. The election of the American-educated Mikheil Saakashvili as president in 2004, and his subsequent efforts to forge closer links with the West in general and NATO in particular, made Putin determined not only to demonstrate to Georgia that – like it or not – it was part of Russia's sphere, but also to use it as an example to larger neighbouring states that might also be thinking independent thoughts.

Under Saakashvili, Georgia's forces were not only modernized but looked above all to the USA for support and training. Georgia expanded its commitment to the US-led coalition in Iraq, and in 2006 publicly expelled four Russians whom it claimed were working for the GRU. Relations steadily worsened – by 2007 there were unconfirmed accounts of a Russian aircraft downed by Georgian air defences; but Moscow wanted to ensure that when it did strike against Georgia it had a solid pretext. For this it looked to South Ossetia and Abkhazia, two rebellious regions of Georgia that had been virtually autonomous since 1992.

A Russian paratrooper, his elite status indicated by his *telnyashka* t-shirt, pictured with a Dragunov sniper rifle during the incursion into Georgia in 2008. The Dragunov has an effective range of more than 600m. (Yves Debay/DPL)

South Ossetia was especially useful for Moscow. It shared ethnic ties with the neighbouring Russian region of North Ossetia; it could be reinforced via the Roki Tunnel cut through the Greater Caucasus range; and its leadership under Eduard Kokoity was fiercely anti-Georgian. Like Abkhazia, South Ossetia was protected by Russian 'peacekeepers', and a failed attempt by Georgian forces to regain the region in 2004 had left a legacy of bitterness and mutual suspicion on which Moscow could capitalize. At its summit in Bucharest in April 2008, NATO held back from offering Georgia a full Membership Action Plan despite the lobbying of US President George W. Bush, but closer relations seemed inevitable. This angered the Russians, and the then-Chief of the General Staff, Yuri Baluyevsky, warned that Moscow would 'take steps' to prevent Georgia or other post-Soviet states from joining the Western alliance.

At that stage Vladimir Putin handed over the presidency to his prime minister, Dmitry Medvedev, as the constitution banned a president from serving three consecutive terms in office. However, no one had any doubt that, even though now technically just Medvedev's prime minister, Putin

Russian paratroopers move into Georgia atop the hull of an infantry fighting vehicle. Although the Georgia incursion was a Russian victory, on the level of individual combat the Georgian soldiers were an equal match for the Russians. (Yves Debay/DPL)

was still quite literally calling the shots, and the Georgian policy he had begun moved towards its endgame. South Ossetian irregulars, egged on and armed by Moscow, began attacking Georgian civilians and government forces across the disputed border. In some cases, Georgians fired back, and on 1 August 2008, South Ossetians began shelling Georgian villages in defiance of a 1992 ceasefire agreement. Their aim was evidently to provoke the notoriously hot-headed Saakashvili into some kind of action that the Russians could use as a pretext. The next week saw claim and counter-claim, ceasefire and ambush, until on 7 August Georgian forces began bombarding the South Ossetian capital of Tskhinvali. Early the next morning the Georgian 3rd and 4th Brigades moved across the border, advancing on the city. Moscow had got the war it wanted.

Georgian forces soon reached Tskhinvali, but this was also the base of Russian peacekeepers, and two were killed and five wounded that first morning. The Georgians claimed that this was in self-defence because the Russians had fired on them, but Moscow immediately claimed that it was an illegitimate act of aggression, and carefully laid plans were activated. Air attacks were launched against Georgian forces in South Ossetia and also airfields and other strategic targets in Georgia proper. The 76th Airborne Division's 104th Regiment was rushed to Tskhinvali, while tactical battalion groups from the 19th Motor Rifle Division's 135th, 503rd and 693rd Regiments (which had been mustered just over the border on the pretext of Fifty-Eighth Army exercises) began moving through the Roki Tunnel, supported by elements of the 10th Spetsnaz Brigade. They were followed by the 70th and 71st Regiments from the 42nd Motor-Rifle Division, and more commandos from the 22nd Spetsnaz Brigade.

By the morning of 10 August, Georgian forces were in control of most of Tskhinvali, but the tide was about to turn. In much greater strength, the Russian task force and their South Ossetian allies pushed the Georgians out of the city during the course of that day, despite attempts to mount several counter-attacks. Saakashvili announced a ceasefire, but the Russians showed no signs of being willing to stop and pushed on into Georgia, heading towards the strategic town of Gori on the way to the capital, Tbilisi. Following airstrikes, government forces abandoned the town on 11 August and pulled back to reinforce Tbilisi, and two days later Russian forces and their auxiliary allies occupied Gori.

Meanwhile, Abkhazia on the Black Sea coast became the focus for a different type of war when Russia committed naval and airborne forces.

1) Scout, Second Chechen War, 2002. This soldier from the reconnaissance company of a regular army unit is calling in an air strike from the Su-25 overhead. He is wearing a SPOSN Gorka-E mountain suit in Partizan SSLeto camouflage pattern, and the black woollen cap informally adopted by many in Chechnya's cold climate. Over his suit he wears a Gorod-2 load-carrying vest, in mismatching camouflage that suggests he may have bought it privately. He is looking through Baigish BPO binoculars and using an R-105M backpack radio. **2)** Honour Guard, Semyonovsky Regiment; Moscow, 2014. The Semyonovsky was one of the oldest guard regiments of the Imperial Russian Army, disbanded by the Bolsheviks in 1918 but re-formed by Putin in 2013 especially for ceremonial duties. This soldier is modelling the so-called 'Yudashkin uniform' by Russian fashion designer Valentin Yudashkin, which was adopted in 2010. The weapon is the 1940s vintage bayonet-mounting SKS rifle, which was retained for ceremonial duties. Officers would carry a sabre. **3)** Soldier with RPO-M launcher, 2010. The RPO-M is a disposable incendiary rocket launcher much favoured for destroying bunkers and similar targets. This soldier's rank of *yefreitor* or senior private would be denoted by a single transverse stripe in subdued green on his epaulet. Typical of the patchy progress of the modernization programme at the time, he wears jacket and trousers in a slightly dated Flora camouflage, but modern lace-up boots, a 6B13 body-armour vest, and a 6B7 composite helmet. **4)** Patch of 2nd Guards

Tamanskaya Motor Rifle Division. One of the elite Moscow-based units, briefly reduced into a brigade before being returned to divisional strength, the 'Taman's' right sleeve patch depicts St George, the patron saint of both Russia and also specifically of Moscow, below the motto 'Motherland – Honour – Glory'. (Johnny Shumate © Osprey Publishing)

On 8 August, ships of Russia's Black Sea Fleet began steaming for the Abkhaz coast from their base at Sevastopol in Crimea, while Su-24 bombers struck the port city of Poti. When four Georgian patrol boats sought to intercept the Russian flotilla, on 10 August the Russian missile corvette *Mirazh* sank one and drove the others away. The Russian ships established a 'security zone' along the Abkhaz coast, blockading what was left of Georgia's small navy; meanwhile, two battalions of Naval Infantry were landed at the southern Abkhaz port of Ochamchire, armoured units from the 20th Motor Rifle Division crossed the border from southern Russia, and elements of the 7th Air Assault Division landed at the capital, Sukhumi. These last joined up with paratroopers already present as part of the 'peacekeeping' contingent and, while Abkhaz forces seized the Kodori Gorge, they moved into western Georgia, seizing the towns of Zugdidi and Senaki. From there they began launching raids into Poti, destroying six Georgian patrol boats in harbour, and even capturing five Humvee vehicles supplied by the United States.

Although they pushed a little way further towards Tbilisi from Gori, and launched a number of airstrikes on the capital, the Russians were essentially content that their point had been made. President Saakashvili had been provoked into providing what Russian diplomats could 'spin' as a defensive war, and Georgia had been shown the consequences of open defiance (such as any thought of NATO membership). On 15 August, Saakashvili signed a ceasefire that had been brokered by European Union representatives, and on the 18th Russia began pulling back its troops. Abkhazia and South Ossetia had become fully fledged protectorates of Moscow.

This victory should hardly have come as a surprise: Georgia's total population was only one-twentieth of Russia's, and Moscow sensibly focused on limited objectives. However, this predictable victory was attended by many unexpected failures. It was noted that, soldier-for-soldier, the US-trained Georgians tended to outfight their opponents. For all their preparations, the Russians made heavy weather of moving through the Roki Tunnel and regrouping in battle order. They frequently failed to co-ordinate effectively and were vulnerable to Georgian ambushes and counter-attacks – including one against an advance column approaching Tskhinvali that left Fifty-Eighth Army commander Lieutenant-General Anatoly Khrulyov seriously wounded, and his troops with no option but to break out and retreat. This lack of co-ordination often reflected patchy and dated communications: at one point Khrulyov even had to borrow a satellite phone from a journalist to give his orders. Units deployed with older T-62 and T-72M tanks, and on the latter many of the canisters for advanced reactive armour were actually found to be empty, leaving them vulnerable to Georgian anti-tank weapons. Maintenance problems were widespread, and failures in satellite targeting inhibited the use of precision munitions.

THE SERDYUKOV/MAKAROV REFORMS

If Saakashvili had given Putin an excuse for war, the poor performance of the Russian forces gave him and Medvedev an excuse to demand genuine military reform aimed at a rapid modernization of the armed forces. Defence Minister Serdyukov, as an outsider – and one reliant on Kremlin support – had no sentimental ties to the old ways, and everything to prove. His new Chief of the General Staff, Makarov, was both determined and a clear thinker, eager to launch such a programme.

On 14 October 2008, Serdyukov announced a 'new stage' in military reform, promising the most radical changes since the end of World War II. The stated aim was to create a flexible, professional army in a permanently combat-ready state, able to mount a whole spectrum of operations, from small-scale interventions to the major engagements that until then had been the sole preoccupation of the High Command. To this end, the establishment strength of the armed forces was to be reduced to one million by 2012, with an increase in the proportion of professionals over draftees. The officer corps was to be pruned accordingly, addressing the top-heaviness of the military (as Serdyukov put it, 'our army today is reminiscent of an egg which is swollen in the middle. There are more colonels and lieutenant-colonels than there

Russian paratroopers at Pristina Airport. The camouflage patterns of their uniforms are one of several new styles of camouflage introduced into the Russian Army in the late 1990s and early 2000s. (Tim Ripley/DPL)

are junior officers'). Meanwhile, a renewed effort would go into creating a corps of professional NCOs, whose lack had been a traditional weakness of the Russian military.

Overall, an army in which the division was the basic building block would be converted to one based on the smaller, more flexible brigade, while a massive procurement programme would ensure that by 2020 some 70 per cent of all weapons systems in use were of the latest generation, and the rest had been modernized. The army would be kept in permanent readiness, compared with the previous situation in which less than 20 per cent of the force was at full combat readiness. This was an ambitious agenda, and some aspects – notably the purging of the High Command, and the closing of redundant and outdated educational institutions – predictably generated considerable opposition. However, in contrast with previous would-be reformers, Serdyukov and Makarov were willing to bulldoze their way through resistance, and were well placed to do so. They had the full backing of Putin and Medvedev, and with it the promise of massive and long-term spending, and after the lessons of Georgia it was impossible to argue that reform was not needed. Thus, 2008 marked the beginning of a new age for the Russian Army.

PUTIN'S ARMY

The Serdyukov–Makarov reforms would indeed be painful for many, especially the 200 generals dismissed as divisions were abolished and administrative structures amalgamated. Overall, nearly 205,000 officers' positions were cut (though 45,000 were actually vacant at the time anyway). The reforms undoubtedly created a much leaner, more effective and responsive military. In 2014, for example, the Russians were able to deploy perhaps 40,000 troops to the Ukrainian border within seven days at the start of their intervention into the south-eastern Donbas region. In 1999, it had taken three times as long to mobilize a similar force for Chechnya.

DIVISIONS TO BRIGADES

Before the reforms, the Russian order of battle in many ways resembled a shrunken Soviet one, with 24 divisions (three tank, five machine gun–artillery, 16 motor rifle), 12 independent brigades, and two separate external task forces – known by this point as 'bases' – in Armenia and

Tajikistan. However, this was still in many ways a paper structure. Only six divisions (five motor rifle and, according to some, one tank) were actually at full strength and operational; ostensibly the others could be brought up to complement through mobilizing reservists, but in fact the reserve system was in disarray. The General Staff's own estimate was that, even given three months to mobilize, only nine more divisions could be stood up, for a total of 15 out of 24.

Russian paratroopers man a vehicular roadblock in Georgia, the man at the front with his Dragunov sniper rifle. The Dragunov was actually developed more along the lines of the designated marksman concept, rather than that of the sniper. (Yves Debay/DPL)

The organizational phase of the reforms would be completed with striking speed. Symbolically, it began with the 2nd Guards Tamanskaya Motor Rifle Division, one of the high-readiness units with a strong historical pedigree and record of loyalty, which was converted largely into the 5th Guards Kalinin Independent Motor Rifle Brigade. (Ironically, this division was later re-formed in a partial rollback of the reforms.) Over the course of the next year all the manoeuvre divisions were re-formed into one or more brigades, with only a single static, defensive 18th Machine Gun–Artillery Division in the Far Eastern Kurile Islands being preserved. The army's fighting force then comprised four tank brigades, 35 motor rifle brigades and a 'cover' (*prikritiya*) or fortifications brigade, supported by nine missile, nine artillery, four MLRS, nine air defence and ten support brigades, including one for electronic warfare. This left the army at a strength of 85 brigades, 40 of which were frontline combat units. As of the end of Serdyukov's tenure in 2012 there were still manning problems because of continuing shortfalls in troop numbers – only 15–17 of the combat brigades were at full strength, the rest being 20–30 per cent 'light' – but this was slowly rectified. The seven Spetsnaz brigades, technically part of the GRU rather than the regular army, survived, and indeed a new brigade and a regiment were established in the North Caucasus. The VDV were at first to go through a similar reform, but after strong lobbying the decision was made to allow them to retain their divisional structure, albeit in reinforced form, as noted below.

The typical motor rifle brigade now has an establishment strength of some 3,800 officers and men. Three motor rifle battalions, each of three companies, and a tank battalion of four companies, make up its fighting force, along with a separate reconnaissance company and a dedicated sniper platoon (an innovation dating from experiences in Chechnya). Fire-support elements include two self-propelled artillery battalions, a rocket battalion, an anti-tank battalion, and two anti-aircraft battalions. Engineer, signals, maintenance and materiel support battalions, and electronic warfare, medical, and NBC companies round out the support component. A tank brigade, with an establishment strength of just under 3,000, is a leaner, punchier force, with one motor rifle and three tank battalions, as well as considerable artillery firepower.

However, since 2015 there has been a partial revival of larger formations geared for major wars. At the beginning of 2016 the First Tank Army was reactivated in the Western Military District, including two re-established

divisions of long and revered history: the 4th Guards Kantemirovskaya Tank Division, and the re-formed 2nd Guards Tamanskaya Motor Rifle Division which had been the first converted to a brigade. Furthermore, it was announced that two new tank and two motor rifle divisions would be formed during 2016, based respectively at Voronezh, Chelyabinsk, Smolensk and Rostov-on-Don. Even so, these are 'light' divisions of some 6,000–7,000 effectives, rather than the 10,000–13,000 men of the old Soviet-model formation.

In part, this change of step reflects an evolution of military thinking and lessons from Russia's operations in Ukraine. There, the army has depended on assembling ad hoc battalion tactical groups from the all-volunteer elements of brigades across the country. This often created serious interoperability problems, as soldiers who had not trained together were thrown directly into battle. While they were generally able to win individual engagements against Ukrainian forces, due not least to greater firepower and a technological edge, they were often unable to exploit these

Russian troops in the Crimea. The man second from the right is armed with a PKP machine gun, fitted with a 100-round ammunition box. (Chris Cobb-Smith/DPL)

1) Chief of the General Staff Nikolai Makarov. His rank as army general is identified by the four stars on his shoulder boards; after 2010 the insignia of this rank became one large gold star plus a wreath-encircled red star. **2)** Cossack major, Volga Host. This veteran wears jacket and trousers in the 'smog' pattern used by the Interior Ministry's security troops. **3)** A soldier from the 135th Motor Rifle Regiment, hefting his 9K338 Igla-S (SA-24 Grinch) shoulder-fired SAM. **4)** Patch of Russia's Fifty-Eighth Army, headquartered at Vladikavkaz in North Ossetia. (Johnny Shumate © Osprey Publishing)

victories effectively. These re-formed divisions will therefore be used not just as rapid-response defensive elements but also as the core of combined-arms formations able to deliver shattering blows quickly, in a reprise of the Soviets' own take on *Blitzkrieg*.

CHAIN OF COMMAND

Truly operational forces and meaningful intervention capabilities depend not just on the quality of individual soldiers and units, but also on flexible and responsive command structures. Bar some minor changes, Russia had largely retained the Soviet model of command, and this was also addressed in the reforms. The president of the Russian Federation is Supreme Commander-in-Chief of the armed forces; he not only sets policy and strategy, he also hires and fires the members of the Glavkomat, the High Command. Beneath him, the Minister for Defence is responsible for the armed forces in general; Sergei Shoigu, Defence Minister since 2012 (still incumbent at the time of writing), is generally considered to be an excellent and effective figure, the most popular Defence Minister post-Soviet Russia has ever had.

The Ministry is more concerned with management – such as logistics, procurement and policy – than operational command. That is the responsibility of the General Staff, from its headquarters at 14 Znamenka Street in Moscow. A high-tech new National Defence Control Centre was finally opened in 2014, within and below the main ministry building on Frunze Embankment. Its Combat Control Centre, packed with computers and walled with massive display screens, is intended as the nerve centre for any future conflicts, and was publicly displayed in use co-ordinating attacks on rebels in Syria in 2015. The Ground Forces themselves have their own commander-in-chief and main staff, although this is not involved so much with field command as with tactics, training, and organizational management. The Main Staff is also responsible for service-specific training and for research establishments. Since 2010 actual operational command has been exerted through four Operational Strategic Commands (VOs), which are also peacetime military districts: West (ZVO), South (YuVO), Central (TsVO) and East (VVO).

The Ground Forces units in each military district are generally subordinated to armies, although some specialist units exist outside this structure, such as the Spetsnaz special forces. The VOs are combined all-arms commands that also include naval, air, and air-defence forces, as well

Russia's Operational Strategic Commands (ex-Military Districts), 2016

as their own intelligence cells (local branches of the GRU), although the release into the field of nuclear weapons is still under presidential control.

The Western Military District incorporates the former Moscow and Leningrad districts, with the First Guards Red Banner Tank Army, Sixth Red Banner Army, Twentieth Guards Red Banner Army, the Baltic Fleet, and elements of the Northern Fleet. This command also includes the 10,000-strong task force in the Russian exclave of Kaliningrad: the 18th Guards Motor Rifle Brigade, 7th Independent Motor Rifle Brigade and 336th Guards Naval Infantry Brigade; and the garrison in Transnistria.

The Southern Military District controls the Forty-Ninth and Fifty-Eighth Armies, the Black Sea Fleet and the Caspian Flotilla. From 2017, the Southern Military District also began the formation of a new Eighth Army, which includes the 150th Motor Rifle Division. The 102nd Base in Armenia also reports to YuVO. This base houses some 3,000 Russian troops, with a powerful air-defence force fielding S-300 missiles (as well as a squadron of

MiG-29 fighters), with the twin aims of defending Armenian and Russian airspace and asserting Moscow's authority in the Caucasus.

The Central Military District, covering a swathe of the country across the Ural mountains and western Siberia, has the Second Guards Red Banner Army and the Forty-First Red Banner Army. It also controls the 201st Base in Tajikistan, a force of 7,000 troops stationed at three military facilities in Dushanbe, Qurgonteppa and Kulob. Their main role is to help defend Tajikistan and its regime in case of insurgency or incursions from Afghanistan, so they are configured as a motor rifle brigade supported by Mi-24P attack helicopters. A small contingent at Kant air base in Kyrgyzstan rounds out TsVO's components.

The Eastern Military District controls not just the Pacific Fleet but also the Fifth and Thirty-Fifth Red Banner Armies and the Twenty-Ninth and Thirty-Sixth Armies. Although this sounds like an impressive total, the VVO mostly has relatively low priority for ground forces elements; not only is it regarded as a distant backwater posting, but its main potential enemy is China. Although the General Staff continues to update its

Supreme Commander-in-Chief of the Russian Armed Forces Vladimir Putin watching the launch of the Avangard missile complex carrying a hypersonic glide vehicle at the National Centre for State Defence Control in Moscow on 26 December 2018. The Avangard can deliver both nuclear and conventional munitions at an astonishing speed of Mach 27. (President of the Russian Federation/ www.kremlin.ru)

contingency plans for a conventional land war on its south-eastern flank, this is increasingly an exercise in futility as the Chinese military continues to modernize. Russia's units are scattered along an indefensibly long land border, and dependent for supply and reinforcement largely on two railway lines which could easily be cut. In practice, any such conflict would quickly escalate to the use of at least tactical nuclear weapons.

In 2014 a fifth Northern or Arctic Command was added. Unusually, this is not a military district; as it is essentially responsible for sea and air space, it was largely built on the basis of the Northern Fleet and attached air units. However, it also fields a small army component, including two specialized Arctic mechanized brigades, initially the 200th Independent Brigade based at Pechenga. The speed with which Moscow can now mobilize forces was evident in 2015 when, shortly after standing up this new command, it mounted a major exercise in the Arctic involving 80,000 troops.

RE-ARMAMENT AND RE-EQUIPMENT

When Putin came to power in 2000, he pledged to spend the equivalent of US $650 billion on the military in the period to 2020. The goal was that by that date 70 per cent of all weapons and systems would be of the most modern standard – in global, not just Russian terms – with the rest soon to follow.

Achievement of this ambitious target has been hampered by considerable waste and embezzlement. In 2013 the Main Military Prosecutor, General Sergei Fridinsky, admitted that corruption and waste had accounted for 4.4 billion rubles (US $134 million) in the previous year alone (for context, that figure is the equivalent of 75 top-of-the-line T-90 tanks 'lost'). Furthermore, even by Western standards the procurement process is often highly politicized, with contracts awarded to keep open factories that otherwise might have to down-size, and to reward support for the Kremlin. In late 2011, for example, Defence Minister Serdyukov announced that Russia had, for the moment, quite enough tanks – at the time its total inventory was some 15,000, greater than NATO's entire combined stock – and that no more would be ordered imminently. Shortly thereafter, Putin publicly rebuked him and reversed the decision, giving UralVagonZavod a US $2 billion order for new T-90s. It was hardly coincidental that at the time Putin was facing massive anti-government protests, and a group of UralVagonZavod workers, with management encouragement, had gone on television to offer to come to Moscow and take on the protesters if need be. Similar political pressure seems to have been brought to bear to ensure that the military ordered the advanced T-14 Armata tank. While apparently an impressive design, it is far more complex and expensive than the High Command had wanted, but again it was a way of rewarding UralVagonZavod and its managers for their wholehearted support for Putin.

For all that, however, the effects of this massive investment have been substantial. Having inherited something that in many ways still looked like a Soviet army, by 2016 Putin had one that looked and fought much more like a modern force. Not only had individual soldiers acquired uniforms, body armour, personal communication gear and weapons that brought them close to NATO standards, Russia had also embraced many of the changes sweeping the world's militaries, from drones to advanced battle management systems. Having become accustomed to seeing the Russians lagging behind, NATO observers had something of a shock when observing their forces in Ukraine and Syria, where they demonstrated not just considerable professionalism but also some unexpected technological 'edges'. These included deploying high-power microwave systems to jam or

The Pantsir-S1 (SA-22 Greyhound) is one of a new generation of air-defence vehicles entering Russian service. It is a self-propelled, medium-range SAM system introduced in 2012, and intended for point air defence. (Vitaly V. Kuzmin/ CC-BY-SA-4.0)

bring down enemy drones, T-90 tanks that have even shrugged off heavy US-made TOW (tube-launched, optically tracked, wire guided) missiles in Syria, and the advanced S-400 Triumf (SA-21) SAM complex.

THE 'TWO ARMIES'

Nonetheless, reform remains a work in progress, which has to a degree seen much of the army cannibalized to create a core of mobile and capable operational units. For example, most battalions have one or two companies made up essentially of professionals, but the others include a high proportion of conscripts who have received relatively limited training. This is a key reason for the creation of ad hoc battalion tactical groups for service in Ukraine; conscripts are not only banned by law from participating in such operations (unless they volunteer), but they are proportionately less capable. By the same token, certain brigades have been granted priority for new weapons and investment in barracks and similar facilities. These brigades are the ones most likely to see action and are thus favoured postings for ambitious and able officers who know that combat duty is a great asset for their career. The result is that a handful of brigades get the pick of the officer corps and volunteer soldiers, while the others tend to get the lower achievers, the ill disciplined, and those who fail to keep up.

There is something of a widening divide between roughly one-third of the ground forces – including, beyond the elite paratroopers and Naval Infantry, such formations as the 15th Motor Rifle Brigade (Russia's dedicated 'peacekeepers'), and the 6th Tank Brigade – and the rest. In the main, these latter units are improving, but at nowhere near the rate of the best. They still suffer more from *dedovshchina* and theft, and generally demonstrate far less combat spirit and readiness. While there is no question of their loyalty in face of a direct foreign threat to the Motherland, it is less clear what enthusiasm and effectiveness they would demonstrate if deployed abroad – especially in politically sensitive operations such as those in Ukraine, where a degree of sophistication may be required.

THE RUSSIAN SOLDIER

Russia has long harboured a belief that it needs a million-man army, given the length of its borders and the potential threats it could face from south, east or west. The same preoccupation with a massive land war – a legacy of the traumatic experience of World War II – has motivated the retention of conscription. That way, a substantial proportion of the male population has some military training and can be called to arms in case of a full mobilization. Both assumptions have been tested, however, both by economic pressures and by the increasingly technical nature of modern war.

THE DRAFT

By 2012 the overall strength of the military was to be fixed at one million, but even then it was becoming increasingly clear that it would be all but impossible to meet and maintain this target. In 2013 the overall strength was only 766,000, including 220,000 professional officers and about 300,000 volunteer *kontraktniki*. Given that since 2008 the length of the draft had been reduced to just one year, in order to keep personnel

A Russian Airborne soldier trains his full-camo AK-I03 during an exercise. The vehicles in the background are Iveco LMVs (Light Multirole Vehicles), an Italian vehicle that the Russian Army has purchased or locally assembled in substantial numbers since 2012. (Ministry of Defence of the Russian Federation/Mil.ru/ C-BY-4.0)

strength at the planned level a quarter of a million conscripts would have needed to be called up during each of the spring and autumn induction seasons, but – due to a shrinking population, ill-health, deferments for educational or other reasons, and simple draft-dodging – no recent drafts had managed to top more than half that number. In 2012, for example, almost as many eligible young men in the target 18- to 27-year age range evaded military service as joined up (and 28 per cent of those who did heed the call-up were subsequently released for medical or other reasons). In 2008, Air Force commander-in-chief Colonel-General Vladimir Mikhailov had controversially and undiplomatically claimed that up to one-third of conscripts were 'mentally unfit, drug addicts or imbeciles'.

Conscription is increasingly unpopular, even more so than in Soviet times: the Soviet-era saying that 'life is a book, and national service is two pages torn from it' is still widely heard. Most Russians do not see a genuine existential threat facing their state, and the experience of the 1990s – when financial collapse led to especially terrible conditions for soldiers, just when a free media was most assiduous in reporting on their plight – has contributed to a widespread and not wholly unreasonable belief that national service is a terrible experience. Serdyukov, in particular, tried to introduce measures to make barracks life more comfortable, including outsourcing catering, but even so the threats of *dedovshchina* and similar abuses faced by their sons still loom large in the public's consciousness. Likewise, although conscripts cannot legally be sent into combat without their consent except in a defensive war, the casualties experienced by draftees sent to Chechnya, as well as a suspicion that officers might coerce them into agreeing to 'be volunteered,' makes this a limited consolation. It did not help when, in 2013, Putin signed a decree allowing soldiers to be deployed to war zones after just four months' training, instead of the previous six months. Chief of the General Staff Valery Gerasimov reiterated that only professional servicemen could be involved in 'combat activities and armed conflicts', but the damage to public perceptions had been done.

Meanwhile, the call-up, pre-training, and reserve systems are all in disarray. Conscription is managed by local military commissariats (*voenkomaty*), but these have become infamous as centres of corruption, and as comfortable exiles to which incompetent or otherwise unfavoured officers are sent. For years there has also been a shortfall of administrative staff to keep their records up to date. In Soviet times, their jobs were made easier by the GTO (*Gotov k Trudu i Oborene*: 'Ready for Labour and Defence') programme that integrated some basic military training into the school curriculum. Under a combination of ideological backlash and financial pressures both GTO and DOSAAF all but vanished, and although Putin decreed the re-creation of the GTO programme in schools in 2014, nonetheless there is a serious problem with the fitness standards of prospective recruits. Likewise, the reserve system is in a shambles, with fewer than one in ten demobilized conscripts ever actually carrying out any of their refresher training in the five years after they leave the ranks. Defence Ministry sources also admitted in 2015 that their records of the whereabouts of ex-soldiers are outdated and often incorrect, meaning that it is difficult to manage anything more targeted than a universal mobilization.

KONTRAKTNIKI

For years there had been talk of recruiting professional soldiers, both in reaction to the difficulty of mustering sufficient conscripts, and also in reflection of the increasing complexity of war. Since 2008, when political pressures forced the Kremlin to shorten the draft to 12 months, the amount of effective training and meaningful service that a conscript can undertake has been very limited. The general assumption is that a Russian draftee is only really operational for at most five, and perhaps only three months of the 12: that short period after he has completed both his basic and unit training, and before his 'demob-happy' final month, when soldiers are distracted, and are anyway logistically and legally hard to deploy in anything other than a declared state of emergency. Against this reality, modern military equipment increasingly demands high levels of technical and professional skills that cannot be acquired during such a brief period of service.

Throughout, the High Command had championed retaining the mass army and conscription, with one eye on a possible land war with China, and another on maintaining a sufficient number of units to justify such a huge establishment of field-grade and general officers. This not only contributed to the malaise of the military, it also ran up against the demographic problems caused by Russia's declining birth rate and parallel qualitative concerns. Serdyukov and Makarov wanted to create an all-volunteer army, one which was also trained to much higher standards especially at the junior officer and NCO levels; a long-term problem within the Russian military was the absence of a seasoned NCO corps, which is the backbone of most Western armies. This ambitious goal proved to be a reform too far, not least because of the huge expense of offering the pay and conditions to

Two Russian soldiers conduct a woodland clearing exercise, one armed with an AK-74M and the other with a PKP Pecheneg, the latter essentially an accurized 7.62×54mmR PKM with a fixed barrel and the capability to mount telescopic sights. (Andrei Ivanov/DPL)

attract and retain a fully volunteer military. Nonetheless, the proportion of *kontraktniki*, volunteers who sign on for three-year terms, has risen steadily.

In 2013, the target was set to recruit 425,000 contract personnel into ordinary soldier and junior NCO ranks by 2017; some sign on for contract service while they are still conscripts or when about to muster out, others join at recruitment centres. Salaries and conditions of service were improved – between 2012 and 2016, for example, salaries for junior officers rose fully six-fold. By 2016, more than half the total military was professional, whether officers or other ranks: 427,000 out of a total of 760,000, with the Ground Forces comprising some 230,000 soldiers, of whom about 130,000 were professionals.

In part, this was facilitated by a 2010 initiative to allow foreign-born recruits to sign up as privates or sergeants on a five-year contract, with the prospect of applying for Russian citizenship at the end. Given the requirement that they speak Russian, this has largely been of interest to young men from Central Asia, where Russian is still taught in schools and income levels are low enough to make a Russian Army salary attractive. Even so, while no firm figures for such recruits are issued, anecdotal accounts suggest that no more than 5 percent of *kontraktniki*, if that many, join from abroad.

TRAINING AND EXERCISES

Training is an issue of considerable importance, and a topic that both Chief of the General Staff Makarov and his successor Gerasimov have tried to address. The key problem is one of time: how to balance training and actual service in a 12-month national service term. The draftees' first three months are spent in accelerated combat training, after which they are sent to their units for further training which, depending on their role and rank (as some are promoted to conscript sergeants), can take another three to five months. Even then, training is still often basic and limited.

Historically, for example, Russians expend far fewer live rounds on the shooting range than their Western counterparts. In 2014, Defence Minister Shoigu expressed his concern that tank gunners simply did not have the

A Russian amphibious BTR vehicle moves ashore during an exercise. Note the elevated exhausts at the back of the vehicle, to ensure that the engine is not flooded in open water. (Andrei Ivanov/DPL)

necessary levels of accuracy due to their lack of live-fire practice; they tend to expend around 20 rounds in training, compared to the 100–160 invested by many other countries. Instead, they spend their time in the classroom or on simulators, and even these are often quite primitive. It was as long ago as 1980 that the US Army introduced its MILES laser-based system that allowed soldiers to train and exercise in the field as if firing live rounds at each other; Russia only began to introduce its equivalent 9F838 Tselik simulator in 2013–14.

On the other hand, Shoigu initiated not only a series of snap inspections meant to test the readiness of forces across the country, but also a steady increase in the size and scale of major military exercises. Mindful of the eighteenth-century Russian general Alexander Suvorov's maxim 'Train hard, fight easy', these exercises test everything from individual soldiers' and vehicle crews' proficiency up to the capacity of the High Command to co-ordinate major combined-arms operations spanning half a continent. The regular *Zapad* (West) and *Vostok* (East) exercises are especially large in scope. *Zapad*-2013, for example, involved some 70,000 troops drawn from every branch of service and stretching from the Arctic to central European Russia. It also war-gamed situations ranging from a simulated terrorist attack through to conventional hostilities. Such exercises demonstrate that Moscow is preparing for the contingency not just of limited but still major deployments in neighbouring post-Soviet states, but also full-scale conventional and even limited nuclear war in the West. Beyond that, exercises also provide potential covers for further adventures: preparations for both the 2008 Georgian War and the 2015 deployment to Syria were masked by major exercises.

OFFICERS AND NCOS

Russia's military has inherited from its Soviet predecessor a structure in which junior officers also often fill the roles of senior NCOs, as junior NCOs tend often to be conscripts selected for the role simply because they show greater capabilities than their peers. The seasoned, veteran NCO of worldwide military legend is notably absent in Russia. This has become recognized as a problem, especially as the old position of *praporshchik* (warrant officer), meant to bridge this gap, was abolished in 2010; it was restored in 2013, though essentially for technical positions. There has been a drive to create a corps of professional NCOs, and in 2015 it was announced that the army would abandon its practice of promoting conscripts to sergeant and would restrict this rank to *kontraktniki*.

This is proving difficult: many *kontraktniki* lack the relevant skills and character, and many of those who do show these qualities tend to be promoted to junior officer rank. Nonetheless, since the end of 2009 a dedicated NCO training centre within the paratroopers' Ryazan Higher Airborne School has put picked NCO candidates though a 34-month programme that is meant to provide such leaders. Even so, with only 2,000 graduates annually, this can only gradually begin to make a difference, and it is proving an expensive project – generous benefits are available to recruits, with further bonuses for the so-called *otlichniki* (the 'excellents') who do especially well. As a result of this shortage of NCOs, junior officers still find themselves filling many technical and professional roles that would fall to NCOs in Western armies, such as basic inventory and supervising drill. In the past most junior and senior lieutenants were graduates who had deferred their national service during their studies and had taken military classes at university, but increasingly today they are volunteers.

As they rise through the ranks, officers receive commensurate further education. Russia inherited a massive military higher education infrastructure from Soviet times, as institutions were then disproportionately located on Russian soil. In fact, almost half the total military education budget was actually being spent on the maintenance and repair of facilities that were often 30–40 per cent under-used. In 2008, Serdyukov announced that of the 65 existing institutions (four universities, 15 academies, 46 colleges and institutes) only ten would survive, with centres of excellence from the others transferred into these survivors. His goal was to replace an old model that meant senior officers would have spent a total of eight years in school, with a Western-style one involving a single military academy posting, followed by short specialized courses to gain the skills demanded by particular positions. Shoigu partially rolled back Serdyukov's

Valery Vasilyevich Gerasimov, at the time of writing the current Chief of the General Staff of the Armed Forces of Russia, and first Deputy Defence Minister. (Andrei Ivanov/DPL)

reforms, pardoning some academies and returning to the older, more academic model, albeit with revised and up-to-date curricula.

Each arm of service has its own specialized colleges, such as the R.Ya. Malinovsky Armoured Forces' Military Academy, and the S. M. Budyonny Military Signals and Communications Corps Academy. High-fliers destined for the top will also pass through the M. V. Frunze Military Academy (typically for captains and majors) and the General Staff Academy (for lieutenant-colonels and up), for education in operational and strategic command respectively. It is an open question whether the Russian model is better than the Western one, but it undoubtedly produces a crop of highly educated military leaders and an extremely intellectual approach to warfare.

SERVICE LIFE AND DISCIPLINE

There have been attempts to make army life more bearable, not least in order to attract and retain volunteers. The worst miseries of the 1990s are now a thing of the past: today's soldiers are fed and paid tolerably well and on time, receive decent medical care, and generally live reasonable lives, even if standards are only slowly catching up with the improvements available in civilian life. It was only in 2013 that conscripts began to be issued socks instead of *portyanki*, the cloth footwraps that had been in use since the sixteenth century, and that showers were fitted in all barracks. Nonetheless, life is often tough, especially in bases away from the cities such as in the far north and east. Efforts to crack down on crime and *dedovshchina* began in earnest under Serdyukov and have continued under Shoigu. While this is still a problem, progress has been made, especially in units which have seen active service, where the value of being able to rely on all one's comrades becomes truly appreciated.

A particular step forward was the decision to create for the first time a professional corps of military police. Previously, beyond serious criminal investigations carried out by the Main Military Procuracy, policing had been handled by local commanders. The so-called 'Commandant's Service' or *komendatura* was essentially a traffic-control and public-order contingent, capable of dragging drunk and disorderly soldiers back to barracks after a rowdy night out but not of any more complex policing. This contributed not only to *dedovshchina* (as soldiers feared to inform on their abusive senior comrades), but also to corruption and embezzlement. The idea of creating a separate military organization was mooted in 2006 but was repeatedly put off. However, in March 2015 the first 2,500 men were inducted into

Russian soldiers sit through a classroom instruction session. The Russian military has steadily been working to remove at least some of the dark shadows of bullying and financial austerity that have overshadowed recruitment to the armed forces. (David Reynolds/DPL)

what is planned to become a 20,000-strong corps, answering directly to the Ministry of Defence rather than to the territorial chain of command. The main role of this *Voennaya politsiya* is to maintain military order and discipline, prevent theft, and stamp out the hazing culture, although it will also have responsibilities in counter-terrorism and force protection. Every military district and fleet headquarters is to receive a VP brigade, which will also contain a psychological operations company.

INTERVENTION FORCES

If the Ground Forces are the Kremlin's hammer, sometimes the state needs military assets that can move more quickly, reach further, and strike perhaps with greater accuracy. This became especially true after 2012, when Vladimir Putin adopted a more openly assertive policy on his return to the presidency, looking to establish Russia's status as both a global power and also the regional hegemon over most of post-Soviet Eurasia. To this end, Russia maintains substantial intervention forces: the Airborne Assault Troops (VDV), the Naval Infantry (MP) and the Spetsnaz special forces. As the best-equipped and most professional elements, mainly staffed by volunteer soldiers (and intended to be all-professional by 2018), these units have been at the forefront of Russian out-of-area deployments, from anti-piracy missions off the coast of Somalia to the recent intervention in Syria, as well as providing the 'test beds' for new tactics and weapons later intended for wider dissemination.

In particular, they played a key role in Russia's annexation of Crimea in February–March 2014, and the subsequent campaign in Ukraine's south-eastern Donbas region. When pro-Moscow Ukrainian President Viktor Yanukovych fled in face of a popular rising in February 2014, the Kremlin was alarmed that the new government might try to take the country in a more pro-Western direction, but it also recognized an opportunity. The peninsula of Crimea was not only strategically important to Moscow as the base of its Black Sea Fleet, but also politically sensitive; it had been a part of Russia from the 1921 aftermath of the Bolshevik Revolution until 1954, when it was passed to Ukraine – in a political gesture to what was then still unquestionably a component of the USSR. For most Russians today,

Russian troops and heavy vehicles in Ukraine. Although Russia has denied the presence of formal combat units in Ukraine since 2014, international observers have put the figure of Russian soldiers in the territory at greater than 10,000. (Chris Cobb-Smith/DPL)

and many of the ethnic Russians living in Crimea, the peninsula is still rightfully theirs.

When the new Ukrainian government was declared in February 2014, VDV and Spetsnaz units were put on alert, and shortly thereafter unidentified men wearing Russian uniforms but no insignia began occupying key locations and blockading Ukrainian barracks. Dubbed by Western media 'little green men' (and by Russians as the 'polite people', for their measured tactics), they were naval infantry from the Black Sea Fleet's 810th Independent Naval Infantry Brigade, as well as Spetsnaz and VDV. The peninsula was soon in Russian hands, and a hurried and not-very-free referendum was staged to provide some cover for Moscow's annexation of Crimea.

The ease with which Crimea was taken – and the unwillingness of Ukrainian troops to fight for it – surprised Moscow, and encouraged it to take a fateful (and, in hindsight, foolish) further step. Its agents started whipping up a largely fake rebellion in the south-eastern Ukrainian industrial region

Russian soldiers in Crimea in March 2014, their uniforms conspicuously stripped of all insignia. They were dubbed, with a grim humour, the 'little green men' by the media. (Chris Cobb-Smith/ DPL)

called the Donbas, populated by a high proportion of Russian-speakers. This conflict with the forces of the Kiev-based Ukrainian government, still ongoing at the time of writing despite an official ceasefire, has largely been fought by local militias organized by Russia's security agencies; however, whenever Kiev's forces looked as if they were about to make progress against the rebels, regular Russian troops were deployed. A mix of army, Spetsnaz, VDV and even some MP formed the battalion tactical groups that Moscow has used in Ukraine. This simultaneously demonstrates the range of intervention capabilities now at the Kremlin's disposal, but also the continuing limitations of military reform, in that it has had to deploy ad hoc units cobbled together for the purpose.

THE VDV

The VDV endured the collapse of the USSR and the transition to the Russian Federation better than many arms of service, in part because of General Grachyov's active patronage. He initially envisaged that they would become the core of a Rapid Deployment Force that never happened, and instead consigned them to Chechnya, mistakenly thinking they would have an easy time of it. Again, as the regular army faltered, the VDV were forced to pick up the slack. Although they had effectively been obliged to unlearn much of what they had experienced in Afghanistan, mainly because nobody

The VDV continues to play a central role in the power projection of the Russian Armed Forces. Note the blue-and-white *telnyashka* t-shirts just visible, a signature item of uniform for Russian SOF. (Andrei Ivanov/DPL)

expected another such war, the lessons of both Chechen Wars have been taken to heart and carefully studied at the Ryazan Higher Airborne Academy. While not abandoning the frankly dated notion of mass parachute drops, the VDV is increasingly configuring itself as a multi-platform intervention force, capable of insertion by helicopter, by aircraft, or on the ground, to conduct strategic missions ranging from special operations – significantly, since 1992 they have had their own Spetsnaz commando unit, the 45th Guards Independent Recon Brigade – through to major offensives. To this end, they are unusually heavily mechanized for airborne forces. As well as light vehicles such as the GAZ Tigr light armoured vehicle, they also use the BMD family of air-droppable light armoured fighting vehicles, including the BMD-4 combat vehicle armed with a 100mm 2A70 low-pressure gun and a 30mm coaxial auto-cannon. As a result, they are much more able to operate as small task forces in their own right – though it would take the entire Russian air transport fleet two and a half full sorties to lift a whole division.

The VDV represents a strategic asset, and although one brigade is attached to each military district, in practice command is exerted through the VDV headquarters in Moscow. They also work especially closely with the GRU Military Intelligence; this has been evident since 2014 in the Donbas, where elements of all the divisions have been identified as present by Ukrainian intelligence sources.

Soldiers of the Russian 137th Guards Parachute Landing Regiment and Belarusian 38th Separate Guards Air Assault Brigade, seen on exercise in Brest in 2018. (Igor Rudenko/ Russian Ministry of Defence/ Mil.ru)

There are also plans for further expansion, with additional brigades. Perhaps most striking has been the decision in 2016 to create armoured units within the VDV: six companies were established by 1 January 2017, later to be expanded to battalion strength. These will be equipped with modernized T-72B3M tanks, which cannot be air-transported like the existing BMD-chassis AFVs; this decision reinforces the prospect that in the future the VDV expects to be deployed not necessarily as light mechanized troops in long-range power-projection missions, but rather as spearhead assault forces within and near Russia's borders.

THE NAVAL INFANTRY

The other main intervention force is made up of the 'black beret' marines of the Naval Infantry, the Morskaya Pekhota (MP). The Soviet Union – like Russia today – was never an especially convincing 'blue water' maritime power, and the MP never had the same opportunities as the VDV to refine their tradecraft and make their name during the Cold War. Since 1992 they have been far more active, however. They served in Chechnya; seized the southern Abkhaz port of Ochamchire in 2008; took the lead in the seizure of Crimea in 2014; played a part in the subsequent operations in Donbas; and were deployed to Syria in 2015 in support of Russia's air campaign to prevent the collapse of the Bashar Assad regime in the civil war. They have also gained a degree of fame – or notoriety –

Soviet naval infantryman kneel with their AK-74 rifles during a demonstration conducted for visiting US Navy personnel in Vladivostok in September 1990. (PHCS Mitchell/PD US Military)

for their ruthless treatment of Somali pirates. In May 2010, for example, Somali pirates boarded the MV *Moscow University*, a Liberian-flagged Russian tanker, forcing the crew to barricade themselves below decks. The Russian destroyer *Marshal Shaposhnikov*, which was patrolling in the vicinity, steamed for the *Moscow University* and deployed a helicopter and MP boarding teams in small boats. The pirates were soon overpowered and the crew freed unharmed, at which point the marines disarmed the attackers and set them adrift some 560km off the coast, in an inflatable boat with provisions but no navigation equipment, thus almost certainly condemning them to die at sea.

Each fleet has at least one naval infantry brigade. These vary in size, but will typically have two to four manoeuvre battalions as well as support elements. Many have a dedicated air-assault battalion, as well as armoured battalions, which are phasing out the last of the venerable PT-76 amphibious light tanks and replacing them with T-80s and T-90s.

THE SPETSNAZ

The final element in the triad of intervention forces is the Spetsnaz units. While undoubtedly an elite, the 17,000 or so Spetsnaz troops of the regular army, navy and VDV are by no means all 'special forces' in the Western sense; for a start, 20–30 per cent of them are short-term conscripts. Rather, they are generally trained for larger-scale and longer-

A Spetsnaz special forces diver in training. SOF troops have become increasingly central to Russian military doctrine and interventions, being well trained in some of the new skills of 'hybrid warfare'. (Andrei Ivanov/DPL)

range reconnaissance and sabotage operations, and are perhaps best understood as spearhead expeditionary light infantry, perhaps equating to the US 75th Ranger Regiment or the British 16th Air Assault Brigade. However, in 2012 a new Special Operations Command (KSO) was established, built around the genuinely elite regimental-strength 346th Brigade, and this asset must be considered as more closely comparable to Western 'Tier One' special forces such as the United States Delta and the British Special Air Service (SAS).

The Spetsnaz thus fill a role similar to, if more covert than, those of the VDV and MP. They too have seen considerable action since 1992 in every theatre of operations in which Russia has engaged, from Chechnya to Syria. Alongside the MP, soldiers of the Black Sea Fleet's 431st Naval Reconnaissance Special Designation Point (as navy Spetsnaz brigades are known) played a crucial part in the seizure of Crimea in February–March 2014. In the Donbas the Spetsnaz have again been a major instrument of the Kremlin's policy; they have been employed to carry out raids on Ukrainian

Alfa Group operatives conduct counter-terrorism drills. The unit is part of the Russian Federal Security Service (FSB), and its official name is Directorate 'A' of the FSB Special Purpose Centre (TsSN FSB). (Andrei Ivanov/ DPL)

forces, to train and support local militias, and – according to unconfirmed but wholly plausible accounts – to eliminate local commanders who proved a little too independent minded.

WEAPONS AND EQUIPMENT

Long known for its dependence on dated but rugged kit of the kind that even the most basically trained soldier can use, today's Russian Army is not only trying to bridge the technological gap with the West, but is also well aware of the speed with which China's People's Liberation Army is pursuing its own modernization programme. The results have not always been smooth, especially given the ten years of near-crisis in the 1990s, but real progress has been made, even if there is still a distinctly Russian approach to many of the design choices made.

PERSONAL AND SUPPORT WEAPONS

Today's Russian soldiers still largely use the 5.45mm AK-74M assault rifle, the 1991 upgrade of a design from 1974. A programme to replace this conventional and generally effective weapon, however, came to fruition in 2018 with the Ministry of Defence announcement that Russian Army forces would receive the 5.45mm AK-12, and the 7.62mm AK-15, with the 5.45mm Degtyarov AEK-971 and 7.62mm AEK-973 procured for special units. The firearms represent the most modern thinking in assault-rifle/battle-field development, the weapons being capable of taking all manner of tactical accessories plus having a degree of modularity and ergonomic adjustment.

The Russian military still relies on a series of other Soviet-era weapons, however, including the 7.62mm SVD sniper rifle and the 9mm PM Makarov pistol. Nonetheless, there is a keen awareness of their limitations, and a slow process is under way to replace them with such weapons as the SV-98 rifle (already standard issue for the VDV) and the PYa/MP-443 pistol. For support, Russian soldiers may fit a GP-25 or GP-30 under-barrel 40mm grenade launcher to their Kalashnikovs, or else rely on a wide range of machine guns and light anti-tank weapons. The 7.62mm PKP Pecheneg general-purpose machine gun has largely replaced the older RPK-74 and PKM as the standard squad automatic weapon, while the 12.7mm Kord heavy machine gun has replaced the older NSV. Beyond that, the venerable but still devastating AGS-30 Plamya ('Flame') 40mm automatic grenade launcher is still a favoured weapon, along with the RPG-22 and -26 disposable anti-tank rocket launchers and the RPG-29 re-usable versions. For specialist purposes, such as clearing bunkers, they use the RPO-A Shmel (Bumblebee) incendiary rocket launcher. Against harder targets, they employ Kornet (AT-14) and Metis-M (AT-13) anti-tank missiles, although some units are still fielding older Fagot (AT-4) launchers. The Igla-S (SA-24) man-portable SAM has become standard issue, although the newer Verba with advanced multi-spectral optical seeker head is beginning to be distributed more widely.

RATNIK: THE FUTURE RUSSIAN SOLDIER

Upgrading weapons is only one part of a comprehensive re-equipment of Russian soldiers' field suite of uniform and personal equipment, known as the Ratnik (Warrior) system. It was formally adopted in October 2014, with serial deliveries beginning in 2015, but many elements of the suite had already been issued to some elite forces for test purposes, as became evident in Crimea in February 2014. Complete conversion to the new uniform and personal equipment will not take place until 2020 at the earliest, especially as some elements (such as new night-vision gear) have yet to come into full production.

Broadly equivalent to the British military's Future Infantry Soldier Technology (FIST) programme, Ratnik is meant to provide all Russian soldiers with personal outfits suited for future combat environments. Its more than 40 pieces of kit include new VKPO camouflage uniforms, 6B45 body armour, a

The NPI-2 wearable GLONASS module for the Ratnik future infantry combat system. This small tactical computer allows the soldier to send and receive secure messages between team members, while also seeing the position of friendly and enemy forces. (Vitaly V. Kuzmin/CC-BY-SA-4.0)

lightweight 6B47 helmet that can be fitted with advanced vision gear (such as a thermal night-vision monocular) and a multi-tool/knife. Modular elements include additional armoured thigh and shoulder trauma plates for infantry, and the modern Strelets (Musketeer) voice, data, and video communications system including a GLONASS satellite navigation module. This last reflects bitter experiences in Georgia, where officers had to resort to using their own personal cellphones or sending orders by motorcycle courier when signals from the US GPS satellite system, which the Russians had been using, were reportedly shut off. The Ratnik outfit, with suitable additions such as a heavy winter coat and facemask for Arctic conditions, is meant to allow soldiers to operate in temperatures of from -50 to +50°C.

Even more ambitiously, initial designs are also being prepared for a follow-on Ratnik-2 suite of equipment, even though this is not expected to be fielded until 2025–35. This may include such high-tech elements as uniforms designed to minimize infra-red and thermal signatures, body armour with the capacity to camouflage itself like a chameleon, and an integral power supply. It may also include advanced computerized sights and laser designators that would allow soldiers to shoot round corners or 'paint' targets for missiles to hit.

ARMOURED VEHICLES

Depending on whom you ask, with the imminent introduction of the Armata AFV series the Russian Army is either about to achieve a breakthrough in armoured vehicle design, or else faces the prospect of an over-hyped and overpriced debacle. Based on a common Armata Universal Combat Platform chassis, this family will include the T-14 main battle tank, T-15 infantry fighting vehicle, Koalitsiya-SV self-propelled 152mm gun, and a series of transport, engineering and support vehicles. Much is promised of this new tracked platform, which began design in 2009 based on the aborted T-95 tank prototype. It will have an advanced powerplant, dual-reactive armour, new-generation sensors, and even a 'semi-stealth' low radar cross-section. The T-14 tank – of which c.100 are meant to be in service as test vehicles by 2020 – has a crew of three housed in a hull fighting position, and an all-automated remote-control turret mounting a 125mm 2A82-1M smoothbore cannon, coaxial 7.62mm machine gun and cupola-mounted 12.7mm Kord machine gun. Its *Afganit* active defence system is designed to detect incoming missiles, and either jam their sensors or destroy them with a radar-triggered shaped-charge blast. The T-15 infantry fighting vehicle

(IFV) uses the same chassis but carries nine infantrymen, and mounts a turret fitted with a 2A42 30mm auto-cannon, a 7.62mm coaxial machine gun and four Kornet-EM anti-tank guided missiles.

There is considerable scepticism even within the Russian military about the viability of the Armata project – it did not help that the first time the T-14 was rolled out, at rehearsals for the 2015 Victory Day parade, one broke down – and even at full production UralVagonZavod will be able to produce no more than 500 a year. Consequently, for some time to come the workhorses of the Russian Army will be the BMP-2 and -3 infantry combat vehicles, the BTR-80/82A personnel carriers, the MT-LB tractor/carrier and the T-72, -80 and -90 tanks.

The BTR-80 and its BTR-82A successor are eight-wheeled, relatively lightly armed personnel carriers; they too have been used as the basis for a wide range of variants, from the 2S23 Nona-SVK fire-support vehicle mounting a 120mm 2A60 rifled gun/mortar, to the Taifun-M, a specialized design used by the Strategic Rocket Force to guard missile bases, mounting a machine gun, radar, and even an onboard observation drone. The BMP-2, by contrast, is a tracked IFV with a low profile, able to carry seven soldiers (albeit in considerable discomfort) and mounting a 30mm auto-cannon and a missile launcher. The larger and more modern BMP-3 is a very heavily

A Russian BMP-I pictured with a crew member in Ukraine. The latest iteration of the BMP family is the BMP-3 fitted with the Bumerang-BM remotely controlled weapons turret. (Chris Cobb-Smith/DPL)

1) A senior lieutenant, commanding a T-80 tank in the Second Chechen War, is taking a moment's break in the ruins of Grozny, 2002. He is wearing jacket and trousers in Dubok ('Little Oak') VSR camouflage pattern. **2)** Drone technician; Donbas, 2014. This technician is carrying out final checks on a Zastava reconnaissance drone about to patrol the battle-lines north-west of the Russian-held city of Luhansk in eastern Ukraine. **3)** Female warrant officer, Signals, 2012. Her rank, typical for advanced technical specialists, is shown by the two metal stars on the chest strap of her field jacket in 'digital Flora' camouflage. **4)** Patch of 251st Pipeline Brigade, Southern Military District. (Johnny Shumate © Osprey Publishing)

armed successor, with a turret mounting a low-velocity 2A70 100mm rifled gun able to fire conventional rounds or 9K116 Bastion (AT-10) anti-tank missiles, a coaxial 30mm auto-cannon and a 7.62mm machine gun, as well as two bow machine guns. However, with the adoption of new IFVs, remaining BMP-3s are likely eventually to be relegated to a fire-support role.

Confusingly enough, the Defence Ministry has also adopted a new Kurganets family of vehicles. In part reflecting a habit of awarding contracts to parallel corporations for political reasons – the Kurganets is built by Kurganmashzavod – this will include the amphibious Kurganets-25 IFV (first seen at the 2015 Victory Day parade), the wheeled Bumerang APC, and the usual array of specialist variants including an anti-aircraft vehicle and a gun/mortar carrier.

Russia's 2,700 current frontline tanks are T-72s, T-80Us and T-90s representing different generations of Russian design, albeit sharing the same basic emphasis on speed and firepower over heavy armour. The venerable T-72, initially introduced in 1973, has been successively modernized, and most currently in use are T-72BA, T-72B2, T-72B3 and T-72B3M versions; these have improved sensors, protection and

The T-14 Armata represents the future of Russia's armoured thinking. It is armed with a 125mm smoothbore cannon and is fitted with the Malachit dual-explosive reactive armour (ERA) system on the front, sides and the top. (Vitaly V. Kuzmin/CC-BY-SA-4.0)

(in the latest T-72B3 and B3Ms) a better 2A46M5 main gun. The third-generation T-80, an evolution of the earlier T-64, promised much but failed to live up to expectations. Fast and agile thanks to a fuel-guzzling gas turbine engine, it also proved temperamental, and after some terrible casualties in the First Chechen War (in fairness, largely due to their foolish deployment in built-up areas with inadequate infantry support) plans to buy more were shelved. Instead Russia opted for the T-90, an effective modernization of the T-72 using the best features of the T-80. The T-90 saw battle in Chechnya (where one famously shrugged off seven hits from RPG-7 anti-tank rockets), in Syria and even in the Donbas, and has a good reputation amongst crews.

ARTILLERY

Russia has traditionally depended heavily on 'the god of war', and artillery remains a strong area of emphasis. In the Donbas war, Ukrainian attacks have often been shattered by extremely heavy bombardments by artillery and multiple-launch rocket systems. For instance, according to observer Phillip Karber of the Potomac Foundation, in July 2014 a combined barrage on Zelenopillya that lasted no more than three minutes virtually wiped out two Ukrainian mechanized battalions.

In line with their mobile approach to war, the Russians largely use self-propelled artillery, such as the 122mm Gvozdika ('Carnation'), and the 152mm Akatsiya ('Acacia'), Giatsint-S ('Hyacinth-S') and Msta-S. The Msta-S is the most advanced of the frontline systems, although it is due to be replaced by the Koalitsiya-SV. The Russians also have a marked predilection for truck-based multiple-launch rocket systems (MLRS), from the venerable 122mm BM-21 Grad ('Hail'), a system dating back to the 1960s, to the newer 220mm BM-27 Uragan ('Hurricane') and 300mm BM-30 Smerch ('Whirlwind'). All three systems are due to be replaced in due course by similar-calibre versions of the 9A52-4 Tornado platform. In addition, the TOS-1 is a tracked launcher for 220mm thermobaric (fuel-air explosive) rockets, which has been used to devastating effect in Afghanistan, Chechnya, Syria and, according to some reports, Ukraine.

For air defence, a handful of ageing ZSU-23-4 self-propelled vehicles are still in service, but mainly because their four rapid-fire 23mm cannon are useful in a direct-fire role, as proven in Chechnya. The real backbones of the army's point air defence are the Strela-10 (SA-13) short-range missile launcher, and the Tunguska (SA-19) gun/missile system and its successor, the Pantsir-S1 (SA-22). Both of the latter mount two 30mm auto-cannon and missiles: 6× 57E6 for the former and 12x for the latter. The Tor-M1 and Kub provide further short-range missile cover, with various models of the Buk ('Beech') SA-11/17 for medium-range capability. A Buk assumed to be operated or supplied by Russian forces gained notoriety in July 2014 when it shot down Malaysian Airlines flight MH17 over the Donbas, killing

1) Arctic warfare clothing. This soldier from the Northern Command's 200th Independent Brigade is wearing a snow-camouflage oversuit over his winter-weight field uniform, a covered helmet and a snow mask, and has also camouflaged his AK-74M rifle with white tape. His tinted goggles help reduce the risk of snow blindness, but he has them up on his 6B7 helmet while he looks through the KPUO sight on his RPG-29 AT rocket launcher. 2) Helicopter pilot; Syria, 2015. With the renewed emphasis on territorial combined-arms commands, the former Army Aviation, which had been transferred to the Air Forces, is being brought back into closer co-ordination with the Ground Forces. This pilot of an Mi-8AMTSh assault helicopter is part of the task force dispatched to Syria in 2015 in support of the beleaguered Assad regime. He wears the regular ZSh-7 helmet and a sand-colour flight suit, with a camouflaged utility vest. He carries an AKS-74U carbine as a personal defence weapon in case he is downed. 3) Bomb-disposal technician, 2016. This sapper is trialling the new OVR-1 suit issued from late 2016; a much more modern design than past versions, it includes heavy trauma plates, a high neck guard, and protective shields on his hands. He is using red flags to mark suspected mine locations; his sniffer dog's protective vest reads *Razminirovanie*, 'Mine Clearing'. (Johnny Shumate © Osprey Publishing)

all 298 civilians on board, apparently in the mistaken belief that it was a Ukrainian Air Force transport. Long-range air defence is provided by the highly capable S-300 (SA-10) and its successor the S-400 (SA-21).

At the time of writing, one new Russian weapon system currently causing concern in the West is the 9K720 Iskander (SS-26 Stone) mobile short-range ballistic missile (SRBM) system. Mounted on the 9P78-1 transporter erector launcher, the Iskander-M can fire hypersonic missiles to a range of 500km with a circular error probable (CEP) of just 5–7m. What is significant about the system is that it can adopt a wide range of conventional warheads – high-explosive fragmentation, sub-munition, penetration, fuel-air explosive – but also low-yield tactical nuclear warheads. To outsiders, the most concerning things about the Iskander-M are not only its mobile presence affecting the balance of strategic firepower in Europe, but also the fact that the ability to switch between different warheads could result, in a conflict situation, in a natural escalation from the conventional to the nuclear option.

'KEEPING UP WITH THE DRONES'

Artillery is most effective when it is well directed. In the Second Chechen War, Russian Pchela-1T and Stroi-P drones had helped vector helicopters and artillery fire on to rebels; although their successes were limited by crude sensors, they had the advantage of fighting enemies with no anti-aircraft capability beyond just shooting into the sky. However, Russia's relative backwardness in this field was then demonstrated during the 2008 Georgian War. In 2012 the Defence Ministry established a specialized drone research and development team, and in 2013 Shoigu ordered a doubling of the speed of the research and procurement of drones. Moscow actually looked abroad at first, buying Israeli Bird Eye-400, I-View Mk 150, and Searcher Mk 2 drones following the effectiveness of these designs when used against them in the Georgian War.

However, since then there has been considerable progress at home. Zala-421 and Gorizont-Air-S100 drones were deployed in the skies over Sochi during the 2014 Winter Olympics. In Ukraine, Russian forces have made considerable use of the Orlan-10, Granat-1, Eleron-3SV, and man-portable Zala-421 drones, especially for spotting for artillery barrages. Although Russia does not at present field an armed unmanned aerial vehicle (UAV), the Altius-M, pitched as an equivalent to the missile-armed US MQ-9 Reaper, is under test. Nor are all Russia's future drone designs airborne: the

Russian ceremonial troops march outside the Kremlin in Moscow. They belong to what is known as the Kremlin Regiment, which in turn is part of the Federal Protective Service (FSO), the equivalent of the US Secret Service. (Iain Ballantyne/DPL)

wheeled Kompas RURS Reconnaissance and Strike Robot is being designed to patrol areas autonomously, engaging enemies in range.

The intensive reforms of the Russian military system over the past decade have indeed transformed the armed forces from a weakened and crumbling organization to a potent and guardedly respected force once again. Faultlines still run through the Russian ambitions, principally economic; as with the Cold War, Russia is struggling to fund the scale of its ambitions. Yet as our Conclusion will show, the Russian Armed Services, together with a more ruthless political intelligence, have become a capable instrument of foreign policy once more.

CONCLUSION: THE FUTURE

TODAY, THE RUSSIAN MILITARY MACHINE has arrested the attention of the Western powers to a level not seen since the height of the Cold War. How it has achieved this status is partly explained by the reforms laid out in Chapter 6, which have turned the Russian Army from a hobbled, corrupt and demoralized force into a forward-looking army equal to many on the world stage. But it is not just professionalization and modernization that are attracting vast amounts of study by the outside world. It is also the Russian leadership in what has been termed 'hybrid warfare'.

The exact meaning of hybrid warfare is not universally agreed, nor in some quarters even accepted. The US Joint Forces command defines a practitioner of hybrid warfare as 'any adversary that simultaneously and adaptively employs a tailored mix of conventional, irregular, terrorism and criminal means or activities in the operational battle space. Rather than a single entity, a hybrid threat or challenger may be a combination of state and nonstate actors'. Similar definitions play about with this concept of blending traditional kinetic force options with a broad simultaneous campaign of cyberwarfare (political and military), disinformation, social and political campaigning, criminality, terrorism, indeed whatever means available to target the vulnerabilities of the opponent. In many ways, this is nothing new. Some see hybrid warfare as little more than linguistically repackaging the traditional combination of warfighting and 'psyops'. Furthermore, we must remember that during the Cold War the efforts of the Soviet Union's ideological machine and its shadowy commitments to various proxy wars and international terrorist networks could easily be perceived as a form of hybrid warfare. I would argue that it is in fact the unprecedented reliance of state and military actors upon networked IT that makes hybrid warfare a valid and new concept. Now, for example, disinformation campaigns can reach literally millions of people almost instantly and globally through online social networking platforms, potentially influencing entire nations to align, unwittingly, with a foreign government's strategic goals. Furthermore, the reliance of almost every nation's infrastructure upon technology makes it critically vulnerable to cyberwarfare, not least so in military forces – take down computers, and much of an army's technology above the level of small arms simply fails.

It is in the practice of hybrid warfare that Russia arguably seems to have taken a lead. The Western world is continuing to scrutinize Russian influence over political events such as the 2016 US presidential election and the UK's Brexit vote (also in 2016). Other countries that have been targeted for Russian cyberwarfare, particularly Denial of Service (DoS) attacks, include Estonia (2007), Georgia (2008), Kyrgyzstan (2009) and Ukraine (2014–16). It is reported, for example, that up to 80 per cent of Ukraine's D-30 artillery pieces were at one point rendered non-operational by their targeting control computers being intentionally infected with malware. Yet many of these cyberattacks cannot be traced directly back to a specific state source, and in that reality lies the potential strength of hybrid warfare. By operating in a shadowy region of deniability, hybrid warfare states leave their opponents in a confused state of response, not knowing when or how to react most meaningfully.

However, at the same time as Russia has boosted its cyberwarfare resources, both within the state security apparatus and the military, its investment in its conventional military has proceeded apace. At the time of writing, the pattern of Russian conventional military deployments perhaps hints at future strategies and tactical possibilities. The Russian Army has established multiple divisional headquarters and three mechanized divisions along the Russian–Ukrainian border, as opposed to just one airborne division near the Baltic. From this some extrapolate that while a large-scale conventional campaign in Ukraine remains perfectly possible, the Baltic is probably threatened more by hybrid warfare-based strategies, and hence the region does not warrant some Western fears of a Russian military campaign in northern Europe.

Russia has also shown its willingness to adopt a new military expeditionary mindset in its recent involvement in Syria. Russian intervention in the Syrian civil war began in 2015, although a physical military presence in Syria actually dates back to the early 1970s, when the Soviet Navy established limited operating facilities at Tartus. The need to preserve this foothold in the Mediterranean certainly informed Russia's 2015 deployments; in 2017, it was announced that Russia had agreed with the Assad regime that the lease of the facility would be extended for a further 49 years. The base is now sheltered under a highly sophisticated anti-access/area denial (A2/AD) umbrella of defences, including S-300 and S-400 SAM systems, on-shore Bastion-P anti-ship batteries, and the shipborne weapons of the Russian vessels within the port, including Kalibr anti-ship/land attack cruise missiles. In addition to its extended presence at Tartus, Russia also established its Hmeimim air base in Latakia province in 2015, from which it would conduct its air operations; in 2016, this air base also became sovereign territory for the Russians through another 49-year lease agreement. It is clear that the Syrian conflict has provided the opportunity for the Russian military to establish a near-permanent and sizeable presence in the Middle East.

There are many other reasons for Russia's willingness to be drawn into a particularly tortured internal conflict. They include projecting international relevance, development of a protective southern 'buffer zone' for Russia and showing dependability to other potential allies. Yet one of the principal benefits to the Russian military is the ability both to test out new weapon systems (also to demonstrate such weapons to potential export markets), refine tactics and blood a new generation of junior officers and professional soldiers. By September 2018, according to Moscow's own figures, 63,012 military personnel had received combat experience in Syria. These personnel range from special operations soldiers conducting small-unit counter-insurgency missions through to Su-34 pilots delivering precision ground-attack missions. What seems particularly advantageous to Russian commanders is having an arena in which to practise modern combined-arms operations, including joint operations with a foreign power (in this case the Syrian Armed Forces) and also private military contractors (PMCs). In terms of weapon testing, the war has seen the Russians even deploy systems such as the Iskander-M, plus the 9A52-4 Tornado-G and 9A52-2 Smerch-M multiple-launch rocket systems. Such actions, taken in their totality, not only enable Russia to refine its firepower delivery and tactics, but also to optimize its command-and-control networks. Syria has in effect become a vehicle for sharpening Russia's military teeth.

The future, in our complex world, is difficult to see. Nor is the strength of the Russian military entirely secure, as Russia staggers under persistent economic hardship. Certainly, the Russian Armed Forces are flexing their muscles for the world to see. During the writing of this book, for example, Russia conducted its *Vostok* (East) military exercises on 11–17 September 2018, a mass demonstration of combined-arms operations involving more than 100,000 troops, 36,000 vehicles and 1,000 aircraft, and which included some 3,200 Chinese soldiers, the latter's involvement hinting at a future power-bloc alliance. Russia still does not have the economic means to create armed services anywhere near equivalent to those of the United States. Yet perhaps making on-paper strength comparisons is missing the point. Russia knows full well that the US military is the greatest on Earth, but by investing heavily in futuristic weapon systems, technologies and tactics of hybrid warfare, and by making global alliances, Russia might conceivably shift the very nature of warfare itself, compelling stronger opponents to fight with their weakest hand. After more than a century of tumultuous history, the Great Bear still commands our respect.

BIBLIOGRAPHY AND FURTHER READING

Abdulin, Mansur, *Red Road from Stalingrad: Recollections of a Soviet Infantryman* (Pen & Sword, 2005)

Akhmadov, I. & M. Lanskoy, *The Chechen Struggle: Independence Won and Lost* (Palgrave, 2010)

Alexiev, Alex, *Inside the Soviet Army in Afghanistan* (Rand Corporation, 1988)

Babchenko, Arkady, *One Soldier's War* (Grove, 2007)

Baev, Pavel, *The Russian Army in a Time of Troubles* (Sage, 2009)

Baker, A. J. & John Walter, *Russian Infantry Weapons of World War 2* (Arco Publishing, 1971)

Baxter, William P., *Soviet AirLand Battle Tactics* (Presidio Press, 1986)

Bocharov, Gennady, *Russian Roulette: Afghanistan through Russian Eyes* (HarperCollins, 1990)

Bradsher, Henry, *Afghan Communism and Soviet Intervention* (Oxford University Press, 1999)

Braithwaite, Rodric, *Afgantsy: The Russians in Afghanistan, 1979–89* (Profile Books, 2011)

Bullock, David, *The Russian Civil War 1918–22* (Osprey Publishing, 2008)

Clark, Alan, *Barbarossa: The Russian-German Conflict, 1941–45* (Macmillan, 1985)

Cohen, Ariel & Robert Hamilton, *The Russian Military and the Georgia War: Lessons and Implications* (SSI, 2012)

Cornell, Svante & S. Frederick Starr, *The Guns of August 2008: Russia's War in Georgia* (Routledge, 2009)

Dunlop, J., *Russia Confronts Chechnya* (Cambridge University Press, 1998)

Erickson, John & E.J. Feuchtwanger, *Soviet Military Power and Performance* (Macmillan, 1979)

Feifer, G., *The Great Gamble: The Soviet War in Afghanistan* (HarperCollins, 2009)

Fremont-Barnes, Gregory, *The Anglo-Afghan Wars 1839–1919* (Osprey Publishing, 2009)

Galeotti, Mark, *Afghanistan: The Soviet Union's Last War* (Routledge, 2001)

Galeotti, Mark, *Russian Paramilitary and Security Forces since 1991* (Osprey Publishing, 2013)

Galeotti, Mark, *Russia's Wars in Chechnya 1994–2009*, Essential Histories 78 (Osprey Publishing, 2014)

Galeotti, Mark, *Spetsnaz: Russia's Special Forces*, Elite 206 (Osprey Publishing, 2015)

Glantz, David (ed.), *Slaughterhouse: The Handbook of the Eastern Front* (Aberjona Press, 2005)

Grau, Lester & Michael Gress, *The Soviet–Afghan War: How a Superpower Fought and Lost* (University Press of Kansas, 2002)

Harris, Catherine & Frederick W. Kagan, *Russia's Military Posture: Ground Forces Order of Battle* (Institute for the Study of War, 2018)

Hedenskog, Jakob & Carolina Vendil Palinn (eds), *Russian Military Capability in a Ten-Year Perspective – 2013* (FOI, 2013)

Howard, Colby & Ruslan Pukhov (eds), *Brothers Armed: Military Aspects of the Crisis in Ukraine*, revised edition (EastView, 2015)

Isby, David C., *Weapons and Tactics of the Soviet Army* (Jane's Publishing, 1981)

Isby, David C., *Russia's War in Afghanistan*, Men-at-Arms 178 (Osprey Publishing, 1986)

Jones, Ellen, *Red Army and Society* (Allen & Unwin, 1985)

Lieven, A., *Chechnya: Tombstone of Russian Power* (Yale University Press, 1998)

Merridale, Catherine, *Ivan's War: Life and Death in the Red Army, 1939–1945* (Metropolitan Books, 2006)

Ministry of Defence, United Kingdom, *Army Field Manual. Vol. 1, Part 10: Countering Insurgency* (MoD, 2010)

Odom, W., *The Collapse of the Soviet Military* (Yale University Press, 1998)

Oliker, O., *Russia's Chechen Wars, 1994–2000* (RAND Corporation, 2001)

Reese, Roger R., *Why Stalin's Soldiers Fought: The Red Army's Military Effectiveness in World War II* (University Press of Kansas, 2011)

Schofield, Carey, *The Russian Elite: Inside Spetsnaz and the Airborne Forces* (Greenhill Books, 1993)

Shalito, Anton, *Red Army Uniforms of World War II in Colour Photographs* (Motorbooks International, 1993)

Sharp, Charles S., *Soviet Infantry Tactics in World War II: Red Army Infantry Tactics from Squad to Rifle Company from the Combat Regulations* (Nafziger Collection, 1998)

Suvorov, Viktor, *Inside the Soviet Army* (Hamish Hamilton, 1982)

US Army, *Handbook on USSR Military Forces*, TM 30-430 (November 1945)

Zaloga, Steven J. & Leland S. Ness, *Red Army Handbook, 1939–1945* (Sutton Publishing, 1998)

INDEX

Note: page numbers in bold refer to maps and illustrations. All military hardware and weaponry is Russian unless otherwise stated.